Rural Recreation in the Industrial World

Rural Recreation in the Industrial World

I G SIMMONS

A HALSTED PRESS BOOK

JOHN WILEY & SONS
New York

© I. G. Simmons 1975

First published 1975 by
Edward Arnold (Publishers) Ltd
London

Published in the U.S.A.
by Halsted Press, a Division
of John Wiley & Sons, Inc.
New York

Library of Congress Cataloging in Publication Data

Simmons, Ian Gordon.
    Rural recreation in the industrial world.

    'A Halsted Press book.'
    Bibliography: p.
    Includes index.
    1. Outdoor recreation. I. Title.
GV191.6.S55 1975   301.5′7   75–4918
ISBN 0–470–79212–4

Printed in Great Britain

Contents

Preface

During the past ten years I have had the chance of seeing rural areas in several of the industrial countries of the northern hemisphere, and in particular the use made of them for recreation by the largely urban populations. This book is thus the outcome of travelling, talking with suppliers and consumers, and of an attempt to digest both official documents and the increasingly voluminous literature of commentary. My purpose is firstly to give some idea of the magnitude of participation in outdoor recreation in the chosen areas together with the types of activities which are pursued, and secondly to see how in particular places the response of both governments and private enterprise has evolved and how the management problems of recreation areas are being faced. The treatment is often brief and spatially extensive rather than concentrating on particular recreation areas in depth: this is in order to give the overall flavour of a particular nation's approach to recreation and its problems, rather than a lot of detail about an especially notable area which may be atypical. England and Wales, Denmark, the Netherlands, USA, Canada and Japan are the source of most of the examples. At this level of resolution, the reader can then begin to make comparisons between the different countries treated, and in this way I hope the book will be useful to two groups of people. The first of these comprises students in resource management, recreational land management, and related subjects, for whom an international perspective may be useful and for whom, so far, no suitable book seems to exist. The second group consists of the resource agencies who are constantly seeking new ideas but whose employers are loth to give them time and money to go see other people's difficulties and solutions. In this way I hope I can repay some of the hours of their time they have given me; though I also expect to confirm their feeling that there is no substitute for a personal visit.

In such a rapidly changing area of resource use and management, the information in such a work as this must age rapidly. Readers should therefore be prepared to treat it as a synopsis of the position in the late 1960s and early 1970s, and as a background against which to view later events about which they may learn.

My interest in this field of study began in 1963 when I was appointed by the then Minister of Housing and Local Government to the Yorkshire Dales (North Riding) National Park Planning Committee, an action instigated by Professor H. C. Darby, then head of the Department of Geography at University College, London. My interest was further encouraged by an American Studies Program Fellowship from the ACLS to study public land use in the USA at the University of California, Berkeley, in 1964–5. In that year and in subsequent visits I have gained much insight (and hospitality) from Jim Parsons and Dan Luten, for which I thank them most sincerely.

In 1968 I prepared a report for NATO on 'Land and Leisure in North Atlantic Countries', and that report, much amended, forms the nucleus of the factual material of this book; without the award of the NATO Fellowship, generously administered by Mr John Vernon, this book would never have come about. The other major chance to improve my knowledge came with the award of a Churchill Memorial Trust Travelling Fellowship, awarded for 1971–2, which enabled me not only to extend my knowledge of Canada but also to visit Japan, and for that opportunity I am extremely grateful.

There are therefore a large number of people to whom thanks are due. Especially, I want to mention the help given by those government officials in bodies such as the Countryside Commission of England and Wales (particularly John Davidson), Naturfrednings-foringen and Landsplanudvalgets in Denmark, Staatsbosbeheer in the Netherlands (particularly Ir W. G. van der Kloet), the National Parks Service of the USA (particularly Mr Fred Pilley), the National and Historic Parks Branch of Canada (particularly Mr Ron Maslin), the Ontario Provincial Parks and Recreation Areas Branch, and Mr Ken Higgs of the Metropolitan Toronto and Region Conservation Authority. In Japan, Tetsumaro Senge (Chairman of the National Parks Association of Japan) and Hiromi Tawara (Prefectural government of Hokkaido) were very helpful.

The penultimate version of the text was completed while I was Visiting Professor at York University, Toronto, in 1972–3, and I want to thank Bill Found, then Chairman, for the undemanding hospitality of his department. Florence Davies, my secretary at

York, produced a complete retyping of the book with maximum speed and efficiency during the spring of 1973. My home department, under its head, Professor W. B. Fisher, has been tolerant of absences and has provided a favourable environment for work, so that here I owe considerable thanks. Most of all, I am grateful to my wife, Carol, for reading and checking the manuscripts of numerous drafts and the proofs and for support and encouragement. This book is dedicated to her, in poor recompense for the many times she stayed at home.

IGS
October 1974

Acknowledgements

For permission to use the following figures, the publishers' thanks are due to:

Resources for the Future Inc. for Figs. 1 and 4; *New Society* for Fig. 2; © The Johns Hopkins University Press for Figs. 3 and 5, published for Resources for the Future Inc.; David and Charles Ltd for Figs. 6, 13, 15, 16, 18 and 19; Ministerie van Landbouw en Visserji, Utrecht for Fig. 7; US Printing Office, Bureau of Outdoor Recreation Surveys for Figs. 8 and 29; Dienst der Publike Werke, Amsterdam for Fig. 9; Civic Trust for Fig. 10; East Bay Regional Park District (Charles Lee Tilden Regional Park) for Fig. 11; Dr Robert M. Newcomb and *Geoforum* for Fig. 12; The Controller of Her Majesty's Stationery Office for Fig. 14; Royal Geographical Society and J. A. Patmore for Fig. 17; Royal Geographical Society and M. F. Tanner for Fig. 20; Hokkaido Government Department of Commerce, Industry and Tourism for Fig. 22; Stanford Research Institute for Figs. 24, 25 and 26; Geodetisk Institut, Denmark for Fig. 27; Landsplanudvalgets Sekretariat, Denmark for Fig. 28; and Parks Canada for Fig. 33.

Part I
Activities Participation and Resources

1 Introduction

This work is mostly concerned with man's use of his rural environment for the particular purpose of outdoor recreation. To this end, the types of terrain which are used, the manipulations of ecological systems which are practised, and the institutional frameworks which have emerged are all studied. The context, therefore, is of human leisure-time activities, as distinct from work; active recreation rather than passive (at any rate active enough to get a person to somewhere outside his home even if he falls asleep at the destination); and rural rather than urban, since outdoor recreation in towns is not discussed although it is no less an important subject than that under examination here. Recreation travel, in terms of origin, pathway and destination of recreation-seekers, is given scant treatment compared with, for example, F. Cribier's *La Grande Migration d'Été des Citadins de France* (Paris: CNRS, 1969, 2 vols.), in order to devote more space to the activities pursued upon arrival and the consequences in terms of resource management.[1] Likewise tourism *per se* is not dealt with, since if tourists engage in rural recreation they need not be differentiated from local people. And although it is often linked with recreation, the protection of visual amenity or landscape conservation is not accorded any particular treatment although it is discussed where directly relevant.

Spatially, this book is confined to industrial countries of the Northern Hemisphere and in particular those in cool temperate climates. Within this framework, certain other contrasts were sought. The availability of space for rural outdoor recreation is very different in the Netherlands and the USA, for example; the scale and distribution of areas of high relief form a strong difference (among

---

[1] F. Cribier also attempts to delineate a distinctive Anglo-American approach to outdoor recreation (as distinct from French) in her 'La géographie de la récréation en Amérique anglo-saxonne', *Annales de Géographie* 81 (1972), pp. 644–65.

1

others) between Denmark and England/Wales. These latter countries can be contrasted on the grounds of space and evenness of population distribution with a huge nation like Canada. Even within the overall climatic zone, there are considerable variations: the lack of really hot summers in Britain and the Atlantic fringe of Europe come to mind, as of course does the fact that within both the USA and Canada are climatic regions which can scarcely be classified as cool temperate. But since rural recreation is culturally so important in the USA, any study which omitted all mention of it would be more prone than ever to accusations of incompleteness. The inclusion of Japan was dictated by the fact that its economy is basically of a free-market industrial type and its traditional culture is heavily infused with western ways. Other Asian states which might have formed parallel examples such as Singapore and Hong Kong exist on too small a land base for any useful comparisons.

Some basic data about the countries from which most of the examples are taken are given in Table 1.1.

Table 1.1   Size and population data

Country	Area (mi²) incl. inland water	km²	Population (1973) million	Rate of population growth (% p.a.)	Yrs to double population
Canada	3,851,809	9,937,667	22·5	1·2	58
Denmark*	16,648	43,043	5·1	0·5	139
United Kingdom	89,736	233,421	57·0	0·3	231
Japan	143,000	370,370	107·3	1·2	58
Netherlands	12,868	34,830	13·4	0·8	87
USA	3,548,974	9,156,352	210·3	0·8	87

* Excluding the Faeroes and Greenland

2 Rural recreation delimited

The activities which are the subject of this work are quite clearly defined in a holistic sense although some of them are difficult to place. But basically, rural recreation consists of leisure-time activities undertaken in relatively small groups. The second of these two conditions are not capable of precise delimitation, for the number-units run from the solitary walker through the couple seeking an ecological niche with maximum protective cover to the members of a sailing club.

Excluded, however, are mass spectator recreations such as football and golf, since these are so closely related to the urban situation;

and tennis, although this is included in data from some investigations. The major activities are included in Table 1.2.

Table 1.2   Major rural recreation activities (no ranking is implied by the order)

Driving for pleasure	
Walking for pleasure ⎱ Hiking ⎰	This is a useful distinction—the latter is the serious version
Outdoor games	These should be of an informal nature, requiring little or no fixed equipment.
Swimming	Includes sub-aqua activities. It is implied that a 'natural-looking' water body is involved, not a 'bath'.
Bicycling	
Fishing	
Nature study, archaeology	
Nature walks	Includes both guided walks and self-guiding nature trails
Boating	This category means motor-boats on inland waters and sea
Sailing	Inland water
Canoeing	
Sea-sailing	Sail only
Sightseeing	Of cultural interests rather than appreciating of views, etc.
Caving	Restricted to limestone pothole country
Hunting	This is an American term, and is used there mainly for deer-shooting. For use in this book it will be taken to be synonymous with shooting and to exclude fox-hunting
Horseback riding	Including pony-trekking
Camping	Including 'day-camping', not easily separable from picnicking; also caravanning: difficult to separate in North America
Picnicking	
Ice skating	Outdoor only, on naturally frozen water
Tobogganing	
Snowskiing	
Mountain climbing	Synonymous with rock climbing: fellwalking and scrambling under hiking
Motor sports	Hill trials, motorcycle scrambles over informal courses
Water skiing	

Sources: ORRRC Recreation for America, 1962, part 1, chapter 2.
    BTA-Keele University, Pilot National Recreational Survey, Report 1 (1967), Section 1A. But this survey also includes activities such as archery, bowls, golf and athletics which are not considered in this work.

Although some of these activities require considerable development of the natural resource or heavy investment in equipment, it can be seen that an important element in every activity is a 'natural' setting, be it fields and forests, water or snow; this is the difference between these forms of activity and the nature-divorced pursuits such as bowls, cricket, and football of all kinds. This means that extra-urban areas are the locations for the activities, particularly since just being out in rural surroundings doubtless forms a major source of attraction, although not one easily susceptible to survey by questionnaire.

The basis for participation is very variable but the family group or friends is the most common. Even where large numbers of people belong to a local club, as in sailing or camping, the actual activity is likely to be on a relatively small number-unit basis: if all the members sailed at once on the club's lake then the crowding would be extreme. Nevertheless, club organization, especially in using scarce resources such as inland water for fishing or sailing in Britain, or in making arrangements with landowners for the use of off-road recreational vehicles in North America, is a significant factor.

Although in geographical terms it is the site of recreation which is most important, for social and economic purposes it must be remembered that this is only part of the total recreation experience. The other parts are anticipation, travel to the site, travel back and recollection. Each of these may be, for example, the subject of expenditure.

3 Leisure in the West

3.1 THE ROLE OF LEISURE

There exists a steadily growing literature on the social anthropology and sociology of leisure. Little of it applies directly to, or is derived from studies of, rural recreation in the sense of this work. One result has been that protagonists of rural recreation have been given a free hand to assert the social benefits derived therefrom without feeling the necessity to quote any evidence. That recreation of all kinds does benefit the community is presumably undoubted, but just who gains, by how much, and to what extent rural outdoor recreation has a particular role needs to be established.[2] Advocates of wilderness have been particularly outspoken in justifying not merely the de-

[2] M. Clawson and J. L. Knetsch, *Economics of Outdoor Recreation* (Baltimore 1967), pp. 267–8.

4

sirability but the need for it in man's welfare. In view of the small numbers of people (mostly of a particular type) who participate, these claims are probably exaggerated.[3] Nevertheless, most politicians and resource managers find it necessary and acceptable to argue for the devotion of resources—both financial and natural—to rural recreation.

This attitude may represent a relatively recent swing away from the idea that work was the chief aim in life and good for you. If you do enough of it then you may have a treat in the form of some leisure. (Margaret Mead uses the analogy of spinach: unpleasant but nutritious.[4]) In such a system, holidays were at the behest of Church or State, or for medical reasons and the Aristotelian idea that we labour in order to have leisure was overlain by the Weberian doctrine that we do not work to live but that we live to work.[5] But in the automated 'hyper-productive' societies of the West, this justification is breaking down[6] and recreation becomes a human right in the same sense as health and education. Although according to Revelle,[7] the question 'do human beings need outdoor recreation?' cannot be answered scientifically, there have been a few attempts.[8] The beneficial nature of exercise, unpolluted air and quietness are thought to be good antitheses to urban living. Although urbanization is not unidimensional and some facets of it affect rural dwellers too,[9] probably more important is the chance that recreation gives for realization of abilities and achievement of satisfactions denied by contemporary working conditions.[10] At any rate, article 59 of the

[3] For example, Sigurd F. Olson, 'The spiritual aspects of wilderness', in D. Brower (ed.), *Wilderness: America's Living Heritage* (San Francisco 1961).

[4] Margaret Mead, 'Outdoor recreation in the context of emerging American cultural values: background considerations', in ORRRC Report 22, *Trends in American Living and Outdoor Recreation* (1962), pp. 2–25.

[5] Quoted by R. Revelle, 'Outdoor recreation in a hyper-productive society', *Daedalus* 96 (1967), pp. 1172–91. See also J. R. Kelley, 'Work and leisure: a simplified paradigm', *J. Leisure Research* 4 (1972), pp. 50–62.

[6] R. Revelle, *op. cit.*, p. 1174.

[7] *Ibid.*

[8] See J. B. Nash (ed.), *Recreation: pertinent readings* (Dubuque, Iowa, 1965), esp. section 3, 'Philosophy', pp. 89–182.

[9] T. B. Knopp, 'Environmental determinants of recreation behaviour', *J. Leisure Research* 4 (1972), pp. 129–38; J. C. Hendee, 'Rural urban differences reflected in outdoor recreation participation', *J. Leisure Research* 1 (1969), pp. 333–91.

[10] P. G. Roads, 'The importance of open-air recreation', First AIT-Congress on Leisure and Tourism, Rotterdam, 1966, Theme I, Report 2, pp. 5–7, 'the time is surely coming when there will . . . be scientific proof to illustrate the medical importance of open-air recreation', p. 7. *Cf.* H. J. Gans ('Outdoor recreation and mental health', in ORRRC

constitutional law of the Republic of Poland stipulates that, 'the citizens . . . are entitled to recreation'.[11] So while no closely documented case can be put for the necessity of rural recreation, it seems to be accepted in the West as an activity which needs no elaborate justification but which must be allotted some of society's resources.

The social meaning of camping in the USA for example has been studied by Burch[12] who regards it as a series of play activities. Symbolic labour involves the provision of tangible but inessential trophies (men tend to cut far too much wood but derive great satisfaction from it); expressive play, such as tree climbing and rolling rocks; subsistence play, in which the altered conditions are important; unstructured and structured play of an obvious kind; and sociability which may gain in intensity in camp settings. (Reserved Europeans might add to the last item, 'whether you like it or not'.) In this specifically American context, it is suggested that traditional historical roles are enacted: the men being the tough, self-reliant backwoodsmen, and the women, sturdy but gentle pioneer mothers. There is little doubt that the 'frontier heritage' motif looms large in American rural recreation (especially in wilderness), but the extent to which it may be important in Europe is doubtful, since the wildlands there were more likely pioneered in the nineteenth century B.C.

The motivations revealed in socio-psychological interviews by Groffen[13] suggest that any emphasis on deprivation is misplaced: desires for fresh air or recreation are seldom uppermost in the recreationist's mind. His stress is not on being in the country but being occupied in the country, with somebody, using one's possessions and gaining fresh experience. His basic question is,

> Does being in the country provide the opportunity for activity . . . with other people, in which he or she can do something for those he or she is with . . . while a number of possessions are used and . . . fresh experience is gained?

Report 22, *Trends in American Living and Outdoor Recreation*, pp. 233–42), 'I do not believe that . . . outdoor recreation . . . can by itself . . . materially aid in the bringing about of mental health', p. 239.

[11] W. Lazuchiewicz, 'The importance of open-air recreation', First International AIT-Congress on Leisure and Tourism, Rotterdam, 1966. Supplement to Theme I, Report 2, pp. 3–4.

[12] W. R. Burch, Jr, 'The play world of camping: research into the social meaning of outdoor recreation', *Am. J. Sociol.* 60 (1965), pp. 604–12.

[13] W. H. Groffen, 'The importance of open-air recreation', First AIT-Congress on Leisure and Tourism, Rotterdam, 1966, Theme I, Report 4, pp. 14–15.

and he thinks that people weigh up the benefits against the costs (patience, attention to others, discord) and choose their recreation relatively rationally. This view accords with the United States' Outdoor Recreation Resources Review Commission's view (Report No. 20, 1962, p. 31) when it says,

> It seems that in many American families leisure time is used not so much for resting and relaxing as to acquire a great variety of skills and interests as well as social contacts,

and again,

> For a minority of people the appeal of outdoor recreation may lie in the possibility of getting away from people to nature and solitude; but for the majority a major attraction of outdoor recreation seems to be the opportunity to be with people and to share leisure activities with others.

These and other studies such as those of Roberts,[14] show that in comparison with information about how people spend their leisure time, very little is known about the motivations of those who indulge in various pursuits or the satisfactions they gain from them, still less anything useful about the social function of leisure for the individual and his society. The relationship between the individual and his or her work, for example, is likely to be strongly reflected in the leisure pursuits sought, especially where these represent an avenue of escape from a boring, arduous or otherwise unsatisfactory job. The values of suppliers are another little explored realm: in particular the possible contrast between the paternalistic (and often elitist) supplier or planner,[15] and the simple democratic aim of providing such facilities as people say they want, which may not be what they would really like if they knew all the available possibilities.

However, the possibility exists that all forms of recreation and play cater to a much deeper-seated need that the re-enactment of a recent pioneering or agricultural past. The irrational element was a prominent feature of the cultures of early man, and the cave-painters

---

[14] K. Roberts, *Leisure*, Aspects of Modern Sociology series: the social structure of Britain (London 1970); and 'Sociology and recreation planning', *Rec. News Suppl.* 4 (1971), pp. 2–6. Also R. Meyersohn, 'The sociology of leisure in the United States: introduction and bibliography 1945–1965', *J. Leisure Research* 1 (1969), pp. 53–68.

[15] I. Emmett, 'Sociological research in recreation', in T. L. Burton (ed.), *Recreation Research and Planning*, University of Birmingham Centre for Urban and Regional Studies, Publication 1 (London 1970), p. 68.

and dancers looked inward to imagination and mystery (albeit with the ultimate aim of propitiating the gods to provide plenty of food) which survives in the irrational and non-purposive elements in our play. In traditional societies, work and play are closely related rather than being the opposites with different moral values which Protestant Christianity assigned to them.[16]

Looking to the future, growing prosperity in the West would mean the expansion of areas of choice, and the chance to opt for more leisure and different forms of it. This may mean, socially that leisure will increasingly have to bear the fulfilment role which work has traditionally provided; and hopefully too that which war has furnished. The role of leisure, including rural recreation, is certainly following the path outlined by Nigel Calder, even if it does not reach his destination.[17]

3.2 LEISURE BEFORE THE TWENTIETH CENTURY

It is perhaps easy to think of the agriculturalist's life as one of unremitting toil, accompanied of course by a closeness to nature which we would all embrace if only we had the time. In medieval England, however, it seems that the husbandman, though at the service of the lord of his manor, was not without leisure time. Some of the feasts of the Church coincided with events of the agricultural year and so there were holidays to mark the beginning of planting, at Michaelmas; the Rogation Days before Ascension Day; Lammastide of the first fruits. As well, there were purely agricultural festivals such as the sheep-shearing and the end of sowing, and throughout the year the freedom of Sunday. Above all this were the three great holidays when the villein was exempt from his lord's service and when a feast would be held—sometimes provided or at any rate organized by the lord—and after which there was a week's holiday. A folk festival then immediately preceded a return to work. The Twelve days of Christmas were the greatest vacation of the year, coming at a slack point in the agricultural calendar; Easter week was ended by Hocktide; and Whitsun week also marked a freedom from customary service. Most of the recreations we know about (with the exception of May Eve) pertain to the gentry rather than the proletariat; the hunting of deer within the park pales or across the wild lands beyond

---

[16] R. Revelle, *op. cit.*, pp. 1172–3. Although agreeing with Revelle's general thesis, I think he underestimates the practical purpose of many early rites.

[17] N. Calder, *The Environment Game* (London 1967).

shared the lord's time with fowling, usually employing the hawk and the bow. Hare-coursing was a common sport and no doubt the digging out of fox and badger occupied countrymen, then as now. Under the later Stuarts in England, the fox replaced the deer as the object of a more ritualized sport and in the eighteenth century hare-hunting began to decline, probably under the influence of increasing enclosures of the open fields. The greater 'edge' created by this movement allowed partridge and pheasant shooting to be important recreations of the aristocracy and gentry, from the eighteenth century onwards. For this group also there were the pleasures of the landscape garden, with its ornamental lakes, tree-lined walks and classical belvederes.[18]

A great contrast is exhibited by the conditions of the urban masses of the nineteenth century in Britain. The rich still had their old pleasures together with such new ones as grouse-shooting and highland deer-stalking, made possible by the breech-loading gun and accessible by the railway. But the urban proletariat worked in increasingly poor conditions. Their places of work—mill and mine—were unhealthy and their homes frequently insanitary. As Mumford says,[19] 'the slavish routine of the mines, whose labour was an intentional punishment for criminals, became the normal environment of the new industrial worker.' All of them—women and children alike—laboured for long hours, and in 1815 a ten-hour day for children and women was regarded as a far-off ideal; it came in fact in 1847. The employment of women and children underground was stopped by the Mines Act of 1842.

Government more and more took a hand in introducing and enforcing measures to improve the conditions of the 'working-poor' and to end the unbridled exploitation which laisser-faire capitalism had practised.[20] Under these conditions it is scarcely surprising that rural recreation opportunities were limited. After work, there was only eating and sleeping, paid holidays were unheard of, and in any case there was nowhere to go other than the beerhall and gin-shop. In 1842 only one town in Lancashire—Preston—had a public park.[21] Sundays provided a possible opportunity, along with public

[18] This section relies on G. V. Homans, *English Villagers of the 13th Century* (London 1941), ch. 23; G. M. Trevelyan, *Illustrated English Social History* (London 1957), vols. 1 and 2.

[19] L. Mumford, *The City in History* (London 1961), p. 446.

[20] G. M. Trevelyan, *op. cit.*, vols. 3 and 4.

[21] L. Mumford, *op. cit.*, p. 463. Professor J. A. Patmore draws my attention to the fact that

holidays such as Easter, for going out into the country and of course the cities were smaller at that time and access to open space was easier. The waggonette was one form of transport used, for example, for the Chapel picnic, and when the railways had become established, cheap excursions provided a rapid means of leaving the towns. The southern part of the Yorkshire Dales thus became a Mecca for people from the West Riding cities who could easily get there for the day by means of the railways to Threshfield, Pateley Bridge, Hawes (where open-air brass band contests were held in a ravine and attracted thousands of people) and Settle.[22] As working conditions became more reasonable and incomes rose, the working class began to look upon the countryside from which they were only a few generations removed in a new light: not in terms of its concrete or economic values, but in aesthetic and emotional terms as a symbol of escape and freedom.[23]

The foregoing account refers only to Britain but it probably reflects the social history of European industrial countries such as France, Germany and Benelux reasonably well; the USA and Canada escaped the worst of the palaeotechnic phase but the history of Labour unions shows that similar progress towards greater leisure and higher incomes was hard fought.

3.3 LEISURE, AFFLUENCE AND MOBILITY IN THE TWENTIETH CENTURY

(a) Decline of working hours and rise of holidays

At the turn of the century, the sixty-hour week was common in the West. In Holland and Denmark, for example, this was the usual figure,[24] and similar hours were worked in most industrial countries. The trend since then has been one of declining daily hours and increasing number of days holiday, with pay. In some countries there are now laws governing the work-time, in others, trade union agreements. In the USA, for example, the fall in hours worked, along with increase in average daily leisure time is given in Table 1.3.

---

other towns in Lancashire at that time had space which functioned as parks, even if not designated as such.

[22] A. Raistrick, *Old Yorkshire Dales* (Newton Abbot 1967), ch. 12.

[23] This classification of attitudes to landscape is found in J. Sonnenfeld, 'Variable values in space and landscape: an inquiry into the nature of environmental necessity', *J. Social Issues* 22 (1966), pp. 71–82.

[24] F. de Soet, 'Groenvoorziening en recreatie', *BOUW* (January 1965), p. 3; personal communication, Cultural Attaché of Royal Danish Embassy.

Table 1.3   Work and leisure in the USA

Date	Work hrs/week	Leisure hrs/day (averaged for year, including vacation)
1920	49·7	5·7
1930	45·9	6·4
1940	44·0	6·7
1950	40·0	7·4
1960	37·5	7·8

Source: S. V. Scheider, The meaning of leisure in an industrial society. In *Recreation in Wildland Management* University of California, Extra-Mural Forestry Field School 1962.

In Britain, the standard working week for male manual workers fell from 44·6 hours in 1950 to 40·5 hours in 1968 and in the same period the percentage of them having over two weeks' annual holiday with pay rose from 2·0 to 44.[25]

The recent situation is summed up in Table 1.4, from a Danish source, which gives for slightly different dates (mostly 1964–6) the relevant figures.

This table provides a standard against which to measure progress towards the forty-hour week declared by ILO in 1962 to be the desired goal for its member states (Recommendation 116). A number of countries have already achieved this and few are far from it; only two have a forty-eight hour level which the ILO Recommendation regards as the absolute maximum. Doubtless in countries not included in this list, there are ILO member-states who do not conform.

The daily hours of work, the annual holiday and the occasional free days mean that individuals are now free to plan a very different time-budget from that which was common earlier in the century. In 1900, Clawson reports,[26] 26·5 per cent of the time of US citizens could be classed as leisure (time after work, sleep, housekeeping and personal care); by 1950 this proportion had risen to 34 per cent and is likely to rise to 38 per cent by 2000 (Figure 1). In Britain, the 1967 proportion is about 31 per cent.[27]

The pattern of leisure that is developing seems to be common to most north Atlantic countries. Daily after-work or after-school

[25] Countryside Commission, *Digest of Countryside Recreation Statistics* (London 1969), Table 1.3.

[26] M. Clawson, *Land and Water for Recreation* (Chicago 1963), p. 5.

[27] BTA-Keele University, Pilot National Recreation Survey, Report 1 (1967), pp. 25–6.

Table 1.4 Working hours and holidays

Country	Normal weekly working hours	Yearly number of holidays	Yearly number of free days (week-days or Holy days)
Denmark	42·5	18	9–10
England	40–42·5	12	6
Netherlands	45	12	7
USA	40	6–24	6–8
Finland	40–45	18	12
Sweden	43·3	24	11
Norway	42·5	24	10
Belgium	42–45	18	10
W. Germany	40–42	15–18	10–12
France	40	18	5–10
Italy	44–45	12	16
Luxembourg	42·5–44	18	10
Iceland	44	18	?
Ireland	48	12	6
Spain	44	7–12	13
Switzerland	44–46	12–24	6–8
Australia	40	18	10
Israel	47	12–18	9–11
Japan	44–48	6–20	?
USSR	41	15–24	?

Source: Arbejdsministeriet Denmarks: *Arbejdstid og Ferie*, 1968, p. 36. Similar figures (for males only) can be found in the UN *Statistical Yearbooks*.

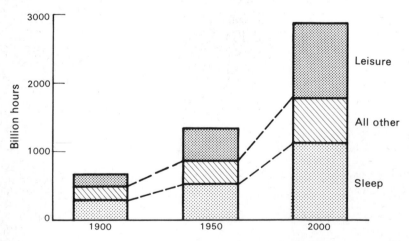

Figure 1 A national time budget for the USA, 1900–2000, showing the increased availability of leisure time (1 billion =1000 million).
Source: M. Clawson, *Land and Water for Recreation*, p. 4.

leisure is currently least important for rural recreation but its contribution is growing, especially with increase in second-car ownership; weekend and special holiday leisure is extremely important and contributes substantially to rural recreation; annual holiday leisure is also very important though this may be modified because it is the time for travel abroad when urban leisure may form a large component of the tourism. Since summer vacations are often within a short space of time, usually in July and August, however, the concentration imposes a strain on resources comparable to that on fine weekends. Forecasts of work and leisure suggest a continuation of present trends. Sweden expects a forty-hour week in the 1970s, with at least four weeks' vacation;[28] in the USA, projections suggested by the ORRRC in 1962 are given in Table 1.5.

Table 1.5   Projected working hours and holidays

Year	Weekly working hours	Weeks holiday	Holidays
1976	35·4	2·8	8·5
2000	30·7	3·9	10·1

Source: ORRRC Report No. 23, Projections to the years 1976 and 2000, Part II, 1962, p. 59.

In Japan, less leisure has been expected by both industrial and white-collar workers, but the national trend is inexorably downwards: the average monthly working hours for the nation in 1955 was 194·8, which had become 187·7 by 1970. Nevertheless, in 1968 89·2 per cent of the total working population received only one day off per week, 5·5 per cent had one-and-a-half days and only 2·8 per cent took two days. No employment category had more than 3·6 per cent achieving a two days off level. Likewise, only 4·4 per cent of the working population had a summer vacation of six days or more in 1968; the modal category was two days, with 37·4 per cent.[29]

[28] H. Sehlin, 'The importance of open-air recreation', First AIT-Congress on Leisure and Tourism, Rotterdam, 1966, Theme 1, Report 1.

[29] H. K. Nishio, 'The changing Japanese perspectives and attitudes towards leisure', Humanitas 3 (1972), pp. 367–88. See also the statistical compilations in Yoka ni Kansura yoron Chosa (Public Inquiry into Leisure, 1971; Office of the Prime Minister, Tokyo, 1972), and the data abstracted from a White Paper of the Japanese Ministry of Trade and Industry ('The present status of and the future prospects for leisure in Japan') in Japan Times (14 February 1973), p. 14.

Unless considerable shifts in social patterns are made, the incidence of leisure is not likely to be changed: merely intensified. The staggering of annual holidays is a constant issue (as are hours of work) but little seems to happen since the rock of the schools' summer vacation seems immovable. Two other trends are however worthy of note. The first of these is the move to a four-day working week, notably in the USA and Canada; in the former, some 500 firms were on this system in 1972.[30] Strongest in the middle-grade office-based occupations, the resulting pattern allows very little or no leisure on working days but compensates for such deprivations by yielding a three-day weekend as the norm; this can expand into a four-day holiday when statutory days-off occur. Acceptance of a 12–15 hour working day is in general high but experience of this pattern is as yet too limited to suggest whether it is the forerunner of a universal pattern. A variant, in which individual workers choose their own hours of work within broad company outlines ('flextime' in English, *gleitende Arbeitszeit* in German) is also popular among those firms,

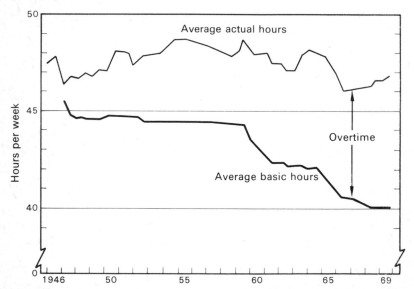

Figure 2 Average actual hours and normal basic hours per week in the UK 1946–69, for adult male manual workers.
Source: J. Gretton, 'The hours we work', *New Society*, 7 January 1971, p. 15.

[30] J. A. Patmore, personal communication.

mostly in the service sector, which have adopted or experimented with it. A second trend is an increase in overtime hours offered by employers to industrial and manual workers (Figure 2) and so affluence is taken in the form of increased earnings rather than more leisure.[31] Thus over the last 25 years the average number of hours actually worked has remained constant at 47 in Britain, 45 in the Netherlands and less than 45 in West Germany, France and Italy.[32]

(b) Affluence

The basic richness of the north Atlantic countries is demonstrated in Table 1.6. For the present purpose, however, the relevant part of the richness is the disposable income: what is left after necessities have been met, which can be given over to such things as leisure pursuits. Most recreation requires the expenditure of some money, either directly, as for equipment, or indirectly, as for food and drink *en route*. Table 1.7 shows the increase in disposable personal income in the USA and its forecasted level for 1976.

---

[31] Although the British national average in 1963 was 42, there was a large group working over 45 hours (BTA-Keele University, *op. cit.*, p. 30):

Actual hours	% adults
35	17
35–9	10
40	14
40–5	16
45	35

There was also a difference between types of employment:

Average actual hours worked		
Manual	Executive	Other
44	41	37

The average projection for 2000 is 30 hours.

In the US, for 1960 (ORRRC Report 23, *Projections to the years 1970 and 2000*, p. 72, Table B-28):

Actual work-week	Hours
Professional and technical	38·5
Clerical	36·0
Operatives	38·2
Farmers	44·5
Labourers	34·2
Average	38·5

[32] J. Gretton, 'The hours we work', *New Society* (7 January 1971), pp. 15–17.

Table 1.6　　Per capita GNP (mostly 1970 data; US dollars)

Western countries		Socialist countries		Non-Western countries	
Canada	3700	USSR	1790	Brazil	420
Denmark	3190	Czechoslovakia	2230	Nigeria	120
UK	2270	Hungary	1600	Indonesia	80
Netherlands	2430	Poland	1400	India	110
USA	4760	Rumania	930	Iraq	320
				Japan	1920

Source: Population Reference Bureau: *World Population Data Sheet—1973.*

Table 1.7　　Disposable personal income, USA

Billions (=000 mill.) 1959 dollars

1946	1950	1957	1976
222·48	246·90	386·00	702·50

Source: ORRRC Report 23, *Projections to the years 1976 and 2000,* 1962, Table F.15, p. 418.

Within the disposable category, expenditure on recreation as a whole appears to vary only within the 4–7 per cent level and is surprisingly constant for all income levels.[33] Definition makes difficult the separation of rural recreation expenditure but it appears that in the USA there is a steeper rise in percentage spent on rural recreation than recreation in general (Figure 3).[34] The World War Two period and the recession of the 1950s are obviously exceptions to the trends. In Sweden, total consumption was 45,000 million Kr in 1962, and of this 13,000 million was on leisure-time consumption;[35] the amount of consumption rose by 45 per cent during 1945–62. In Canada, the average expenditure per family in 1969 on travel, tourism and rural recreation was $1158 out of a net income before taxes of $8026.[36] The sum includes travel abroad and car purchase as well as the recreation activities discussed in this book. If only those items directly related to rural recreation (thus excluding autos) are included, the sum spent is roughly $142 (1·8 per cent of income) which suggests an under-calculation.

[33] Alfred Politz Research Inc., *Life Study of Consumer Expenditures—A Background for Marketing Decisions* (New York 1957), vol. 1.
[34] M. Clawson and J. L. Knetsch, *op. cit.,* p. 107.
[35] H. Sehlin, *op. cit.,* p. 1.
[36] Statistics Canada, *Travel, Tourism and Outdoor Recreation. A Statistical Digest* (Ottawa 1972), Table 9.8A.

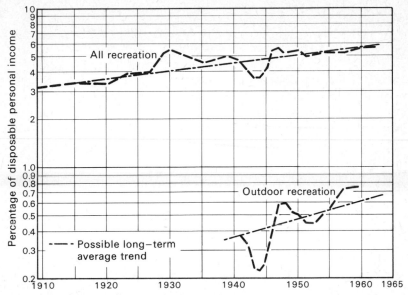

Figure 3 Percentage of disposable personal income for all recreation and for outdoor recreation in the USA, 1909–62.
Source: M. Clawson and J. L. Knetsch, *Economics of Outdoor Recreation,* p. 107.

Nobody expects that the rate of expenditure on leisure activities will do anything other than rise. In Britain, for example, real income per head in 1985 was expected to be 175 per cent of the 1960 figure, and disposable personal income at 1970 prices rose in the UK from £19,710 million in 1951 to £35,131 million in 1971.[37] Senge forecast[38] that per capita income in Japan would rise from a 1965 level of $690 to $1500 in 1975 and $2500 in 1985, but as Table 1.6 shows, the 1970 level was already $1658. Actual leisure expenditure rose from 19·2 per cent of total expenditure in 1965 to 22·7 per cent in 1969.[39] Here, as in the Western countries, continual rises are forecast, war, monetary system collapse and ecocatastrophe permitting.

[37] T. L. Burton and G. P. Wibberley, *Outdoor Recreation in the Countryside,* Wye College Studies in Rural Land Use, Report 5 (1965), p. 39; Department of the Environment, *Report of the National Park Policies Review Committee* (London 1974), p. 124.

[38] T. Senge, 'The planning of National Parks in Japan and other parts of Asia', in J. G. Nelson and R. C. Scace (eds.), The Canadian National Parks (Calgary 1969), pp. 706–21.

[39] H. K. Nishio, *loc. cit.* He also quotes absolute figures in Yen which are in the magnitude of 10⁵ and hence seem rather low.

17

(c) Mobility

As far as rural recreation in north Atlantic countries is concerned, possession of a private motor vehicle is a paramount factor in participation (Table 1.8). In Eastern Europe and Japan, public transport is still the most important conveyer of recreationists but in the West the outdoors is visited largely in the company of an individual's internal combustion engine. The car is dominant but in Holland and to a lesser extent in Denmark the power-assisted bicycle (*hulpmotor* or *bromfiets* in Dutch) is important as well. Elaborations of increases in numbers which may not be very accurate are not particularly helpful here since they all tend in the same direction: to the point where ownership will be so widespread that only those who never share in economic growth such as the old and the indigent will be debarred from rural recreation for this reason: it simply will not be considered as a factor in demand changes,[40] although such reckonings always omit the needs of the young without access to private cars. In terms of impact on resources, of course, it will be a considerable influence and later reference will be made to problems thus created. Of all the three factors of leisure, affluence and mobility, this one is most likely to change radically, due to technological innovation: the gasoline engine may be a museum-piece within the span of projections now being made.

Table 1.8   Passenger cars in use (thousands)

	1953	1963	1970	persons per car 1970
Canada	2,513·8	4,788·9	6,602·2	3·03
Denmark	157·5	605·0	1,076·1	4·52
Great Britain	2,797·7	7,482·6	11,666·0	4·62
Netherlands	187·6	865·5	2,500·0	4·58
USA	46,460·1	68,683·0	88,840·5	2·28
Japan	114·7	1,234·0	8,779·0	10·18

Source: United Nations Statistical Yearbook *1971*, 1972, Table 148.

[40] In ORRRC Report 20, *Participation in Outdoor Recreation* (Washington 1962), only 5 per cent of respondents said that the lack of a car prevented their taking part. For a British view, see J. M. Hall, 'Leisure motoring in Great Britain: patterns and policies', *Geographia Polonica* 24 (1972), pp. 211–25.

3.4 RURAL RECREATION AS A FACET OF LEISURE

As hinted in Figure 1, open-air recreation in the countryside is only one of the possible uses of leisure time. The home and the environs of the place of residence compete for time and for money too. We have seen that rural recreation in the USA seems to account for 4–7 per cent of disposable income; here we shall briefly consider its role in disposable time. The Outdoor Recreation Resources Review Commission background study suggests that about one-fifth of leisure time in the USA is spent this way (Table 1.9). The absolute figures show, however, that 21 per cent of weekday leisure only amounts to forty-five minutes and even with American standards of mobility, little enough activity can be undertaken in that time.

Table 1.9   Leisure spent on rural recreation (USA June 1961)

	Weekday	Weekend	Public Holiday
Percentage	21	29	38
Absolute hours (1) Leisure (2) Rural recreation	4·00 0·75	4·75 1·5	5·25 2·0

Source: ORRRC Report 19 *National Recreation Survey*, 1962, Table 4.34, p. 360. Averaged over a year (Table 1.10) the figures are, as might be expected, slightly lower and Clawson and Knetsch suggest that a national figure of 3–4 per cent for the USA is the correct one for rural recreation.[41] In Sweden, people living in towns of population 10,000 and over disclosed that on a year-round basis about 24 per cent of their leisure time was spent on recreation.[42]

Obviously, accurate figures are difficult to obtain and the variables many, although the correspondence between the official US and Swedish figures is remarkable. Whatever the actual amounts, there seems to be considerable potential for growth if the other factors

Table 1.10   Percentage of leisure spent on rural recreation

USA August 1960–July 1961			
All 20	Weekdays 17	Weekends 23	Holidays 24

Source: ORRRC Report 19, *National Recreation Survey*, 1962, Table 5.35, p. 360.

[41] M. Clawson and J. L. Knetsch, *op. cit.*, pp. 24–5.

[42] *Friluftslivet i Sverige* (1964), del I, p. 33. No comparable figures are provided by the BTA-Keele Survey.

concerned in demand permit or encourage a shift from more passive and home/urban-based recreations to open-air rural activities.

3.5 VARIABLES IN DEMAND

We have seen in very general terms that leisure, affluence and mobility are constraints on recreation. It is interesting to examine more closely the effect of these and other factors such as education on demand for recreation at the present time. All factors operate within the context of population: in the west this is rising relatively slowly although with a high population even a small annual increment means a large absolute number. In countries like the Netherlands there is a larger summer influx of visitors who may specifically come for outdoor resources: the inhabitants of the Ruhr, for example, for whom the Dutch coast is the nearest. In 1964, 12·3 million private cars and 1,773 million people entered the Netherlands, of which a large number were doubtless from West Germany.[43] Since demand varies with age, the proportion of young people in the population is important too, although there is evidence from Britain to suggest that it is families with young children and people whose children have grown up that are the major participants in activities such as driving, picnics and walking for pleasure: the teenagers are missing.[44] US evidence shows that income affects participation up to a certain, relatively low, level (Table 1.11), beyond which there is little appreciable effect except for the most expensive activities and the richest people. A similar trend is noted with education: the completion of High School seems to be a significant threshold (Figure 4).

In Britain it was found that, 'the higher the income level, occupational class and educational status of contacts, . . . the greater the importance of the "active" recreations.'[45] Car-ownership outside North America is still a sector with opportunity for growth; public transport is little used for outdoor recreation in Britain but appears to be more so on the Continent: in Holland the division of those going into the country was car 50 per cent, public transport 7 per cent (the bicycle and moped account for the rest).

[43] A. Haulot, 'Évolution et prévisions du mouvement touristique dans les régions tempérées', IUCN 10th Technical Meeting, Lucerne 1966, *Towards a New Relationship of Man and Nature in Temperate Lands* (Morges 1967), pp. 60–71.

[44] J. Furmidge, 'Planning for recreation in the countryside', *J. Town Planning Inst.* 55 (1969), pp. 62–7.

[45] BTA-Keele University, *op. cit.*, Report 1, p. 49.

Table 1.11   Family income and selected recreation activities, USA, 1965

Income group	Percentage of all participants in activity													
	Bicycling	Outdoor games, sports	Fishing	Canoeing	Sailing	Swimming	Water-skiing	Camping	Walking for pleasure	Picnicking	Driving for pleasure	Hunting	Skiing	% respondents in income category
<$3,000	11	9	13	3	2	8	5	6	14	13	13	14	4	19·0
$3–6,000	27	27	29	24	12	27	24	28	27	29	29	34	18	29·0
$6–8,000	21	20	19	23	17	21	16	23	19	20	19	20	17	18·0
00–10,000	10	14	12	10	17	10	10	14	12	12	12	0	11	10 0
$10–15,000	18	19	17	21	26	19	23	17	17	16	17	14	26	14·0
$15–25,000	5	6	5	11	13	6	8	6	6	5	5	4	14	4·5
$25,000 +	2	2	2	1	7	2	3	2	1	1	1	1	5	1·5
Other	3	3	3	4	6	4	5	4	4	4	4	4	5	4·0

Source: BOR, The 1965 Survey of Outdoor Recreation Activities, 1972. Ch. 5 and Table A, p. 52.

3.6 PARTICIPATION IN RURAL RECREATION

The integration of all these variables is the rate of participation: this is usually measured from a home survey by post or interview, and so is a sample from which the rate for the population is calculated. Absolute numbers at a particular site are not relevant at this particular time. The data from different countries are not, of course, comparable since different sampling standards and different recreation categories may be used.

(a) Relative popularity of different activities in Britain

A good deal of research on demand, both by means of home interviews and on-site questionnaires, is currently being conducted. No large body of data, nationally applicable, have yet been assembled, and so there is no sophisticated analysis of demand patterns for the present or as a basis for projections. A comprehensive body of information is the survey carried out by the British Travel Association and Keele University[46] by means of a household interview of 3167 respondents. The survey included indoor recreation as well as outdoor pursuits. Thirty activities were ranked and the most popular, in order, were team games, swimming, cycling, athletics, tennis, camping and hiking (Table 1.12). All these are relatively inexpensive and many of them continue interests established during the school years. This trend may well be intensified now that so many

[46] Ibid., p. 49.

21

Table 1.12 Great Britain: participation in recreation 1960–64 and 1965

Activity	Rank	% Reporting participation 'at least once', 1960–65	% Participation in 1965
Swimming	1	10	11
Inland sailing	2*	6	3
Camping	2 =	6	4
Fishing	2 =	6	5
Cycling	5 =	5	2
* Tennis	5 =	5	4
Hiking	5 =	5	5
† Bowls	5 =	5	2
Sea sailing	5 =	5	3
* Team games	10 =	4	4
* Skating	10 =	4	1
† Golf	10 =	4	3
* Athletics	13 =	2	1
Riding	13 =	2	1
Hill walking, climbing	13 =	2	1
Natural history	13 =	2	2
* Motor sports	13 =	2	
Youth hostelling	18 =	1	
Sub-aqua sports	18 =	1	sample not
Winter sports	18 =	1	significant
* Archery	18 =	1	

* Is likely to have a large urban-based component
† Not in the scope of this book

Sources: BTA-Keele University, *Pilot National Recreation Survey,* Report 1, 1967, Table 1.4, p. 18; and Report 2, 1969, table 5.1, p. 26.

education authorities maintain outdoor centres in the wilder parts of Britain. It is a curious reflection on the survey that although such eclectic sports as go-karting (which only 1 per cent of the sample had ever experienced)[47] were included, driving for pleasure and picnics were not. It is worth pointing out that during 1960–64, the, most popular activity, swimming, was reported by only 10 per cent of the sample, and thus all other activities were carried out by smaller numbers of people.[48] Within the national sample, regional variations can be detected, leading to certain 'regional specializations'[49] in participation in rural recreation. Dwellers in metropolitan England and in south and west England, for example, report above average participation in camping and fishing (not necessarily carried out in

[47] BTA-Keele University, *op. cit.,* Report 1, p. 9.
[48] *Ibid.,* p. 18.
[49] BTA-Keele University, *op. cit.,* Report 2, Table 5.2, pp. 30–31.

their region of residence, presumably), and the north shows an above average interest in hill-climbing and walking, hiking and sailing, while being below the national average for most other activities. The differences can be quite large (for example, deviations of +90 per cent and −75 per cent from the national average are recorded) and probably reflect a combination of the availability of suitable environments and the differences in demand in different parts of Britain.

The material allows a rough estimate of trends as expressed by statements of intention to participate: rapidly climbing in popularity are winter sports, archery, rallying or motor-racing, salt-water sailing, golf and riding. A moderate rise is shown by inland sailing and fishing, and a moderate drop by youth hostelling, hiking and tennis. A considerable fall is suffered by team games, cycling and athletics, whereas a large group, including swimming, camping, hill-walking appear to remain static.[50] Since this measures future aspirations against past experience, it is an extreme comparison and not one which can be used with confidence for planning ahead. The ownership of recreational equipment is very clearly related to income, which would suggest that as this level rises, a strong increase in rural recreation demand is to be expected. This is provided that extra free time is spent on rural recreation as distinct from other leisure pursuits, or even on leisure at all, rather than in seeking overtime working or another job, a social characteristic which shows some regional variation: 12 per cent of northern workers in a survey were reported as desiring more overtime, compared with only 5 per cent in the Midlands and 7 per cent in metropolitan England.[51]

As elsewhere, rural recreation is only a minority use of total leisure, since activity in and around the home occupies most spare time. Sillitoe notes that all rural occupations amounted to 23 per cent of leisure for men and 16 per cent for women, figures which fluctuate through the year and during the life cycle.[52] However, the cumulative picture is firstly that there is a great potential for growth and secondly that small increases in the frequency of use will generate considerable increase in the demand, so that many more facilities

[50] BTA-Keele University, *op. cit.*, Report 1, p. 20.
[51] J. Gretton, *loc. cit.*
[52] K. K. Sillitoe, *Planning for Leisure*, Government Social Survey Report SS388 (London 1969), pp. 37–9; BTA-Keele University, *op. cit.*, Report 2, Table 4.4, p. 25.

23

will come under considerable pressure, especially at summer weekends.[53]

J. F. Wager has compiled a table of 'known demands for recreation',[54] which is really more a table of consumption since it measures the rise or fall in the numbers of participants during a decade (Table 1.13). The categories of this report do not of course coincide with

Table 1.13   Participation in rural recreation

Changes in 1954–64	
Main holidays in Britain	+11%
Additional holidays in Britain	+200%
Sailing	+80% membership in clubs, 50,000 people 1,280 clubs
Mountaineering	c. 30,000 attend courses each year
Cycling	−50% 35,000 serious cyclists
Skiing	+220% 100,000 ski in Britain. Increase 10% p.a.
Riding	+130% 150,000 ride.
Camping and caravanning	+370% membership of national club, 240% increase in caravan members.
Fishing	+50% 3 million participate.
Nature study	+257% membership of RSPB. Council for Nature has 100,000 members of affiliated bodies.

Source: J. F. Wager, 'Known demands for outdoor recreation', in *The Countryside in 1970*, Proceedings of the 2nd Conference, 1965, Report 6: 'Outdoor recreation: active and passive', pp. 6.16–6.18.

those of the BTA survey, but there appears to be little contradiction between them. The Wager figures suggest rather more strongly than those of the BTA the burgeoning demand for certain activities, and they are confirmed by the Countryside Commission's digested statistics on participation, some of which are presented in Table 1.14. The figures for future car ownership suggest that by 1980 car ownership will have doubled from its 1968 level, to 20 million vehicles.[55]

The only countryside resources which are likely to undergo relative decline, according to Burton,[56] are rambling and cycling, and

[53] J. A. Patmore, *Land and Leisure in England and Wales* (Newton Abbott 1970), pp. 49–50.
[54] *The Countryside in 1970*, Proceedings of the 2nd Conference (London 1965), Report 6: 'Outdoor recreation: active and passive'.
[55] Countryside Commission, *Digest of Countryside Recreation Statistics* (London 1969), p. 5.
[56] T. L. Burton, 'The shape of things to come', in T. L. Burton (ed.), *op. cit.*, p. 266.

it may be noted that these are in general low impact activities which do not at present make heavy demands upon the available resources with the exception of the most highly popular walking tracks, such as Sty Head Pass in the Lake District National Park. But even a relative decline will most likely mean an absolute increase.

Table 1.14   Participation in rural recreation: changes 1950–68

	1950	1960	1965	1968
Number of visitors to ancient monuments (thousands)	5,762*	6,844	8,907	10,808
Membership of the National Trust	25,000	95,000	155,000	160,000
Membership of County Naturalists' Trusts	825	3,006	—	33,272
Membership of the Camping Club	13,800	52,000	91,500	120,000
Membership of the Caravan Club	11,000†	44,000‡	—	95,276
Membership of the Ramblers' Association	4,600**	11,300	13,771	17,193
Number of clubs affiliated to the British Mountaineering Council	36**	92	135	152

* 1954 figure   † 1951 figure   ‡ 1961 figure   ** 1948 figure
Source: Countryside Commission, Digest of Countryside Recreation Statistics, 1969, Table 2.2.

Although no good bases exist from which to project demand, there can be no doubt that it will be heavy.[57] The social factors underlying demand are without doubt going to be in a situation of explosive potential, and the rate of annual increase of demand over the next 40 years is likely to be more than the 2·8 per cent forecast quoted by Rubenstein and Speakman,[58] and nearer to the BOR's forecasts for the USA of 3·5 per cent over the same period. Indeed, since Britain does not appear to be very far along the road of participation in rural recreation activities, it could be argued that an even higher rate may be likely over any period in which the economic situation allows a resumption of a range of consumer expenditure. Precise prediction of either the growth of leisure time or the use made of it is impossible but there is a clear indication of the general direction for the

[57] Ibid., pp. 242–68.
[58] D. Rubinstein and C. Speakman, Leisure, Transport and the Countryside, Fabian Research Series 277 (London 1969).

near future and it contains no assurance that the increasing demand for leisure facilities in the countryside is a transient phase.[59]

(b) Relative popularity of different activities in Canada

A nation-wide survey for Canada yielded the results shown in Table 1.15. Only 10 per cent of the 5992 Canadians of 18 years and older reported no participation in any of the activities listed.[60] The classification has some very fine distinctions, for example, between bird-watching and nature study, but the possible overlaps such as between driving and looking at scenery make it a little difficult to use. The summer cottage is not mentioned unless the 'relax and get away from it all' category includes this activity. The report draws attention to the popularity of the 'casual' recreations which require little preparation or equipment.

Table 1.15   Canada: adults participating in rural recreation 1966–7

Activity	% participating away from urban areas	Rank	Total (%) participation all areas	Rank
Just driving around	47	1	52	1
Relax and get away from it all	39	2 =	44	2
Picnics	39	2 =	42	3
Looking at scenery	35	4	37	5
Swimming	34	5	39	4
Seeing new places	29	6	31	6
Fishing	26	7	27	7
Photography	16	8	18	8
Visits to historic sites	14	9 =	16	9
Power boating	14	9 =	15	10
Tent camping	13	11 =	14	11 =
Hunting	13	11 =	14	11 =
Hiking	11	13	14	11 =
Boating (excluding canoeing and power boating)	7	14 =	8	14
Water-skiing	7	14 =	7	15 =
Trailer camping	6	16 =	7	15 =
Power tobogganing	6	16 =	7	15 =
Nature study	6	16 =	6	18 =
Snow-skiing	6	16 =	6	18 =
Canoeing	5	20	5	20
Climbing	4	21	4	21 =
Bird-watching	3	22	4	21 =

Source: Canadian Facts Co. Ltd, *Park Visits and Outdoor Activities of Canadians,* 1967.

No survey comparable to the ORRRC or Swedish surveys have been carried out, but the similarities of culture with the USA are

[59] J. A. Patmore, *op. cit.,* p. 16.
[60] Canadian Facts Co. Ltd, *Park Visits and Outdoor Activities of Canadians* (Ottawa 1967).

probably such that most of the ORRRC work, and subsequent Bureau of Outdoor Recreation predictions, apply. Modifications for level of income doubtless have to be applied, but as far as tastes go, there is probably no great difference, and large numbers of people cross the border both ways in search of recreation. At the outset, it must be stressed that most of Canada's population lives within a short distance of the USA border and so may seek some of its recreation there and likewise the mid-west and New York State, for example, contribute a great number of participants to Canadian recreation. This is particularly noticeable in second home ownership on the proximal parts of the Canadian Shield, and in such areas as the north-east corner of Lake Erie which functions as a resort area for Buffalo, NY.

As Table 1.21 shows, Canadian and US participations show the same order of magnitudes, with a slight Canadian edge for active sports such as sailing, skiing and hiking. The data from a 1966–7 Survey[61] confirm the general trends of North American activity in this field. The most common rural leisure activities are the casual ones: driving, looking at scenery, and the 'relax and get away from it all' category used in the Survey—in which 44 per cent of the adult Canadians (n = 4992) participated. A 40 per cent participation rate was achieved by picnics and swimming and the active recreations fell clearly into a range of 4–8 per cent participation by adults.[62] Fishing is predominantly a male occupation, being done by about one-third of the men; and power-boating is an activity of some 15 per cent overall.

Later statistics (Table 1.16) show consistent increases during the period 1967–9, and there is little reason to think that any levelling-off has subsequently been experienced, except perhaps in snow-mobiling, where the build up of dealers' inventories and cutbacks in production during 1972–3 suggest that saturation has been reached. Tent camping is declining because of the popularity of trailers and motor homes.

Some regional variations in participation are evident (Table 1.17), though not perhaps on as large a scale as might be expected. The economic nature of the Atlantic Provinces shows in its generally

---

[61] *Ibid.*

[62] 'Adults' were defined in this survey (see footnote 60 above) as people over 18 years; this seems a curious cut-off level, since it excludes a large group who might be expected to be important in the active recreations.

Table 1.16 Percentage of Canadians participating in rural recreation, selected activities (persons over 18 participating at least once in year; NWT and Yukon excluded)

Activity	1967	1969
Swimming	39	44
Power-boating	15	19
Canoeing	5	8
Sailing	8	3
Water-skiing	7	7
Skiing	6	7
Snow-mobiling	7	14
Fishing	27	n.a.
Hunting	14	13
Tent camping	14	12
Trailer camping	7	6
Climbing	4	5
Hiking	14	37
Driving for pleasure	52	67
Sightseeing	31	43
Picnics	42	54
Relax and get away from it all	44	n.a.
Looking at scenery	37	n.a.

Source: Statistics Canada, Travel, Tourism and Outdoor Recreation. A Statistical Digest, 1972, Table 8.1.

Table 1.17 Regional variations in Canada; selected activities, 1969 (percentage of persons over 18 participating at least once in year; NWT and Yukon excluded)

Activity	Atlantic Provinces	Quebec	Ontario	Prairies	BC	Metropolitan Montreal, Toronto, Vancouver
Picnics	50	48	56	58	58	55
Tent camping	11	13	10	13	14	12
Trailer camping	4	5	4	8	7	6
Swimming	14	14	23	17	24	22
Hiking	28	41	39	28	45	47
Snow-skiing	4	8	9	4	5	9
Hunting	15	12	10	15	16	7

Source: Statistics Canada, Travel, Tourism and Outdoor Recreation. A Statistical Digest, 1972, Table 8.1.

lower rates, as does Ontario in its high levels of participation. Elsewhere, variations are small (although the relatively poor skiing facilities in the prairies are manifest) and conform to general expectations such as the lower number of hunters in the big cities and the popularity of swimming therein: some of this activity may in fact take place within the cities, rather than in the countryside; the statistics do not differentiate.

Canada being the size that it is, there is no doubt that the highest demands for intermediate and resource-based recreation are generated relatively near to population centres. As far as the National Parks are concerned, ready availability to population centres seems to determine the number of visits they receive: thus Banff is visited by about 5 per cent of Canadian adults in the year, but most of these visitors are from the Prairie Provinces and British Columbia and 31 per cent had visited it more than once in the year preceding the survey, which indicates the nature of the demand.

In recent years the visitor numbers, where counted, have increased very rapidly. Since the Parks are not so crowded as those of the US, it may perhaps be thought that the rate of increase is unlikely to level off yet, especially since more and more US visitors are coming to them. So that although there is no base from which to make reasonable predictions about future demand, it is safe to say that it is in an escalatory phase and unlikely to enter an equilibrium state yet. An increase in visits of c. 10–12 per cent p.a., which has characterized recent years in the US and Canada,[63] is not an unreasonable thing to expect during the next few years.

(c) Relative popularity of different activities in Sweden and Denmark

The majority of the data in the Outdoor Recreation Report for Sweden are for a sample of 2700 dwellers in towns of over 10,000 people and for adults aged 18–65. The high rates of participation (Table 1.18) must also be seen in the context of a country where 15–20 per cent of the population were spending most of their annual holiday abroad. In Sweden about 20 per cent of the population stated that rural recreation was their most important leisure time activity; 25 per cent were indifferent to open-air activities.

No surveys on demand have been carried out in Denmark, nor are there any systematic data about participation rates. The trends probably follow those of the West in general and perhaps Sweden more particularly. The possession of a private car is one of the first

[63] L. Brooks, 'The forces shaping demand for recreation space in Canada', in *Resources for Tomorrow* (Ottawa 1961), vol. 2, pp. 957–68. Apart from the visitor figures to National Parks, no other time-series statistics on demand or participation are given. A press release of 1967 by the Minister of Indian Affairs and Northern Development gives a 15 per cent rise in National Park campers 1965–6; and in 1966–7 numbers of visitors to the Atlantic Parks rose by 17 per cent.

priorities in spending disposable income but after that a private summer cottage on the coast ranks highest: usually before items of consumer hardware. This is thus an outstanding feature of the Danish demand pattern to which special attention will be given. In this feature, Denmark and Sweden are very similar: the second home is a characteristic of Swedish rural recreation patterns also.[64]

Table 1.18   Sweden: participation in rural recreation, 1963

Activity	Percentage of population taking part
Swimming	65
Walking	73
Fishing	37
Wood walking (e.g. hiking)	79
Sailing or motorboating	24
Cycling	26
Ball games	26
Car driving	73
Camping	19
Running, orienteering, gymnastics	6
Skiing	41
Skating, ice hockey	19

Source: *Friluftslivet i Sverige*, Del 1, 1964, pp. 46–7.

Nevertheless, in spite of a relatively low population the pressures for other forms of recreation are building up. A significant element is the desire of the urban dweller (74 per cent of the population) to be in open country. The rural landscape in which he wishes to motor or walk or sit must not only be varied but also have a significant content. The significance depends upon expectation—people must find familiar elements which they expect. As Bjerke puts it,[65]

The individual forms his own impression of the Danish landscape, and this impression is influenced by impressions from the landscape of his childhood and later connections. . . . The impression of landscape formed by an individual rests upon past experience, and often also upon knowledge of the dynamic composition in what was experienced. Expectations are thus generally limited to existing landscape forms and often restricted, when compared to

[64] *Friluftslivet i Sverige* (1964).
[65] S. Bjerke, *Landscape Planning and Nature Parks* (mimeo, Copenhagen 1967).

the expectations an individual may have towards landscapes in other countries.

This has led, *inter alia*, to a strong movement for the preservation of antiquities as part of the 'expected landscape'. In an urban context, old buildings have been reconstructed in a 'living museum' fashion. In Aarhus, 'Den Gamle By' (the Old Town), and in rural areas many monuments are officially scheduled so that they may escape destruction. At Lejre on Zealand a historical-archaeological research centre has an outdoor reconstruction of an Iron Age village which attracts much attention, and a similar museum at Hjerle Heide in Jylland contains material from several prehistoric and later periods. The assembly of museum-parks where 'historical landscape units which will both preserve discrete features and cast them in a context that satisfactorily reveals their historic geographical characteristics,' can be constructed[66] is and no doubt will be, a major recreative focus in the light of the revealed tastes quoted above. It does not mean, however, that increasing recreation pressures, including numerous visitors from Germany, will not impinge heavily on other parts of coast and countryside.

(d) Relative popularity of different activities in the Netherlands

Insights into recreation demand in the Netherlands can be gained from some of the work of the Central Statistical Office although it is not strictly comparable with the US and Swedish studies. However, no special characteristics seem to stand out in the Dutch pattern of demand: as many as 50 per cent in one sample stated a preference for rural recreation on Sundays.[67] This demand is translated into a participation rate of 39 per cent of the population sampled going to rural areas on Sundays; on dry sunny Sundays it was 45 per cent, whereas a rainy day depressed the figure to 30 per cent. On Whit Sunday 1965, even six hours of rain did not stop 59 per cent of the sample going out to the countryside.[68] On Saturdays, the proportion fell to about 10 per cent.[69] About half the people used cars for their recrea-

[66] R. M. Newcomb, 'Geographical aspects of the planned preservation of visible history in Denmark', *Ann. Assn. Amer. Geogr.* 57 (1967), pp. 462–80.

[67] R. Wippler, *Open Air Leisure Activities: the demand for outdoor recreation in the province of Groningen* (1966), p. 14.

[68] Netherlands Ministry of Culture, Recreation and Social Work, *Increased Leisure, What Use is Made of It* (1966), p. 1.

[69] Netherlands Central Statistical Office, *Leisure Activity in the Netherlands*, part 6 (1965), pp. 4–5.

tion and only 7 per cent used public transport.[70] The difference is made up by bicycles and mopeds, both of which limit the range of the recreation seeker. The concentration of demand upon Sundays and holidays is emphasized by the influx of visitors from abroad at these times, especially from Belgium and West Germany.[71] These people doubtless share the general preferences for activities demonstrated by the inhabitants of Groningen Province[72] set out in Table 1.19.

Table 1.19   Groningen: participation in rural recreation, 1966

Activity	Frequency of participation: % of sample		
	Never	1/week	>1/week
Country walks	62	25	13
Cycling	44	34	22
Motoring	29	50	21
Camping or cottage	85	11	4
Outdoor sports	73	9	18
Spectator sports	54	35	11
Pools or beach	51	29	20
Angling	79	14	7
Gardening	18	13	43
Going for walks	24	24	52

Source: R. Wippler: Open air leisure activities: the demand for outdoor recreation in the province of Groningen, pp. 12–13.

The singular features of the recreation scene of the Netherlands are firstly the distribution of population and secondly the relatively short distance at which most of them seek their rural experience. The cities of west Holland—Randstadt Holland—form a densely populated area, and parts of the ring have population densities of over $1000/km^2$, most of it being over $500/km^2$. The open space—mainly polder, dune and river-bottom land—is under considerable pressure from urban-industrial demands. Yet the majority (c. 60 per cent) of urban dwellers want to stay within 20 miles of their homes when on day recreation. This means, especially, that Sunday afternoon is a high peak, since with increased car use (although bicycle and moped account for 30 per cent of Sunday rural recreation transport) the recreation can be made in the afternoon. This is likely to be

[70] Netherlands Central Statistics Office, op. cit.
[71] Ibid.
[72] R. Wippler, op. cit.

intensified in west Holland by a proportion of the 80,000 foreigners making for the Dutch coast on a day-visit, especially those from the Rhine-Ruhr area.[73] Thus west Holland becomes a distinct problem, which will be examined later in the total context of rural recreation in the Netherlands.

The annual vacation adds greatly to the load of recreation areas. In 1960, 5·9 millions spent their holidays in their own country but outside their home towns. Twenty-two per cent of these went to the coast, 49 per cent to the land vacation areas, 4 per cent to the lakes and 25 per cent to the rest of the country, including the cities. The 4 per cent figure seems low in view of the great use and popularity of sailing and boating, but it seems to be in the same order as most Western participation rates. One other recreation which has been investigated is 'Roadside Recreation'. Motorists go into the country-side, park just off the main road (less than 50 per cent sat over 20 m from the road in spite of opportunities to go further) and observe the traffic. Nearly 80 per cent of respondents in a survey had camping gear with them. Eighty per cent of them agreed that theirs was a recreation which was inimical to road safety and to personal health but cognitive dissonance seems to have been strong.[74]

(e) The relative popularity of different activities in the USA

No other country has so thoroughly investigated the participation of its people in rural recreation, and the twenty-seven volumes of the Outdoor Recreation Resources Review Commission (ORRRC)[75] stand as a monument to the seriousness with which the subject is treated at all levels of concern. In connection with the present topic, the final report[76] and the study volume on demand are especially important sources.

The National Recreation Survey,[77] a sample of 16,000 persons

---

[73] The dune-coast between Hoek van Holland and Alkmaar is not spatially closest to, for example, the Ruhr, but the E36 highway links Köln and the Ruhr with Den Haag (The Hague). It is c. 220 km (140 minutes) from Essen to Den Haag.

Of the foreigners camping in the Kennermerduinen National Park in 1959 (33 per cent of the total camper-nights), West Germans comprised 96 per cent (E.C.M. Roderkerk, *Recreatie, Recreatieverzorging en Natuurbescherming in de Kennermerduinen* (Delft 1961), Table XXV, p. 87).

[74] J. C. Heytze, *Recreation on the Roadside*, abstract in English of publication of Sociological Institute of the State University at Utrecht (mimeo, 1965).

[75] ORRRC, *Outdoor Recreation for America* (Washington, DC: 1962) and 27 Study Reports (Washington, DC 1962).

[76] ORRRC, *Outdoor Recreation for America*: Study Report 26, *Prospective Demand for Outdoor Recreation* (Washington, DC 1962).

[77] ORRRC, Study Report 19, *National Recreation Survey* (Washington, DC 1962).

aged 12 or over, indicated about 90 per cent of American adults engaged in some form of outdoor activity during the course of a year. Within this overall statistic, the variation is immense. There are, of course, strong differences by age group but also between white and non-white, city dwellers and rural people, and between regions. North-easterners are especially involved in swimming, skiing and walking; southerners do the most hunting, Lake States folk the most sailing. Inhabitants of the west just do more of everything. All figures for the USA as a whole, therefore, have to be interpreted in the light of these variables.

Before the ORRRC surveys (made in 1960, published 1962), changes in involvement in recreation could only be estimated from a number of indices. Some of these for 1951–9 are given in Table 1.20.

Table 1.20   USA: rural recreation (indices of change, 1951–9)

	% increase over 1951
Visits to National Parks	86
Outboard motors in use	94
Visits to selected recreation areas	143
Intercity travel	46
Fishing licence holders	25
Per capita disposable income	15

Source: ORRRC, Outdoor Recreation for America 1962, Table 3, p. 213.

The high rate of participation estimated for 1960 and later for 1965[78] must therefore be seen in the context of a surging consumption dating at least from 1950. One of the few reliable time-series statistics is visits to National Parks (which all have gates); these are available from 1904 onwards. They show a very vigorous rise from 1920 onwards interrupted only by World War II, so that the rural recreation 'boom' although large in absolute terms cannot be interpreted as a totally recent phenomenon.

In terms of activities, comparable data for two dates exist: 1960 and 1965. The 1960 figures clearly show that 'automobile riding for sightseeing and relaxation' was the most popular activity and one in which 61 per cent of the sample participated during the study period giving rise to 20·73 'activity days' per person aged 12 and over.[79] By 1965, this had fallen in rank, when measured

[78] Bureau of Outdoor Recreation, *Outdoor Recreation Trends* (Washington, DC 1967).
[79] ORRRC, *Outdoor Recreation for America*, Tables 1 and 2.

by the number of summer occasions on which people participated in them—this being the most useful measure for planning.[80] The most popular activity became walking for pleasure and the latest statistics (for 1965) give a slightly different ranking of involvement from the 1960 figures (see Tables 1.20a, 1.21). Most remarkable are the percentage increases for 1960–5 (Table 1.21), which range from 8 per cent (driving for pleasure) to 105 per cent (bicycling), and which average at 64 per cent. Cycling, outdoor games, walking for pleasure, and outdoor concerts and plays were all above this average in their increase.[81] Some changes in reporting bases make comparison with the 1970 figures more difficult,[82] but if comparability is assumed, then a certain downward trend in many activities can be seen (a phenomenon which could of course be due to more accurate collection of statistics and which in a growing population means no lessening of absolute demand), with the exceptions of nature walks, bicycling and camping. Here it may be surmised that the environmentalist movement is producing a shift in tastes, although much of the camping is accompanied by large enough quantities of hardware

Table 1.20a   USA: Number of occasions of summertime participation (million times)

Activity	1960	1965	Increase %
Walking for pleasure	566	1030	82
Swimming	672	970	44
Driving	872	940	8
Outdoor games	474	929	96
Bicycling	228	467	105
Sightseeing	287	457	159
Picnics	279	451	62
Fishing	260	322	24
Outdoor sports events	172	246	43
Boating	159	220	38
Nature walks	98	117	19
Camping	60	97	62
Riding	55	77	16
Water-skiing	39	56	30
Hiking	34	50	47
Outdoor concerts, plays	27	47	74

Source: BOR, Trends in Outdoor Recreation, 1967.

[80] BOR, op. cit., p. 15.
[81] Ibid., p. 19.
[82] BOR, The 1970 Survey of Outdoor Recreation Activities, Preliminary Report (Washington, DC 1972), Table A.

Table 1.21   USA: participation in rural recreation (% population 12 years +
participating)

Activity	1960	1965	1970
Picnics	53	57	48
Driving	52	55	n.a.
Sightseeing	42	49	n.a.
Swimming	45	48	44
Walking for pleasure	33	48	30
Outdoor games	30	38	33
Fishing	29	30	28
Outdoor sports events	24	30	35*
Boating (including sailing and canoeing)	22	24	24
Nature walks	14	14	17
Hunting	13	12	13
Bicycling	9	16	19
Sledding	9	13	n.a.
Outdoor concerts, plays	9	11	see note*
Camping	8	10	20
No participation	n.a.	n.a.	25

* In the 1970 figures this category includes outdoor concerts and plays also.
Sources: BOR, *Outdoor Recreation Trends*, 1967; and *The 1970 Survey of Outdoor Recreation Activities*, Preliminary Report, 1972.

(including the kitchen sink) to make close *rapport* with nature some-what improbable. An interesting statistic is the 25 per cent of the population over 12 years of age who reported no participation in rural recreation.

A much more accurate guide to the relative popularity of summer outdoor activities is given by the figures for the number of occasions in which people participated, so that the inaccuracies which are inherent in the 'at least once' category of frequency employed by so many classifications are eliminated. The figures are given in Table 1.20. Notable in this table is the change in status of driving for pleasure, which has fallen from first place in 1960 to third in 1965, having been overtaken by swimming and walking for pleasure. This may well reflect increased opportunities in the form of pools and trails, and the popularity may have shown a lack of alternative opportunity. Later statistics (Table 1.22) are on a year-round basis and put the playing of outdoor games or sports in first place; since informal games (like the ubiquitous American frisbee-throwing) are included. The same source[83] omits driving for pleasure and its relative status *vis-à-vis* walking cannot be determined. Both walking and

[83] BOR, *op. cit.*, Table B.

swimming remain in positions of eminence, and there is a break of a magnitude of nearly three times before sports events and concerts, fishing, picnics and other less significant recreations. The contrast between days/person and days/participant shown in this table for occupations such as fishing, nature walks, hunting, riding and above all bird-watching emphasize that although these activities are pursued by a relatively small number of people, those that participate are very keen.

Table 1.22   USA total and average days of participation (persons 9 years +, 1970)

Activity	Number of recreation days (000)	Days per person	Days per participant
TOTAL	12,126,000	72	95
Playing outdoor games or sports	2,673,362	16	45
Walking for pleasure	1,860,540	11	37
Bicycling	1,735,916	10	47
Swimming	1,721,996	10	22
Sports events and concerts	628,471	4	11
Fishing	562,052	3	11
Picnicking	542,161	3	7
Birdwatching	432,515	3	58
Boating	421,530	3	10
Camping	397,162	3	11
Nature walks	374,394	2	12
Hunting	216,704	1	10
Horseback riding	207,831	1	13
Wildlife and bird photography	40,048	<0·5	8
Other reported activities	311,321	2	29

Source: BOR, The 1970 Survey of Outdoor Recreation Activities, Preliminary Report, Table B.

Table 1.23 shows the 1965 situation in absolute terms for the whole USA. In somewhat more concise terms, these and later statistics[84] mean that in 1970 three out of every ten persons over 9 years old participated at least once in the 5 most important activities (see Table 1.22), that 20–30 per cent of the population enjoyed

[84] *Ibid.*, p. 1.

fishing, boating, bicycling and camping, and that 10–20 per cent took part in nature walks, hunting and horseback riding.

Table 1.23   USA: rural recreation participation 1965 (million occasions of summer participation)

Activity	Rank	Rank 1960	Million occasions	Occ/capita (total pop)
Walking for pleasure	1	2	1030	51·5
Swimming	2	4	970	48·5
Driving for pleasure	3	1	940	47·5
Outdoor games	4	3	929	46·5
Cycling	5	6	467	23·35
Sightseeing	6	5	457	22·85
Picnics	7	9	451	22·55
Fishing	8	7	322	16·1
Sporting events	9	8	246	12·3
Boating (not canoeing or sailing)	10	11	220	11·0
Nature walks	11	10	117	5·85
Camping	12	14	97	4·85
Riding	13	13	77	3·85
Water-skiing	14	18	56	2·8
Hiking	15	17	50	2·5
Outdoor concerts and plays	16	19	47	2·35

Source: BOR, Outdoor Recreation Trends, 1967, pp. 14–19.

The ORRC and its successor, the Bureau of Outdoor Recreation, have made a number of projections of demand into the future. The basis for projection was twofold: first the present relation between participation rates and socio-economic factors such as age, income and occupation was established; secondly the probable future change of the socio-economic factors was estimated and from this the probable demand established. The major assumption is that the association between socio-economic characteristics and recreation desires established for 1960 will hold good for projection dates such as 1976 and 2000, two years for which BOR has made projections. If this is so, then although the projections may well be wrong, the magnitude of error will be of a different dimension from that which will pertain should the relationships change. Such relativities are much more difficult to predict than variables like population growth (itself subject to considerable forecasting difficulties), income levels and leisure time. As Clawson and Knetsch point out,[85] this type

[85] M. Clawson and J. L. Knetsch, *Economics of Outdoor Recreation*, pp. 130–31.

of analysis is of greatest value if repeated at regular intervals with compatible data.

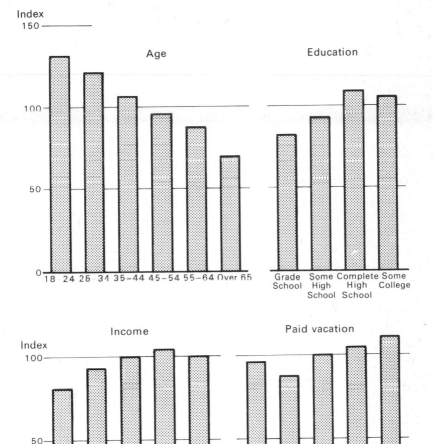

Figure 4   The apparent net effect of socio-economic factors on relative participation in outdoor recreation in the USA.
Source: M. Clawson, *Land and Water for Recreation*, p. 50.

A feature of the ORRRC projections made in 1962 is that they are too low. An overall 20 per cent increase for 1960–5 forecast by the ORRRC in fact came to 51 per cent when it was measured[86]— 4282 million occasions escalated to 6476 million in 1965. On this basis the projected increase for all activities 1960–2000 is 293 per cent, whereas the original ORRRC estimate, assuming the 1960 quality and quantity of facilities on a per capita basis, was 184 per cent.[87] With improved opportunity, a 228 per cent rise was forecast.

There is no reason to suppose, therefore, that the 1965–2000 projections will turn out to be very accurate. It is possible that they will be too low, but on the other hand there may be satiety before those levels of participation are reached: mere extension of some trends would ensure that in the not far distant future every inhabitant spent 365 days/yr engaged in rural recreation. Presumably rates of participation will follow an S-curve, but nobody seems willing to predict when the upper asymptote will be reached.

As a practical matter, resource managers in the USA appear to take it for granted that there is to be increased demand for recreation at any rate over the period for which plans can be made and investment calculated. Some of the ways in which adjustments to this demand are being made will be outlined in the next section.

(f) Comparisons

Meaningful comparisons are very difficult to make since few of the categories employed in the various surveys are discrete, and only the 'per cent participating at least once' measure is common to them all; as we have seen this is not a very satisfactory measure for practical purposes. Some categories which appear to be sufficiently distinct for some comparisons are given in Table 1.24, which is compiled from earlier tables. The remarkable feature of the figures is their homogeneity for any given activity, which suggests that here may be a cultural trait in the forms of preference for outdoor activity. Notable exceptions are the Swedish figures for sailing, skiing and swimming which doubtless reflect a national orientation towards an abundance of water and snow. Apart from driving and sailing, Britain lags behind in most activities. Were it not for the com-

---

[86] BOR, *op. cit.*, p. 7.

[87] *Ibid.*, pp. 4–12. There is a discrepancy between the 187 per cent increase quoted on p. 12 and the 184 per cent printed in Table 23 of *Outdoor Recreation for America*. This is scarcely significant.

parability of those two categories, the validity of the statistics might be thought to be questionable. If these figures really are comparable then it means that for planning purposes, figures from other countries can, with adjustments for local resource opportunities, be used with fair confidence in the absence of nationally-gathered data.

Table 1.24   Comparisons of participation (selected activities: per cent of population sampled)

Activity	USA		Netherlands	Sweden	Canada	GB
	1960	1965	1966	1963	1966–7	1965
Walking for pleasure	33	48	25	73		
Swimming	45	48	29	65	34	11*
Camping	8	10	11†	19	13	4
Sightseeing	42	49			29	
Driving	52	55	50	73	47	56‡
Fishing	29	30	14	37	26	5
Hiking	7	9			11	
Sailing**	2	3		24	7	3
Skiing	2	4		41	6	

* Will include some use of urban facilities
† Includes use of country cottage
‡ An estimate for Whitsun 1963, quoted by T. L. Burton, 'Outdoor recreation in America, Sweden and Britain', Town and Country Planning 34 (1966).
** Not motorized, (Sweden: motorboats included) includes rowing where this is separated.

Rank comparisons can also be made from the statistics already given and a summary of rankings for the most popular activities is given in Table 1.25. This table confirms the scattered evidence of previously discussed tables: that walking for pleasure, swimming and driving form the most popular activities wherever reliable measurements of participation are taken. Outdoor games also come very high and so the relatively informal recreations, as a whole, are the most popular: apart from the car (which may be purchased basically for non-leisure use), little or no equipment is required and relatively little preliminary organization, although to get even two small children organized for a 'drive and walk' afternoon is not a negligible feat of preparation. The recreations requiring expensive equipment all figure lower in ranking lists, with camping as a possible exception.

The patchiness of the data make many comparisons difficult: the British position for sailing seems hard to believe set against the North American figures, but the role of fishing is much more credible. Spectator sports come relatively high in the USA and the Nether-

41

Table 1.25   Comparisons of popularity by rank (selected activities)

Activity	USA 1965	Netherlands 1966	Sweden 1963	Canada 1966–7	GB 1960–4
Driving	3	1	1 =	1	—
Swimming	2	4	3	5	1
Walking for pleasure	1	5	—	—	—
Outdoor games	4	8	—	—	5 = *
Bicycling	5	3	—	—	5 =
Sightseeing	6	—	—	4/6†	—
Picnics	7	—	—	2	—
Fishing	8	6	5	7	2 =
Power boating/sailing	10/—	—	–/6	9/14	—/2‡
Camping	12	7	7	11**	2 =
Water-skiing	14	—	—	14	—
Hiking	15	—	—	13	13††
Skiing/Winter sports	17/—	—	4/–	16/—	—/18
Spectator sports	9	2	—	—	—

* Tennis only
† 'Looking at scenery'/'Seeing new places'
‡ 'Inland sailing'
** Tent camping only, not trailer (=caravan) camping
†† Hill-walking and climbing.

lands, but are not considered further here. Beyond their interest value, comparisons of rank are not very useful for planning.

From the data assembled, a few generalizations can be made in summary:

1 Participation rates for rural recreation activities only rarely involve more than 50 per cent of the population, and only driving for pleasure achieves this.

2 For informal, low equipment cost activities, the rates of participation average at 38 per cent without driving, 44 per cent with motoring; when equipment is a factor as in sailing, skiing and fishing (and the activity may be more structured), the average is at 15 per cent. Hiking is low in cost but high in effort and comes out at 8 per cent. These figures cannot be translated into total participation rates, however, because no idea of the net frequency of involvement is given.

3 Though particular national differences in popularity exist, sufficient similarity is found to suggest that some of the variations in rates of participation are due to 'lag' and lack of opportunity rather than lack of interest in the activity.

4 With the exception of motoring, the most popular recreations are not very demanding on resources. Even with swimming, the facilities required can be very basic: a simple sand-hole and some

toilets will suffice. Moreover they can relatively easily be integrated into multiple-use schemes since few of them—roads and water apart—require exclusive use of large surface areas. On the other hand, sailing and fishing, for instance, are less easy to fit in; skiing presents far less difficulty because of its off-season nature. Of the middle-range popularities, camping (especially trailer (caravan) camping) is probably the most demanding of resources, both natural and financial, in relation to the number of people involved.

5 In view of the growing volume of international travel for recreative purposes, it might be worthwhile to see if definitions of activities, and other measures for collecting data, could be standardized, so that valid international comparisons can be made. At the very least, this should now be possible within the EEC.

3.7 TRENDS AND PROJECTION OF PARTICIPATION AND DEMAND

The reverse of the coin of studies of participation is the observation of the number of visitors to a particular site, from which certain general trends can be ascertained.

The 'explosion' of rural recreation, and the difficulties of measuring visitor numbers, means that few time-series data on recreation use are available, especially for places where records of users are not kept or cannot be kept.. In the latter category is Britain, where only recently have any data on participation and use been collected. Using the numbers of people belonging to clubs and taking part in various activities, Wager has collected some information on the rise in participants during a recent decade (Table 1.26). As in Britain, other European figures are rather scattered and not of great value. In the Netherlands the total number of 'overnights' in Staatsbosbeheer (Forest Service) campgrounds rose from 763,741 in to 1,092,272 in 1966.[88] In the Kennermerduinen National Park the overnights rose from 1000 in 1951 to 105,300 in 1959; day visitors over twelve years rose from 187,000 in 1957 to 256,900 in 1959.[89]

Better time-series data on use are available for parks in North America, especially the National Parks. In the post-1945 period the annual growth rate has been of the order of 10 per cent (see Figure 5). Some activities show even higher climbs—bicycling in the USA is one —and the figures quoted for Britain in Tables 1.26 and 1.27 exceed

[88] Staatsbosbeheer, *Jaarverslag 1966* (Utrecht 1966), p. 65.
[89] E. C. M. Roderkerk, *op. cit.*, p. 57.

Table 1.26   Participation in rural activities (Great Britain: 1954–64)

Activity	Trend	Absolute number 1964
Royal Yachting Association	+80% people in affiliated clubs	500,000
British Cycling Federation	−50% people in affiliated clubs	35,000
National Ski Federation	+220% people in affiliated clubs	100,000 ski in Britain
British Horse Society	+130% people in affiliated clubs	150,000
Youth Hostels Association	+6% members	960,000 overnights
Camping Club of Great Britain and Northern Ireland	+370% members	Estimated 1½ million campers
Caravan Club	+240% members	34,370 own caravans
Anglers' Co-op. Association	+50% people in clubs	3,000,000
Royal Society for the Protection of Birds	+257% members	15,000

These can be roughly related to the 1952–62 increases in demand quoted by Dower in Table 1.27.

Source: J. F. Wager, 'Known demands for outdoor recreation', in The Countryside in 1970, Proceedings of the 2nd Conference, Report 6: 'Outdoor recreation: active and passive', pp. 6.16–6.18.

Table 1.27   Increases in leisure demand (Great Britain: 1952–62 (%))

Value of sports equipment purchased	40
Visitors to National Trust properties	50
Overnight camping in forest parks	130
Overseas visitors to Britain	167
Expenditure on cars and motorcycles	600
Number of sailing dinghies	1200

Source: M. Dower, The Fourth Wave: the challenge of leisure, Architects J., January 1965, p. 124.

the 10 per cent per annum rate, suggesting that Britain is probably at the beginning of an immense surge in demand (Figure 6). The result of the rates of participation for various activities is fully confirmed, therefore, in the amount of use of the resources.

If the principles underlying demand are properly understood then using both types of data, accurate projections of future demand should be possible. There are complicating factors since for example

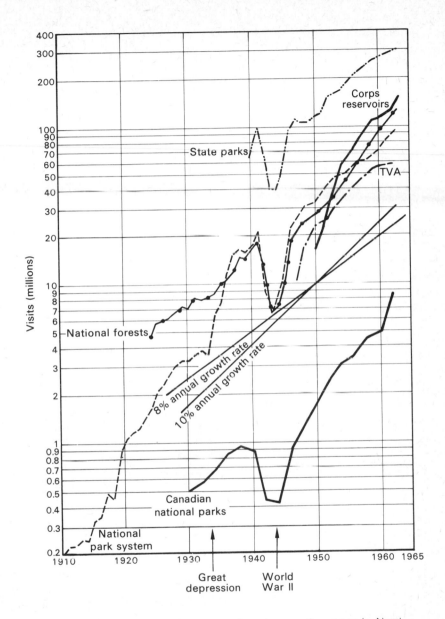

Figure 5 Attendance at major types of rural recreation areas in North America, 1910–62.
Source: M. Clawson and J. L. Knetsch, *Economics of Outdoor Recreation*, p. 44.

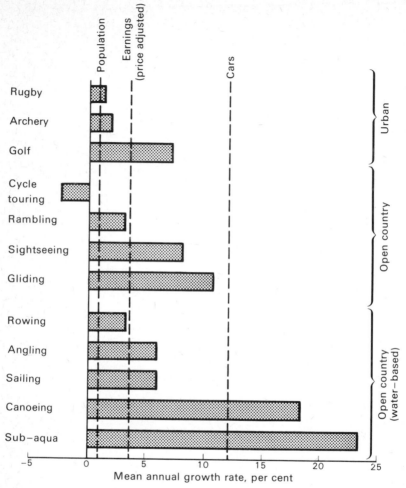

Figure 6 Growth rates for various types of recreation in the UK during the mid-'50s to mid-'60s decade, together with other relevant measures. Cycling may well have picked up again in the early '70s.
Source: J. A. Patmore, *Land and Leisure*, p. 68.

the role of opportunity in stimulating demand is strong but not easily forecast. Basically, two forecasting methods may be used:[90]

[90] This section relies heavily upon M. Clawson and J. L. Knetsch, *op. cit.*, chs. 6 and 7. A concise criticism of demand surveys, together with suggestions for improvement is given by R. Burdge and J. Hendee, 'The demand survey dilemma: assessing the credibility of State outdoor recreation plans', *Guideline* 2 (1972), pp. 65–8. See also E. L. Shafer and G. H. Moeller,

1 *Demand factor extension.* This is based on analysis of the economics of individuals and on the costs involved to them, i.e. money, time and travel; basically, the causal forces of population, leisure, income and mobility and the known relationships between these and participation in open air recreation are extended into the future.

But trends in these basic factors cannot be extrapolated directly into terms of people hammering at the park gates in 1984. New factors and new relationships may become significant, as in the growth of boating because of developments in boat-building techniques. Also although there is a correlation between educational level and participation at present, if the educational level of the whole population rises, will this affect the ratio of participation?

Overall, therefore, there are considerable pitfalls in projecting population, leisure-time and the like and multiplying by the appropriate factor for the relationship with demand.

2 *Trend extension.* This involves the extension of use data for specific areas or types of area into the future. With the US data, simple extension of trend lines, for example, 2000 would involve an average citizen in 150 visits/year to a National Park. Obviously, this method can only be used for short-term projections.

Where actual projections have been made, as by the ORRRC[91] these have been exceeded in the short term:[92] the 1960–5 increase in total number of rural recreation occasions was predicted to be 20 per cent but actually was 51 per cent. On the basis of this, the Bureau of Outdoor Recreation has revised its year 2000 projections for individual activities considerably (Table 1.28); overall a 184 per cent increase is converted to 293 per cent. In view of these obvious deficiencies it is not surprising that efforts to construct more sophisticated models for demand have been made. Clawson[93] has prepared a demand curve for individual facilities which has as its basis the total monetary cost of visiting the area from a number of tributary

'Predicting quantitative and qualitative values of recreation participation', in Northeastern Forest Experiment Station, *Recreation Symposium Proceedings* (Washington, DC 1972), pp. 5–22.

[91] ORRRC, Report 26, *Prospective Demand for Outdoor Recreation*, 1962. The method used was (i) establishment of relationship between socio-economic factors and participation and (ii) projection of socio-economic variables and hence of demand for outdoor recreation.

[92] BOR, *Outdoor Recreation Trends* (1967), pp. 7, 12.

[93] M. Clawson, *Methods of Measuring the Demand for, and Value of, Outdoor Recreation* (Washington, DC 1959).

Table 1.28   Changes in projections (USA per cent increases expected)

Activity	ORRRC 1962 1960–2000	BOR 1967 1960–2000
Walking for pleasure	177	356
Driving for pleasure	154	146
Swimming	243	344
Outdoor games	251	520

Sources: ORRRC, *Recreation for America*, 1962, Table 23; BOR, *Outdoor Recreation Trends*, 1967, pp. 14–15.

zones. A demand schedule is constructed by multiplying these costs by the number of actual visits and this gives the amount of recreation demanded at various prices. Thus the effect of an increase in entrance fees could be predicted. But it cannot be used for new facilities unless comparison with a similar area already in existence were made. Knetsch has elaborated the Clawson model by adding such variables as availability of substitutes and a congestion factor.[94] At this regional level also, the Michigan Department of Conservation has developed, to deal with individual areas and travel in that State, a computerized systems-based model called RECSYS.[95] It uses three basic components: destinations, origins and interconnections and these are linked to resource inventories, use statistics and origin of visitors. A subjective element enters in the assignment of 'attraction indices' for particular recreation areas. This programme can then be used to evaluate new demand patterns resulting from changed circumstances. It is, however, useful only for predicting the results of change (planned or unplanned) and does not evaluate criteria for plans.

It is clear that in recreation, as in most of the social sciences, prediction is essential but difficult. The methods of demand projection chosen will depend upon the extent of data available, the time and money that can be used for collecting new data and the time and money for analysis at the disposal of the commissioning body. In general, it appears that trend projection is the most useful for short-term estimates and for local and regional recreation systems; for

[94] J. L. Knetsch, 'Outdoor recreation demands and benefits', *Land Economics* 34 (1963), pp. 387–96.

[95] *Outdoor Recreation Planning in Michigan by a Systems Analysis Approach, Part I—A Manual for Programme RECSYS, Technical Manual 1* (Michigan Department of Conservation 1966).

long-term and nationwide forecasts the socio-economic based projections, provided the data are adequate, are probably best.

3.8 TIMING OF DEMAND

Collections of data confirm the obvious fact that demand is not evenly spread throughout the year. Apart from the obvious summer/winter dichotomy in the countries under discussion (with the exception of

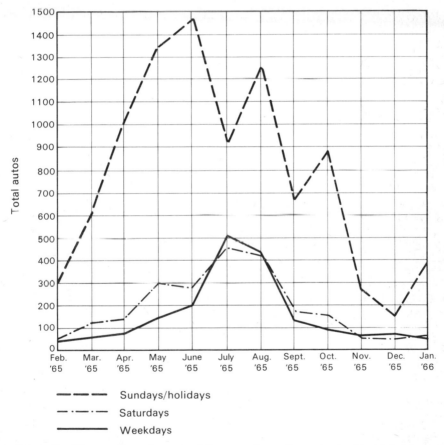

- - - - Sundays/holidays

- · — · — Saturdays

———— Weekdays

Figure 7   The number of automobiles at a State Forest in the Netherlands during one year.
Source: J. C. Heytze, Het recreatieverkeer in enkele boswachterijen van het Staatsbosbeheer (SBB 1968), p. 9.

49

parts of the south and south-west USA), there are concentrations of demand: at weekends, at long weekends where a national holiday is added, at holidays such as Easter, and in the period of annual holidays in the summer. Staggering has spread the summer load a little but the peak months remain (see Figure 7). What is less obvious is whether this pattern will change during the period for which planning is being done. It is generally assumed that no major shifts will occur and policy decisions have to be made about whether it is desirable to plan for a peak capacity that is reached only on a few weekends in the year.

3.9 CONCLUSIONS

No serious study of rural recreation comes to any conclusion other than that it has increased explosively, and will continue to increase. The rate at which increase will occur is taxing the ingenuity of many bodies and universally applicable predictions are unlikely, except that present rates of increase will lead to astronomic participation rates if projected over the long-term, i.e. forty years or more. The countries in this study are probably not all at the same stage in the recreation surge, if we accept for a moment the assumption that they are likely to follow a common pattern of expansion. The USA and Canada are obviously in the lead, with the USA having a distinct edge; in the Netherlands, participation is high but likely to go further (for example, the car-ownership rate is quite low); in the UK participation is relatively low and there is likely to be a great deal of expansion; Denmark (except in the particular area of summer cottages) is probably just at the beginning of the take-off, and Japan has a great potential for expansion if current trends continue. These are subjective estimates and it is naturally likely that particular national patterns may evolve which do not follow a set course. More accurate prediction of the demand for rural recreation and hence of the resource requirements must follow upon investigation of the social and psychological influences acting upon both participants and non-participants, and the development of economic models for the forecasting of demand which incorporate more of the social and demographic variables involved. To what extent these aims can be regarded as high priorities in Western societies with other pressing social problems is difficult to assess in terms with any wide applicability.

4 Recreation resources

4.1 THE ATTRACTIONS OF THE COUNTRYSIDE

'Natural resources are cultural appraisals' and although the environments of a country may provide what appear to be an obvious set of recreation resources, it must be remembered that the recreationist is viewing them through the lenses of his culture. Part of the lens is wrought from the basic and rational facts of income, leisure and mobility that have previously been discussed. Another part, surely, is less susceptible to investigation by the techniques of economic analysis than by environmental cognition research. In this way can be introduced the tastes, history, irrational motivations and intangibles that may well strongly influence peoples' recreational preferences. The different meanings of landscape, as categorized by Sonnenfeld,[96] are useful here: the concrete, the useful or economically productive, the aesthetic and symbolic. Recreation is largely interested in the latter two: the emotional reactions of visitors to particular landscapes, and the deeper-seated values which may be sought—freedom, escape and 'the land beyond'. And Sonnenfeld's distinction between the attitudes of natives and non-natives of a particular area may be remembered as a useful clue to some of the conflicts encountered in planning.

Since culture is held to be so important in the matter of aesthetics and symbols, we need not expect that people from different countries will exhibit the same attitudes. In the absence of a large-scale international research project designed to produce comparable information about such things, a few subjective impressions by the present writer will have to suffice. Some of the English attitudes have been discussed by Lowenthal and Prince,[97] although it should be stressed that their printed sources derive largely from the articulate end of the middle classes and above and cannot be representative of all strata of society. Their headings, 'the bucolic', 'the picturesque', 'the deciduous', 'the tidy', 'Facadism', 'Antiquarianism', 'Associations' and 'Genus loci', lead them to conclude that the main strands in tastes are firstly the acceptance of what is said by authorities to be

[96] J. Sonnenfeld, 'Variable values in space and landscape: an inquiry into the nature of environmental necessity', *J. Social Issues* 22 (1966), pp. 71–82; and 'Environmental perception and adaptation level in the Arctic', in D. Lowenthal (ed.), *Environmental Perception and Behaviour*, Univ. Chicago Dept of Geog. Res. Pap. 109 (1967), pp. 54–9.

[97] D. Lowenthal and H. C. Prince, 'English landscape tastes', *Geogr. Rev.* 55 (1965), pp. 186–222.

51

good, on the basis of historical or other (for example, literary) associations and secondly the 'nostalgic but firm commitment to the old, the tried, the worn . . . as long as it is uniquely and unyieldingly itself'.[98] One facet which they mention is of immediate relevance in recreation: the dislike of coniferous trees and the desire for deciduousness. The plantations of spruces and pines, in upland Britain especially, have been scourged in print for many years, despite the efforts of the Forestry Commission to gain their acceptance. Nowhere is the opposition more vehement than when open moorland is affected,[99] for the bare windy spaces of the uplands have a very devoted band of lovers who feel confined by the new forests. 'The implacable and immutable conifer blanket is foreign to our experience', wrote a protagonist group with more fervour than ecological accuracy, and phrases such as 'numbing predictability', 'endless precision of trunks and bottle-green foliage'—and 'serried ranks of conifers' have been vigorously wielded:[100] The Welsh poet R. S. Thomas writes of

a landscape sour with spruce [101]

The value of trees in recreation planning and use is intuitively recognized everywhere and future developments for recreation in the emptier parts of Britain will be harder to make if afforestation cannot be undertaken. Judging by the increased use of Forest Park campgrounds and trails, the prejudices are breaking down and it will be interesting to see if the dislike survives the present adult generation. Indeed, it would be valuable to know if the anathema is currently widespread outside the articulate.

The Dutch, on the other hand, are like most continental Europeans in being very fond of forests. The pine, spruce, fir and larch forests are extremely popular in recreation even where obviously planted as in the Amsterdam Forest. Subjectively, the forests in the Netherlands do not look so orderly and lacking in diversity as those in Britain (it is possibly significant that the Netherlands Forest Service (Staatsbosbeheer) is also the national landscape and amenity authority), but we may also remember that practically all the landscapes of the Netherlands are man-made and look man-made.

[98] D. Lowenthal and H. C. Prince, *op. cit.*, p. 222.
[99] 'Moorland' is used in its English sense of high, above 900 feet (275 m) open bog, heath and grassland and not in the continental sense of peat-land.
[100] Quoted by D. Lowenthal and H. C. Prince, *op. cit.*, pp. 197–8.
[101] 'Afforestation', in *The Bread of Truth* (London 1963), p. 17.

Therefore it is possible that 'artificiality' has a much weaker-impact on the Dutch than the British, most of whom think for example that the upland moors are natural, which in fact they are not. Attitudes to landscape in the Netherlands appear to be conditioned by practicality: acceptance of high densities of people seems to be as common in the rural recreation scene as it is in the urban environment. In Denmark, a distinct thread has pervaded some of the planning for landscape amenity which is discussed later in this book. This is based on the maintenance of the present content of the rural landscape and the demands for recreation

> concentrate on the landscape elements which are familiar and which people expect to find. . . .
> Expectations are thus generally limited to existing landscape forms and often restricted, when compared to the expectations an individual may have towards landscapes in other countries.[102]

This usually means that protected areas, and those popular for open-air recreation have a combination of natural and anthropogenetic landscapes. Lakes, woods, farmlands and farmsteads, villages and churches all form a holistically perceived scene in which simple presence forms a recreation. Whether this will survive the present middle-aged generation is a question which springs to mind.

In West Germany, a survey[103] found that 43 per cent of interviewees thought that 'hilly country' was an ideally suited holiday area, whereas only 32 per cent opted for mountains (34 per cent for lakes, 31 per cent for the seaside, 21 per cent for forests, 9 per cent for towns, 4 per cent for flat country and 18 per cent for 'generally healthy and beautiful areas'). Here the *zusammenhang* of landscape elements sounds as if it conforms to a particular type of expectation.

It is difficult for Westerners without an intimate knowledge of Japanese language and culture to comment on their attitudes to countryside areas. Two themes can be stated, at a superficial examination, to have relevance to rural recreation, the first of which is an identification of man and nature as one whole, without the dualism fostered in many strands of Western intellectual history. This leads, among other things, to an acceptance and indeed high valuation of cultural features of interest as recreation resources,

[102] Sten Bjerke, *Landscape Planning and Nature Parks* (mimeo, Copenhagen 1966), p. 2.
[103] W. Leutzbach, 'Traffic and transport for touring', AIT-Congress, Rotterdam 1966, Theme IV, Table 2.

53

especially when in a pleasant setting. Such an outlook is not exclusively Japanese, for it leads to the high visitor numbers to the ruins of Cistercian monasteries in Britain and the Mesa Verde cave dwellings in the USA, but appears to be intensified in Japan. Its impact is increased by acceptance of change as a normal feature of the passage of time which, coupled with an ability to 'screen out' unpleasant things, leads to acceptance of environmental degradation, crowding, visual disamenity and litter at recreation areas which would in the West be subjects for comments, complaints and letters to *The Times*. It is sometimes difficult therefore for a *gaijin* to see why a particular area is attractive to so many people: the answer is probably bound up in the subtleties of Japanese culture although if near a city the simplest explanation of it being the only available open space may be equally valid.

Attitudes to land and water in North America must of necessity be conditioned by different perspectives of time and space from those found in Europe. The exploitive history of resource use seems to be nearing its end in the USA, though less so in Canada, and new attitudes towards the quality of environment are rising. Alongside these are such dominant themes as those of wilderness and the frontier, and it is clear that in these outdoor experiences, many Americans are re-creating pioneer living, as a tribute perhaps to their not-far-distant predecessors who tamed the unknown land. Thus even highly developed campgrounds in fairly densely populated New England, seemed to the campers to be basically a 'wilderness experience', and this was particularly so to those with more than $1000 invested in camping equipment.[104] The pioneer theme should not be taken too far: as Burch has suggested,[105] there are other needs to be satisfied by camping, and forms of recreation which require seashore resources are scarcely likely to owe much to the days of the Conestoga wagon.

What happens to be common to all countries is that attitudes to landscapes and to recreational uses of them are basically sets of conventions. The British convention expects long walks over open land; the American convention is to use wildlands to satisfy a need for wanderlust and so there needs to be in the very wildest lands few

---

[104] W. F. LaPage, *Camper characteristics differ at public and commercial campgrounds in New England*, US Forest Service Research Note NE-59 (1967), p. 6. See also the section 'Characterizing the recreation user', in Northeastern Forest Experiment Station, *op. cit.*, pp. 105–48.
[105] W. Burch, Jr, *op. cit.* (note 12).

reminders of the security of the twentieth century world like tele-phones or roads.[106] But the conventions vary with the beholders: Lucas found differences in wilderness perceptions in the Quetico-Superior canoe area between those who paddled and those with out-board motors.[107] So no studies of recreation resource classifications which ignore the conventional behaviour and requirements are likely to form an optimal basis for planning. In this context the per-ception of recreation resource accessibility, people's evaluation of the quality of experience they are likely to gain and their attitudes towards environmental quality are all important and are worthy of considerably more research.[108]

4.2 NATIONAL COUNTRYSIDE RESOURCES

(a) The Netherlands

The small size of this country (12,868 sq miles, 3·6 million ha) is accompanied by a low diversity of environments suitable for re-creation. Built-up land accounts for about one-quarter of the surface, and most of the agriculture is highly intensive. The basic land use statistics are given in Table 1.29. The classification employed is rather strictly agricultural in its point of view and the figures in Table 1.30 give more information on the forests, dunes and heaths which make up the most important environments for recreation. The forests are mainly of coniferous trees (75 per cent Scots pine, 12 per cent larch) and are plantations. Deciduous forests are of oak and beech and are more common in South Limburg, on the hilly country of that Province. The heathland areas are open communities dominated by heather (*Calluna vulgaris*) but a fair amount of self-sown pine and birch may occur in them. As with the coniferous forests, a

---

[106] D. B. Luten, 'Engines in the wilderness', *Landscape* 15 (1966), pp. 25–7.

[107] R. C. Lucas, 'Wilderness perception and use: the example of the Boundary Waters canoe area', *Nat. Res. J.* 3 (1964), pp. 384–411, reprinted in T. Burton and R. W. Kates (eds.), *Readings in Resource Management and Conservation* (Chicago 1965), pp. 363–74.

[108] For example, K. K. Sillitoe, *Planning for Leisure*, Government Social Survey Report SS 388 (London 1969), ch. IX; M. L. Barker, 'Beach pollution in the Toronto region', and D. Swanson, 'Public perceptions and resources planning', in W. R. D. Sewell and I. Burton (eds.), *Perceptions and Attitudes in Resource Management*, Dept of Energy, Mines and Resources, Resource Paper 2 (Ottawa 1971), pp. 37–47 and 91–7; G. L. Peterson and E. S. Newmann, 'Modeling and predicting human response to the visual recreation environment', *J. Leisure Research* 1 (1969), pp. 219–45; D. Mercer, 'The role of perception in the recreation experience: a review and discussion', *J. Leisure Res.* 3 (1971), pp. 261–76; F. Newby, 'Understanding the visual resource', in Northeastern Forest Experiment Station, *op. cit.*, pp. 68–72.

Table 1.29   Netherlands: land use (ha, 1960)

1 Settlements	305,000
2 Horticulture	75,000
3 Perennial crops	55,700 Inland water: 476,500
4 Cropland	881,600
5 Improved grassland	1,326,800
6 Unimproved grazing:	
heathland	82,300
moorland	26,900
7 Forests	259,600
8 Swamps and marshes	11,100
9 Unproductive:	
sandy areas	7,990
dunes	43,700
mudflats	50,700

Source: L. D. Stamp (ed.) *Land Use Statistics of the Countries of Europe Occ. Papers No. 3, World Land Use Survey,* 1965, p. 21.

Table 1.30   Netherlands: recreation resource potential (ha, 1965)

1 Woodland	260,000	72% of area of Netherlands
A Coniferous	154,000	59% of woodland
B Broadleaved	29,000	11% of woodland
C Not fully stocked	35,000	14% of woodland
D Other	42,000	16% of woodland
2 Natural Areas	156,000	43% of area of Netherlands
A Moorland*	82,000	53% of natural area
B Dunes and shifting sands	44,000	28% of natural area
C Peatbog and fen	30,000	19% of natural area

* Heathland is the English equivalent.
Source: Staatsbosbeheer *Jaarverslag* 1966, p. 10.

podsol soil is usual. The dunes are mostly coastal, although semi-stabilized sand areas occur inland on the heaths, and have an ecology of hills and slacks which seems to be common wherever this eco-system is found. Peatbogs and fens are more important for wildlife conservation than recreation except where extensive cutting has left a large contiguous water body.

Agricultural land is not to be ignored however since the planting up of polderlands to make picnic and camp sites is practised, as will be discussed later, and polders next to water bodies may be given over to parking space. The inland water is of course very extensive in all parts except South Limburg and can be qualitatively classified into:

1 large canals, canalized rivers and rivers where recreation must share with commerce
2 smaller canals where recreation use predominates; many of these are being converted to roads and their continued use for recreation presents problems since it cannot pay for their upkeep
3 large water bodies formed from former sea inlets by diking as in the IJsselmeer and Delta projects
4 water bodies (all sizes) formed from former sand pits and peat diggings; as on (3) recreation is a dominant use.

The resources are not equally distributed over the country: the dunes are of course a coastal feature and the coniferous forests and heaths tend to be associated with each other on the higher parts of Western Holland. Elsewhere, patches of wildland in a matrix of farmland form the major resources. Except in South Limburg, water is more evenly spread.

(b) Denmark

Denmark is another small country, where total area, including inland water is 4,304,300 ha (16,619 sq miles). Of all the countries studied, it is the most dependent upon agriculture for its economy although the traditional bacon and dairy produce image of Denmark is now yielding (except in the tourist literature) to the reality of an export trade over half of the value of which is now produced by industry. The rural nature of much of the country is summed up in Table 1.31 and it must be remembered that metropolitan Denmark

Table 1.31   Denmark: land use (ha, 1960)

Land use type	Area
Built-up land, communications	332,600
Horticulture and gardens	33,100
Perennial crops	10,100
Cropland	2,751,000
Improved grassland	140,600
Unimproved grazing	202,400
Forest	444,000
Scrub and heath	100,000
Swamps and marshes	20,000
Dunes	100,000
Other unproductive land	129,000

Source: L. D. Stamp (ed.), *European Land Use Statistics, Occ. Papers No. 3, World Land Use Survey,* 1965, p. 9.

(i.e. excluding Greenland and the Faeroes) includes 482 islands, only 99 of which are inhabited. The highest point in Denmark is only 568 feet (173 m) above sea-level but the terrain is quite diverse, being largely founded upon glacial deposits. Moraines, kame deposits, and tunnel-valleys are all common features of the landscape and the land use is arrayed upon this diverse topography in an equally diverse mixture. Many of the rural settlements are very attractive—half-timbered buildings and white-washed churches are common—and so the whole forms a distinctly attractive environment, particularly for foreign visitors and for the inhabitants of large urban agglomerations such as the Greater Copenhagen region.

As might be expected, the coast is a major recreation resource. The estimated length is 7500 km, which is about 1·6 m of coast per inhabitant. Not all this coast is uniformly suitable for recreation, since different landforms create varying conditions. Combining the natural resources with the existing land use pattern, a classification of coastal quality has been produced. Group 1 coasts are suitable for intensive use, and consist of sandy beaches with plenty of water movement, suitable for bathing or for building summerhouses; together with a narrower beach type, sometimes undergoing erosion, which is also serviceable for bathing and quite suitable for building. Group 2 includes combinations of intensive-use coasts with poor beaches of mud, with shallow or stagnant water which are unfit for bathing and, sometimes, for building too because of boggy con-

Table 1.32   Coastal zones: Zealand and Møn

Unit	Km	%
Group 1 (suitable for intensive use)		
(a) good for bathing	155	10
(b) less important for bathing	55	4
(c) with urban area inland	5	1
Group 2 (less suitable for intensive use)		
(a) good for bathing	70	5
(b) less important for bathing	245	16
(c) with urban area inland	25	2
Group 3 (poor coasts)		
(a) unsuitable because of natural conditions	665	44
(b) monopolized by urban area	295	19

Not included in survey: 190 km

Source: Landsplanudvalgets Sekretariat, Strandkvalitet og Fritidsbebyggelse, 1966, pp. 9–15.

ditions at the rear of the shoreline. The amounts of these types in a survey of Zealand and Møn[109] are given in Table 1.32.

This classification was later extended to the whole country for the major groups of units and the regional results are summarized in Table 1.33. Bornholm apart, it is apparent that high-quality shore-

Table 1.33 Coastal quality: Denmark (major groups, by regions)

Region	Group 1		Group 2		Group 3		Not class		Total km (100%)
	km	%	km	%	km	%	km	%	
Zealand and Møn	240	13	359	19	712	39	546	29	1857
Lolland and Falster	53	9	287	49	95	16	152	26	587
Bornholm	58	41	51	36	0	0	32	23	141
Funen and adjacent islands	97	9	366	33	333	29	333	29	1121
East coast of Jutland Limfjord	381	14	810	31	956	36	491	19	2638
West coast of Jutland	360	37	65	7	466	48	73	9	964
Whole country	1189	16	1938	26	2562	35	1627	23	7316

Source: Landsplanudvalgets Sekretariat, *Datakort Danmark 12: Strandkvalitet,* 1967.

line is not so widespread as might be expected and that it is unevenly distributed: the west coast of Jutland is of course farthest from the areas of densest population. Further reference to the coast will be made in due course.

Other than the shoreline, there are no startling inequalities in the distribution of resources although differences exist: in Jutland most of the forests are coniferous plantations, whereas beech (*Fagus sylvatica*) predominates in the east; Jutland also has most of the dune-coasts and the heathlands, although these are only remnants of the great stretches that existed before the reclamation operations of the Danish Heath Society since the nineteenth century.

(c) England and Wales

The total area for England and Wales is 15,117,100 ha (including inland water), which makes them approximately 30 times the size of Holland or Denmark. The figures (Table 1.34) do not show the inequality of distribution of the types of land use shown. The north and west have much more of the extensive types of land use, especially the unimproved grazing, in what is known as the Highland Zone;

[109] Landsplanudvalgets Sekretariat, *Strandkvalitet og Fritidsbebyggelse* (Copenhagen 1966).

Table 1.34   UK: land use (ha, 1961)

	England and Wales	UK
Settlements	1,605,169	1,902,700
Horticulture	156,246	176,000
Perennial crops	5,275,790	6,118,110
Cropland	4,351,473	6,954,580
Improved grassland	2,007,183	5,171,300
Unimproved grazing: private	1,399,920	
common land	607,263	7,541,400
Forest	1,034,400	1,735,400
Unproductive (unaccounted for)	498,779	501,620

Source: L. D. Stamp (ed.), *Land Use Statistics of the Countries of Europe, Occ. Papers No. 3, World Land Use Survey*, 1965, pp. 29–30.

the south and east contain most of the intensive agriculture and the bulk of the population. Within the lowlands the resources are mainly woodlands, a lot of which are privately owned, and patches of lowland heath which are usually common land with *de facto* access. In the highland zone, the terrain is mostly coniferous forest of fairly recent origin (i.e. post-1920), open moorland and unimproved grassland. This is used for hill farming, overwhelmingly of sheep and in drier places for the production of grouse (*Lagopus scoticus*) which is shot for sport by a very small group.

Leaving aside agricultural land, since it has a low potential for active recreation, though not as scenery, the potential public recreation resource for England and Wales is set out in Table 1.35.

The lands tabulated are mostly in private ownership. In National Parks, the public have *de jure* access only to limited areas, which are either the subject of special agreements or, as in the Lake District, for example, where common land falls within a pre-1974 Urban District administrative unit. Elsewhere, in National Parks as outside them, the public may have *de facto* access to large areas of land (generally unimproved and unfenced moorlands and grasslands) but they have no legal right to be there. The ownership of Common Land is vested in the Lord of the Manor and the various usage rights are let to tenants. Nature Reserves belong to or are leased by the Crown but variable access rights exist: some are closed completely, in others access is restricted to public rights of way through them. A great proportion of the woodland belongs to the Forestry Commission which is the national government body and this land is now, after long years of closure, being opened to public access, generally on foot or horseback

Table 1.35   England and Wales: recreation resource potential (land) (ha, 1968)

TOTAL AREA	152,659,800	
National Parks	13,621,800	9% of land surface of England and Wales, mostly private land.
Areas of Outstanding Natural Beauty	11,119,100	7·35% of land surface of England and Wales, mostly private land.
Green Belt	4,899,000	Mostly private land, but increasing small amounts of public ownership.
Defence Land (freehold and leasehold over 3 years) (foreshore)	221,980 15,398	Publicly owned land where freehold, but Defence Depts reluctant to relinquish. Some usable part-time for recreation.
Derelict land	45,533	A very narrow official definition—real amount much greater. Reclamation often for purposes other than recreation.
Long-distance routes (1969, km)	576	Public right of way along these routes.
National Trust: gardens and open spaces owned	144,196	Open to public.
Forestry Commission (forest parks)	72,965	Areas where special attention paid to recreation.
National nature reserves	30,931	Recreation not always compatible with nature conservation in these places.
Local nature reserves	3,171	
Common lands	897,990	Excepting Urban Districts, public access is de facto.

Sources: Countryside Commission, Digest of Countryside Recreation Statistics, 1969, Table 3.1; T. L. Burton and G. P. Wibberley, Outdoor Recreation in the British Countryside, Wye College Studies in Rural Land Use 5, 1965, p. 8.

only. The water bodies (Table 1.36) exhibit great variation in terms of public access: most rivers and canals have open navigation, although mooring and lock fees are payable, but lakes, ponds and pits are generally controlled by the shoreline owners. Additions to the countryside resource are rare, since most land-use changes create additional urban or industrial areas, but it may be noted that the policy of contraction adopted by British Rail has meant the availability of 5618 miles (8989 km) of railway right-of-way between

Table 1.36   England and Wales: recreation resource potential (water) 1968

Coastline: total length	4,386 km	
Protected coastline:		
NNRs and SSSIs	843 km	Public access may be restricted since some of land is private.
National Parks and AONBs	1,684 km	
National Trust land	245 km	
Navigable inland waterways	2,290 km	
Reservoirs (impounding and storage)	26,494 ha	Not all open for all kinds of recreation.

Source: Countryside Commission, Digest of Countryside Recreation Statistics, 1969, Table 3.2.

1948–68. Usually sold piecemeal to farmers and other landowners, a government report [110] has suggested that local authorities should be given first choice of disused lines and encouraged to develop them as linear recreation facilities for riding and walking; a number of studies have appeared, [111] and in north-west Co. Durham the Derwent Valley line has been converted to a 9-mile (14·5 km) bridleway and walking track.

(d) Canada

Canada is the second largest country in the world and has a relatively low population, 22·5 million in 1973. The land-use statistics (Table 1.37) belie the immense variety of landscapes which form the background to any consideration of outdoor recreation resources in Canada. The coasts of both the Atlantic and Pacific are splendid, the Rocky Mountains justly famed, and even the Canadian heartland along the St Lawrence has good mountain country in the Laurentides as well as the river itself which at Thousand Islands forms an international sailing and resort area. If they were not so badly polluted, Lakes Erie and Ontario would be even more sig-

[110] *Disused Railways in the Countryside of England and Wales.* A report to the Countryside Commission by J. H. Appleton (London 1970).

[111] For example, *Disused railways in Lindsey—Policy for After Use* (County Planning Department, Lindsey County Council 1972); DART, *Exmoor Greenway. The recreational use of disused railways.* A report by the Dartington Amenity Research Trust for the Exmoor Society (1970).

nificant in the pattern of resources than they are; and in addition to them the country has millions of small lakes, some forest-girt, others in open country, which are summer magnets.

Table 1.37 Canada: land use

	Million acres	mill. km²
Arable	91·2	0·37
Pasture	78·6	0·32
Forest	837·2	3·38
Unused but potentially productive	208·6	0·84
Built-up, waste land, other	178·4	4·75
Total	2389·7	9·66

Source: F. S. and S. Woytinsky, *World Production*, 1950, Table 216.

In its own way, the north also forms a considerable resource. Although very difficult of access and increasingly of economic importance, it is very wild country and thus is important for hunting, and increasingly for naturalists who wish to observe wild animals. In the far north, the Polar Bear is an animal of considerable interest. No rapid capsulated description of resources can thus be given for Canada, whose motto in this respect might be 'you want it, we've got it'. The qualifications to be entered are firstly those of distance: there may be a lot of resource A in one place, but it is likely to be a long way to resource B, so that variety may be an attribute at a national, rather than a regional or local, scale; and secondly of climate, particularly the lengthy and severe winters. (F. K. Hare is reputed to have said of Canada, 'it's too darn big and too damn cold.') The Department of Indian and Northern Affairs has taken an inventory of the major natural environments of Canada, with a view to including examples of all of these in the National Park system. (Recreation is not the only, nor even necessarily primary, function of such areas, however.) Some 39 natural terrestrial regions are delineated, but those in which rural recreation demand is likely to be greatest number only about 15: the rest cover the remotest parts of the nation.[112]

[112] Canada, Dept of Indian and Northern Affairs, National and Historic Parks Branch, *National Parks System Planning Manual* (2nd edn, Ottawa 1972).

(e) USA

The size and variety of environments to be found in this nation defy rapid description, as do the bewildering complexities of human uses of them. The land-use details in Table 1.38 provide a skeletal key to

Table 1.38   Forty-eight United States—land use (million acres: 1950)

		km^2
Cities—2500 population and over	17	68,850
Agriculture:		
Crops	409	1,656,450
Pastured Cropland	69	279,450
Non-providing agricultural land	45	182,250
Forestry	484	1,960,200
Grazing	700	2,835,000
Transportation	25	101,250
Reservoirs/water management	10	40,500
Primarily wildlife	14	56,700
Public recreation areas, excluding city parks	46	186,300
Deserts, swamps, mountain tops, non-commercial forest and miscellaneous	85	344,250
Total	1,904;	7,711,200
with inland water	1,934	7,832,700

Source: H. Landsberg, R. Fischman and J. L. Fisher, Resources in America's Future, 1963.

the fact that many of the major world biomes are represented in this part of the North American continent. Thus in Florida there are tropical-type swamps and swamp forests, deserts in the southwest, and an abundance of forests, especially on the mountain chains of Appalachia and the west. If Alaska is included, then tundra is present too. Within this framework, the inhabitants have, in a relatively short space of time, effected numerous transformations of land use, many of which favour recreation while others are inimical to it. Some of the land in the residual category of Table 1.38 is of importance for recreation: for example, deserts are used for second homes in southern California and for four-wheel drive vehicle expeditions; and the high mountain tops and non-commercial forests provide wilderness by reason of their lack of interest to other potential users.

Water is, on the whole, well represented. The Great Lakes provide an inland sea system of considerable magnitude but Erie especially, and Ontario and Michigan to lesser extents are regrettably heavily polluted. Most rivers are tamed somewhere along their course, to the point where the Congress passed in 1968 a Wild Rivers Act to preserve parts of streams which have not yet been harnessed or altered in some way. Small lakes are commonest in formerly glaciated territory, especially in the western mountains and in northern states such as Minnesota; elsewhere the small impoundments for water or soil conservation have an important secondary purpose in providing a recreation resource.

In short, almost every type of terrain and every activity can be found at some place in its due season. The difficulties arise because there are 210 million people, many of whom wish to use the resources, and most of them live where the resources are scarcest. Here, as with Canada, lies a fundamental tension behind the imbalance of population distribution and resources.

(f) Japan

The rural recreation resources of Japan are dominated by the mountainous terrain, often volcanic, which forms so high a proportion of each major island. The lower and middle slopes are usually forested (Table 1.39) but the upper parts present a truly high-altitude landscape in which alpine flora combine with long and deep snow-lie to

Table 1.39   Japan: land use (million ha)

Forest land	22·6
Cultivated land	14·3
Waste land	3·6
Scrub and grassland	2·6
Meadows, pasture and grass	1·6
Swamps, bogs and inland water	0·7
Communications	0·6
Built-up	0·4

Source: E. A. Ackerman, *Japan's Natural Resources*, 1949, p. 14. Since that date, shifts have taken place resulting in expansion of the latter two categories at the expense of the others.

form at different seasons, an attractive region for recreationists from the crowded cities. The forests absorb much of the recreation of family groups, clubs from educational institutions and the excursions laid on by firms for their own employees. Thirty-two per cent of the forests are state-owned and thus managed by the Forestry Agency; some are owned by prefectures and municipalities; yet others belong to temples and shrines and as such are open for public recreation

65

(Table 1.40). There is thus no problem of public access to these resources. Mention of the religious establishments is a reminder that much rural recreation in Japan is conducted in and around such places, particularly where extensive gardens are attached; there is thus a focus upon cultural phenomena as recreation resources as well as natural or seemingly-natural countryside. The coasts of Japan are

Table 1.40   Japan: forest land

Ownership	Type (%)	
Private forest (57% of total)	Planted	31
Includes temples and shrines.	Natural	60
	Mixed	9
National forest (32% of total)	Planted	19
Owned by government.	Natural	70
	Mixed	11
Public forest (11% of total)	Planted	24
Ownership by municipalities.	Natural	66
	Mixed	6

Source: *Japan Statistical Yearbook 1965*, p. 127. Bureau of Statistics, Prime Minister's Office, Tokyo.

also much sought, especially during the heat and humidity of summer. There is no shortage of coastline, nor difficulty of accessibility (except in parts of Hokkaido), but competition for shoreline use is severe. Industry, urban uses and reclamation projects all demand priority upon the flatter land behind the shores which are of course the most accessible areas for swimming and sailing since the rocky coasts and headlands are too intractable for such purposes. In south-west Hokkaido, even the coastal plain is being industrialized in a great swathe between Muroran and Tomakomai, without thought for the alternative uses. Considerable amounts of land in Japan are being released from agriculture because of intensification, but little of this is suitable for recreation because of its fragmented nature and miniscule plot size: until land consolidation is completed over all the islands, no additions to recreation area can be expected from that source.

Because there are so few parks in and at the fringes of cities, and because agricultural land contains few if any niches for casual, unstructured recreation, the importance of forests, mountains and coast is magnified. Emphasis has therefore been laid upon development and protection of those areas in planning for rural recreation.

4.3 CLASSIFICATIONS OF RECREATION RESOURCES AND USE

Most classifications have been compiled by planners for a particular purpose and not by academics for their own amusement. There are two basic types: (a) those which deal with physical resources only, and (b) those which try to incorporate both resource and user characteristics.

(a) Classifications of physical resources

On a national scale the ORRRC classification[113] is a typical example and one from which many others have been adapted according to local circumstances. The units of the classification are:

1   High Density recreation areas. A wide variety of recreation uses involving substantial development. Such resources as are at hand are used.
2   General Outdoor Recreation areas. Again, there is a wide variety of uses for which substantial development is undertaken but choice of resource is likely to be excercised.
3   Natural environment areas. These are suitable for recreation which is fitted to the particular area; opportunities for multiple use are frequent.
4   Unique natural areas. Places of scenic splendour or natural wonder or scientific importance where observation is the primary form of enjoyment.
5   Primitive areas. Undisturbed roadless areas, including wilderness zones.
6   Historic and cultural sites.

At a smaller scale, recreation departments may use very detailed classifications which attempt to inventory resources for a particular recreation use. Land and water facets may be classified and ranked in terms of their suitability for different activities, and an attempt made to assess the significance of special features on local, regional or national scales. The landscape units which are delineated in the Ontario classification[114] are:

[113] ORRRC, *Recreation for America* (1962).
[114] Ontario Department of Lands and Forests, *Methodology for Ontario Recreation Land Inventory* (mimeo, Toronto 1968).

1 *Shoreland units*
   a Bathing and camping
   b Cottages and deep water activities
   c Wetland wildlife: viewing or hunting
2 *Water units*
   a Boating and viewing
   b Angling
   c Wetland wildlife
3 *Land units (general)*
   a Travelling and viewing
   b Upland game viewing or hunting
   c Wetland wildlife: hunting or viewing
4 *Special features*
   a Viewpoints
   b Ski hills
   c Waterfalls and other special features

Each of these is ranked from 1 to 7 according to the relative capability of a unit to attract and sustain intensive recreation use. This 1–7 ranking is the central feature of the Canada Land Inventory (ARDA) Land Capability for Outdoor Recreation classification.[115] This is a reconnaissance survey to indicate the comparative levels of recreation capacity for non-urban lands based on present popular preferences. The basis of the classification is the quantity of recreation which may be generated and sustained per unit area of land per year under perfect market conditions, i.e. assuming uniform demand and accessibility throughout the area. Thus class 1 lands have very high capacity to engender and sustain very high total annual use based on intensive activities. On the other hand, class 7 lands have very little capability for popular rural recreation activities: they may have some capabilities for very specialized activities, or may provide open space. For planning purposes a map on the scale of 1:50,000 is prepared; coloured maps at a scale of 1:250,000 are published.

Both the ORRRC and the ARDA classifications, however, are solely resource suitability classifications, which assume that the initial characteristics of the environment are those which will be sought by users. Where spatial considerations such as proximity to urban centres are also taken into account, such capability constructs,

---

[115] Canada Land Inventory (Dept of Forestry and Rural Development), *Field Manual: Land Capability Classification for Outdoor Recreation* (Ottawa 1967).

although not now totally unimportant, lose much of their significance beside the ability of people to accept high degrees of environmental manipulation where urban-fringe recreation is concerned. Far better, for the present purpose, is a classification which aims to integrate both the qualities of the environment and some of the temporal and spatial characteristics of the user.

(b) User-resource methods

These methods attempt to classify resources not only in terms of their physical nature and potential but also with regard to their use. Thus accessibility from large urban areas is often taken into account as a major factor determining recreation demand for and impact upon a particular region. Some California studies[116] delimited a series of TIM (Time–Income–Mobility) zones around the major urban complexes of the State, especially the Los Angeles and San Francisco Bay Area metropolitan areas, in which T and M were the dominant factors.

The zones established for California were:

Zone 1   up to 2 miles from the dwelling
Zone 2   an area accessible on one-day round trips: up to 40 miles
Zone 3a   an area accessible on overnight trips of 1–3 days, up to 125 miles
Zone 3b   an area accessible on vacation trips of 4–9 nights, within 250 miles
Zone 4   an area extending beyond Zone 3, for vacation trips of 10 nights or longer.

The delineation of such zones means that impact within them can be estimated and unsuitable use of resources avoided: it is obviously impossible to have primitive areas within the Zone 2 areas of a large city unless there are plenty of alternative developed areas or an inescapable environmental factor. This type of classification has the advantage of adding a social factor to the natural resource factor and can fairly readily be applied outside the areas for which it was devised.

The most flexible classification of all was developed by Clawson[117] and, while applying to recreation areas as individual locations (or

[116] California Resources Agency, *California Public Outdoor Recreation Plan* (1960), part II; California Dept of Park and Recreation, *California State Park System Plan* (Sacramento 1968).
[117] M. Clawson and J. L. Knetsch, *op. cit.*, p. 37; but Clawson uses this classification in most of his writings.

sets of them), integrates accessibility and resource features. The three basic categories are *user-oriented areas* of highly intensive development, near to large population centres; *resource-based areas* where the type of resource determines the use of the area and development may be at a low intensity; and an *intermediate* category. Table 1.41 amplifies some of the characteristics; this classification

Table 1.41   Classification of rural recreation uses

	User-oriented	Resource-based	Intermediate
General location	Close to users or whatever resources are available	Where outstanding resources are found: may be distant from most users	Best resources within limited distance from users
Major type of activity	Games such as golf, tennis, swimming, picnics, riding, children's play areas	Major scenic and historical sightseeing. Hiking, mountain climbing, camping, fishing, hunting	Camping, picnics, hiking, hunting, fishing
Period of major use	Daily leisure	Vacations	Daily outings and weekends
Typical size of areas	1–100 acres	Some to many thousand acres	100–several thousand acres

(100 acres = 40·5 ha)
Source: After M. Clawson and J. L. Knetsch, *Economics of Outdoor Recreation,* 1967.

will be the one most used in the rest of the present work. The general validity of this type of classification, for the USA in particular, is shown by statistics for the size classes of rural recreation areas according to management agency (see Figure 8). The concentration of the holdings of County governments within the smallest size classes is complemented by the greater representation of the Federal government in the larger units (its strong showing at the lower end is mainly due to historical sites and buildings), with the States in between.[118] As with many classifications, the reality is a continuum

[118] BOR, *1965 Survey of Outdoor Recreation Areas,* Table 2A.7, p. 54.

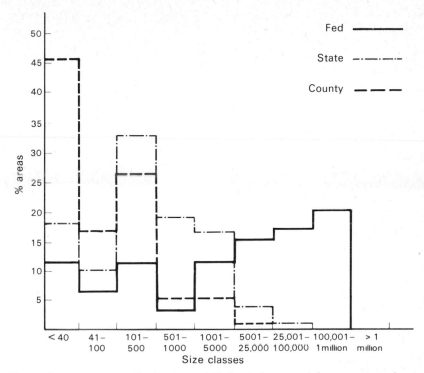

Figure 8 Percentage distribution of Federal, State and County recreation areas by size classes. The dominance of the Federal government in the larger classes, the Counties in the smaller areas, and the States in between, is shown. A representation of <0·5 per cent of the States is present in the 100,001–1 million class, and of the Federal and State areas in the >1 million class.
Source: BOR, *1965 Survey of Outdoor Recreation Areas,* p. 54.

and it is not always possible to categorize distinctly; the recreation areas of any region form a system which will have different demands placed upon it as changes in leisure patterns and recreation preferences come about.

In comparing the two types of classification, one point can be re-emphasized. The resources-only classifications can be made, as an inventory of potential, without knowing about the socio-economic characteristics and recreation choices of users. Thus where no large-scale survey of the latter exists, it is still possible to embark on the beginnings of recreation planning and undertake useful work until the necessary knowledge about consumer behaviour is acquired.

Part 2
User-Oriented and Intermediate Category Recreation

1 Introduction

1.1 THE USEFULNESS OF THE USER-RESOURCE CLASSIFICATION

Since this classification was developed in the USA, its applicability elsewhere needs some examination. In Europe, access to the immediate countryside for recreation is likely to be more difficult than in North America because the city fringe may not contain areas dedicated to recreation as do most Canadian and US cities and freeway access is likely to be lacking. On the other hand, public transport may be better in Europe and so those lacking a car or having only one, are not debarred from participation; in Holland and Denmark the usefulness of the bicycle and moped are emphasized. Equally, the provision of public open space within the suburbs is likely to be better in Europe than North America so that demand for countryside resources may be less; in Japan neither cities nor suburbs have much open space unless there has been large-scale replanning as in Nagoya or there is an abundance of temples and shrines as at Kyoto, so that people are therefore forced into the rural and coastal areas beyond the conurbations.

The relatively compact nature of many European countries means that the city fringe recreation zone and the intermediate zone are not easily separable: the emphasis in the user-oriented zone is upon sites that can be reached for part of a day but *de facto* this could often be stretched to include most of what would usually be called the intermediate area. However this latter is also characterized by its heavier use at weekends and short holiday periods.

1.2 ACCEPTABILITIES WITHIN USER-ORIENTED AND INTERMEDIATE ZONES

In the user-oriented zone, it is generally axiomatic that the activity is paramount over the characteristics of the resource. Activities focus on swimming, informal games, day-camping, picnics and walking for pleasure over short distances. If present, children's playground equipment is heavily used. There is a heavy summer emphasis in the cool temperate climates and indeed some designated areas may be closed in winter or have equipment such as picnic tables removed; winter-use centres round toboggans and children's variants of this occupation, with perhaps some snowmobile use demanded in larger parks; ponds or artificial water bodies may also be used for skating in northern North America.

Since the activities are paramount, the environment can display many artificial characteristics, and the examples described later in this Part show this quite fully. Swimming areas can be extremely tidy, surrounded by manicured lawns and having elaborate changing facilities, for example, even if not quite made into 'baths' by having structured edges. There is often sufficient trade at a given point to establish a refreshment kiosk or perhaps even a restaurant; paths are asphalted or gravelled and may have drainage channels on either side; planted shrubs may create the appearance of an urban park in some places. Above all, children are the main reason for the establishment and use of these areas[1] and they are notably uncritical in their recognition of, and demands for, pristine environments.

In general, acceptances in the intermediate zone are several degrees more strict: a recognizably 'natural' environment is sought (even though it may in fact be a cultural landscape, it is essential that natural things such as soil, plants and water should predominate) and activities may be moulded to that pattern. The kiosk and the swings are less frequently seen, fishing and walking become more popular and in winters, where there is abundant snow, skiing and its associated developments are strong features of the landscape. Parts are almost certain to be kept as natural areas and may even be designated as wilderness areas, although they will be rather different from the larger wildernesses of resource-based recreation areas.

The popularity of camping in the intermediate zone enforces an acceptance of very crowded conditions at weekends (sometimes to the point of refusal of entry, for example to State Parks in parts of the USA), which in turn brings about high degrees of wear in and around camp sites so that the mature trees are the only natural phenomena left. This price is apparently paid so long as there are

[1] In southern Scotland, two surveys placed children's amusements first in the list of priorities they wished to see in the countryside. B. S. Duffield and M. L. Owen, *Leisure + Countryside =* (Dept of Geography, University of Edinburgh 1971).

opportunities for the desired recreation activities amid a largely natural setting.

2 User-oriented recreation

This section deals with recreation just at or outside the fringes of cities, starting with two developments in the Netherlands, and proceeding through an examination of a regional park in the UK to a cursory discussion of the situation in Japan. An example of a regional park system in the USA concludes the material on user-oriented parks.

2.1 THE AMSTERDAM FOREST

A most striking example of municipal enterprise is the Amsterdam Forest (Het Amsterdamse Bos), which is near Schiphol Airport on the outskirts of the city. It was started in the 1930s in an area of open polderland, some 13 feet (4·3 m) below sea level. The woodlands are interrupted by playing fields, a riding school, open-air theatre, a farm and bird sanctuary, and joined by 137 km of footpaths, 51 km of bicycle paths and numerous canals (Figure 9), and in summer 100,000 visitors a day is not unusual. As an example of diversity in a user-oriented facility, it could scarcely be better and Amsterdam has been negotiating for three other sites to develop in the same manner.

2.2 LAND CONSOLIDATION IN THE NETHERLANDS

An important arm of the State government concerned with recreation is the Department of Land and Water Use (Cultuurtechnische Dienst) of the Ministry of Agriculture.[2] Its responsibility is to ensure adequate provision for open-air recreation when rural planning is being undertaken and its most important area of activity is in land consolidation schemes, where old and outmoded land holdings inhibit modern farming. Distances between parcels are often excessive and accessibility to them and the farm itself is poor. The recreation aspect of consolidation programmes comes from the 1954 Land Consolidation Act whereby 5 per cent of the land involved may be used for public purposes; the government may also

---

[2] Ministry of Agriculture and Fisheries, Foreign Information Service, *Land Consolidation in the Netherlands*, Pub. E125 (1965); *Open-air Recreation and Rural Development*. AIT-Congress 1966; Cultuurtechnische Dienst, *Jaarverslag 1967* (Utrecht 1967); Ministry of Agriculture and Fisheries, Service for Land and Water Use, *Rural Development in the Netherlands* (text in French, German and English; n.d.); R. J. Benthem, 'Changing of the countryside by land consolidation', *Biol. Cons.* 1 (1969), pp. 209–12.

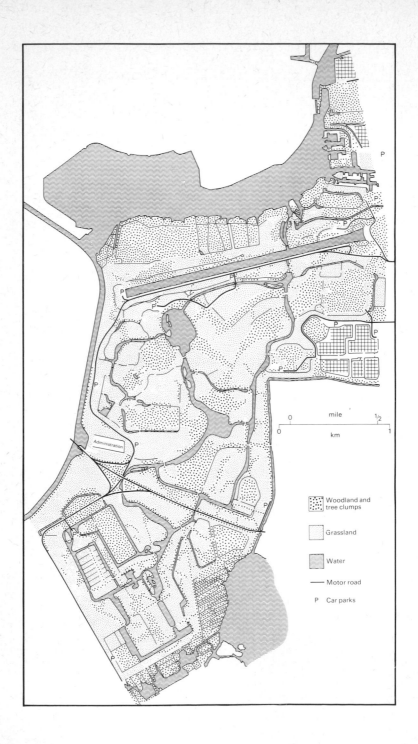

Administration

mile
0   1/2

km
0   1

Woodland and
tree clumps

Grassland

Water

Motor road

P   Car parks

buy land during the consolidation process. The Netherlands Forest Service (Staatsbosbeheer) prepares a landscape scheme for the whole project and so is frequently involved with the planning of recreation areas. The types of development undertaken vary in character but are generally accepted to be fairly intensive developments of a user-oriented character, not least because of the economic strengthening they may bring to rural communities, especially those easily accessible from towns. Picnic sites, trails in wooded areas and nature reserves are all acceptable but a good example is the Maarsseveense Plassen near Utrecht, a former peat-digging centre with numerous transverse baulks, surrounded by agricultural land with uncertain drainage. The baulks have been eradicated, leaving an uninterrupted water area, lawns and formal gardens laid out at one side, changing rooms and refreshment facilities built, and the whole planted and landscaped. The scheme has resulted in a large lake with intensive-use swimming area (there is an entrance fee) expecting 30,000 users/yr, surrounded by 120 ha of horticultural land. In addition, the project yielded 6 million cubic metres of sand for a housing project in Utrecht, which is only a cycle-ride away. The project is a distinctly useful addition to the recreation resources of Utrecht and its surrounding area and was well used even on a weekday afternoon in early September.

Cultuurtechnische Dienst has its own budget (Dfl. 4 million in 1966) but can use money from the Ministry of Culture, Recreation and Social Work as well, a contribution of 10–15 per cent being usual for recreation schemes; in its planning for landscape and recreation it is the most advanced in Western Europe, and by 1964, over 220,000 ha of agricultural land had been consolidated, resulting in a notable addition of recreation space to the resources of the Netherlands.

2.3 REGIONAL PARKS IN ENGLAND

In Britain it is difficult to differentiate between day-use and weekend-use areas near cities, but some examples of regional developments involving local governments will be given at this point, separate from the account of Country Parks on pp. 113–15.

Figure 9   The land-use layout of Het Amsterdamse Bos (see plate section). A totally artificial landscape uses trees to divide off areas of grass; motor access is very limited.
Source: Dienst der Publike Werke Amsterdam.

The valley of the River Lee slices through the eastern suburbs of London, in a north–south direction. Its use has been highly fragmented and has included recreation in the form of team pitches but is mostly devoted to reservoirs, communications (railway and canal), gravel pits, refuse dumps and small industries like scrap-metal reclamation. The distribution of most of these activities is rather random and the whole swathe unsightly. In 1964 the Civic Trust launched a scheme for a regional park (Figure 10) under an authority delegated by the numerous local government units with an interest in the valley. By 1972 the first tangible results were appearing. The plan[3] calls for some 'natural' features such as nature reserves but in general specifies a high degree of development with more playing fields, indoor-sports halls, water-sport pools, restaurants and features such as animal collections of particular interest to urban children such as sheep and cattle.

The reception of the idea of a regional park has been reasonably favourable, considering its transgression across the boundaries of local hegemony, and a similar concept for the Colne in west London has been put forward. River valleys often form suitable sites for linear parks but suffer from being natural boundaries for local governments reluctant to submerge their authority. New and larger units from 1974 will in some cases promote more integrated planning so that the plan for the Tyne corridor in the urban parts of the Tyneside conurbation is thus more likely to be put into effect under the aegis of a single metropolitan authority,

Another example of co-operation is given by the plans put forward in 1974 by the Greater Manchester Council and Stockport District Council for leasing a 1300-acre (526 ha) hall and park from the National Trust (see pp. 116–18) at Lyme Park. They propose an intensive-use plan with a golf course, ski-slope and boating, but with sufficient undeveloped area for a deer park and nature trails. Visitor numbers in the early 1970s to the hall and grounds were 280,000/yr but an eventual capacity of 1 million/yr is envisaged. A comparable merging of local authorities is suggested by a plan for a South Pennines Regional Park which would provide recreational space for the inhabitants of cities like Manchester, Burnley, Halifax and Bradford, and would link the Peak District and Yorkshire Dales National Parks (see Figure 14). Within the Regional Park, there

[3] The Civic Trust, *A Lee Valley Regional Park* (London 1964).

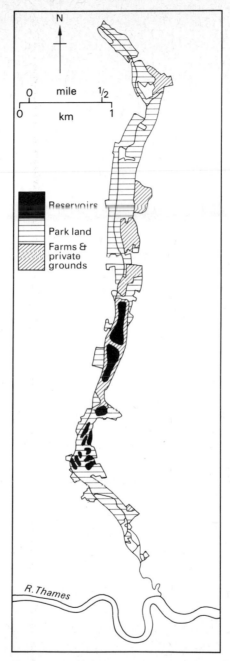

Figure 10 The outline plan for the River Lee valley in East London, combining water storage with recreational and private use. The valley is set in a context of continuous urbanization on the west side.
Source: Civic Trust, *A Lee Valley Regional Park.*

would be scenic roads, more than forty picnic sites, six country parks, and the development of new footpaths and bridleways, camping and caravan sites and second home developments. Run-down farms are also expected to be improved.[4]

2.4 CITY-FRINGE RECREATION IN JAPAN

The destruction of many cities in 1944–5 provided opportunities for rebuilding at lower densities which were in general not taken except where open boulevards with formal gardens as a centre strip were constructed, as in Nagoya. It remains generally true that open space in urban areas is connected with temples and shrines, as in Tokyo's Ueno Park. Other parks in cities like Tokyo and Osaka tend to be connected with palaces and castles (for example, Hibya Park in Tokyo, the Castle of Osaka) and the equivalent of Boston Common, Central Park and Hampstead Heath are missing. The profitability of land speculation and the absence of a physical planning infrastructure have militated against parks in suburban areas, and the Tokyo Metropolitan government is just beginning to formulate a programme for the acquisition of land as public open space. In association with the Construction Bureau it is directing its initial concern at the seashore of Izu Bay which is the favourite summer bathing area for the inhabitants of the Kanto.

The important role of religious establishments in open space is emphasized in cities which have a particular concentration of them such as Kyoto and Nara, where temples and shrines provide gardens not only within the city but also at the edge of it. The Nanzenji temple in Kyoto, for example, lies at the eastern edge of the city where the alluvial plain meets the encircling hills. Behind the temple buildings, the wooded hills are the property of the temple and available as public open space. Trails are maintained of two types: those leading to small subsidiary shrines, usually alongside streams; and others purely for recreational use. Apart from numerous warnings about fire risk, there appears to be no management either of the woodland or of recreationists. An analogous situation is found at Nara where the hill beyond the Kasuga shrine

---

[4] The proposals for these developments may be found in: D. J. Thomas and J. T. Roberts, *Tyne Recreation Study 1969* (University of Manchester Centre for Urban and Regional Research 1970); 'Intensive-use plan for park' and 'Running of park to be shared', *The Guardian* (21 August 1974 and 5 September 1974); West Riding Planning Committee, *The South Pennines: an interim report* (Wakefield 1974).

complex is kept as public open space, partly wooded and partly grassland, there being a fee for entry to the latter. As in most parts of the world, heavy recreational pressure is more easily absorbed by the deciduous woodlands, whereas the grassed areas show considerable signs of wear (especially bare soil) even in April. Even woodlands become stripped of all but mature trees where the people are concentrated, as in parts of Nara where visitors gather to feed the deer which roam much of the town. The same process is exemplified at a forested mountain (Takasakiyama) near Oita in Kyushu where sacred monkeys are found and can be watched and fed by the public at one particular spot in the woods.

The regarding of city-fringe parks as exceptional events rather than routine acquisitions by local government during urban expansion is typified by the Nopporo Forest Park on the edge of Sapporo in Hokkaido. The only park of its kind in the island, it was acquired in 1968 as part of a Hokkaido Centenary programme, in association with a nearby museum. A small artificial lake is a focus for picnics and the trails through the mixed forest are gravelled, have drainage channels on either side, and have the shrub vegetation cleared for 2–3 m either side of the path, creating a manicured effect. In 1969, 92,500 visitors were recorded to the park's 2040 ha, so that such manipulation may well be necessary to avoid more far-reaching damage.

The inadequacy of shoreline resources for bathing is also a concern of some levels of government and some prefectures are undertaking acquisition programmes in order to strengthen the roster of available areas since private occupance of shorelines has eliminated huge areas from public use and threatens to engulf more. This is particularly so along the east coast of Japan between Tokyo and Osaka, and around the Inland Sea; in south-western Hokkaido the few beaches that are suitable for bathing have already been placed under Quasi-National Park status to try and prevent undue development of them.

2.5 INTRA-STATE PARK PROVISION IN THE USA

Three main levels of government are concerned here: the counties, which are the main local government units outside the cities; the cities themselves, which may organize parks outside their limits; and regional associations, which are compacts of counties or cities and counties which join together to form a special district for recreational purposes, analogous to a Soil Conservation District, for example. Recreational use may also be a by-product of other special districts as on the impoundments created by flood control districts.

(a) County parks

The criteria for the selection of resources for this use are similar to those for State Parks but their major purpose is to serve local people so there is considerable orientation towards user-oriented facilities, catering for local people, rather than out-of-county visitors. The levels of provision vary greatly.[5] Alabama, Vermont and Maine counties, for example, had none in 1968; whereas Michigan counties had 114 areas totalling 19,629 acres (7944 ha) and the County Conservation Boards of Iowa had dedicated 12,421 acres (5027 ha) to recreation in a total of 226 park and recreation areas. All these had grown since 1957, when Conservation Boards were created to fill in the gaps of the inadequate State Park system.

Planning at county level frequently means the re-use of abandoned areas rather than the emparkment of 'natural' areas as in the case of State and Federal provision. It is at this level of government that gravel pits, abandoned strip mining areas, or a railroad grade and other disused lands, become identified as potential rural recreation resources. United in a national association, the future role of the counties in user-oriented or intermediate types of recreation looks secure, not the least because counties will be able to draw on a large fund of local goodwill and energy.[6]

(b) Extra-urban city parks

It is not surprising that, having both people and money, cities should buy or lease land outside their limits for park use. This is done by many cities in the USA, and in Arizona, for example, only two counties have parks which total 2866 acres (1160 ha), whereas Phoenix operates 5 parks and one recreational area together making 111,955 acres (45,308 ha) and Tucson has two parks totalling 18,280 acres (7398 ha). In Colorado, Denver operates 25 areas of mountain parks and Colorado Springs 4 areas. As in Arizona, the aim is to provide mountain terrain in contrast to the lower situation of the cities. In the East, the lack of public or wild land from which such parks can be created generally limits this type of development, but Detroit and

---

[5] Totals for each State are given in NPS, *Parks for America* (1965).

[6] National Association of Counties, *County Parks and Recreation* (Washington and New York 1964).

Boston have both been responsible for organizing non-urban parks beyond city limits. In the case of Detroit, the Huron-Clinton Metropolitan Authority was created as a city-county compact in 1940 specifically to provide recreation facilities. These are within 45 minutes' drive of the centre of the Detroit conurbation, and the fact that 95 per cent of the visitors come from the five-county district emphasizes the user-oriented status of the district. Water resources are the usual focus, either at the banks of the Huron and Clinton rivers or at Lake St Clair, and artificial lakes have been created at two of the parks. The visitor rate is highest at weekends but is also considerable on summer weekdays, reflecting the attractiveness of the parks on warm evenings.[7]

(c) Regional Park districts

An outstanding example of this type of organization is the East Bay Regional Park District (EBRPD) which serves 955 square miles (2473 km[2]) and two counties (population estimated at 1·6 million in 1967) bordering the eastern shore of San Francisco Bay. The district operates 9 regional parks, 4 regional recreation areas and one wilderness camp. It also owns some land which is not yet open to the public. The largest park is 4750 acres (1922 ha) in size and the smallest recreation area only 45 acres (18 ha); the wilderness camp is 240 acres (97 ha).

Of its total of 21,000 acres (1214 ha), the EBRPD has maintained most of it in a wild condition. That is not to say 'natural' for there are large areas of eucalyptus woodland, but a feeling of wildness persists in most of the parks, except in the developed areas. These latter attract most of the people and are very intensively used. Besides camping and picnic areas, such features as fishing lakes, a merry-go-round, miniature railway and golf course are provided in one park (Figure 1), and an equestrian school and marksmanship range in another. These facilities are generally in the part of the park nearest the cities so that the interior is left wild.

Financing of the system is through a property tax levy on the citizens of Alameda and Contra Costa Counties (10¢ per $100 assessed value) and through Federal and State matching grants. Donations of land have also been received, and the District has power of eminent

---

[7] Data from Huron–Clinton Metropolitan Authority for mid-1960s, quoted by J. A. Patmore, *Land and Leisure in England and Wales* (Newton Abbott 1970), pp. 286–7.

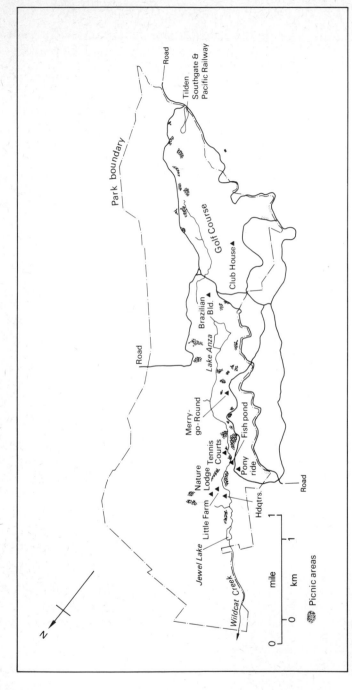

Figure 11 Tilden Park, one of the EBRPD units. Access, and the major area of urban population, is concentrated along the south-western side, and so many of the developed facilities are found there also.
Source: EBRPD leaflet.

domain (compulsory purchase), which it has recently used to acquire park lands. It can also combine with other public agencies for multiple-use projects.[8]

Regional Park districts of this kind are not particularly common: among other things they demand the relinquishing of sovereignty of counties over certain affairs, and 'regional government' is looked upon with suspicion by many local authorities. Nevertheless, the saving of administrative costs and the multiplicity of different resources which can be provided in a regional system make this form of provision extremely attractive if viewed rationally.

3 Intermediate zone recreation

The order of treatment follows that of the previous section. The important role of the Forest Service and of a particular institutional arrangement in the Netherlands is followed by material on Denmark. Then there is a discussion of the situation in England and Wales, where both structured and unstructured recreation is mentioned; this is succeeded by some information about Japan, Canada and the USA, with California being selected as a particular example in the last nation. Finally, the role of private enterprise in the intermediate sector is examined, as is the demand for second homes and the use of unconventional recreational vehicles.

3.1 THE STATE FOREST SERVICE (STAATSBOSBEHEER, SBB)[9] OF THE NETHERLANDS

The work required of this Service covers several fields of environmental relations and the Service comes under both the Ministry of Agriculture and the Ministry of Culture, Recreation and Social Work. The Service was established for the growing of timber and this is still carried on, but its economics are very marginal. Prices for timber have been low and it has been easier to import from outside. (In 1962, imports exceeded production by a factor of twelve.) The

[8] East Bay Regional Park District, *Stewardship Reports* (Oakland, California, annually); D. S. Prayn, 'San Francisco's East Bay Regional Parks', *Local Government Chronicle* (13 May 1967).

[9] The source of much of this section is personal inspection in 1968. Some useful printed sources are the *Jaarverslagen* (Yearbooks) of the SBB, Utrecht, in Dutch; the AIT-Congress pamphlet *Staatsbosbeheer* (1966); and the Report by J. W. Zaaijer at the same Congress; *The Task of the State Forest Service in the Netherlands* (Utrecht 1966), an SBB booklet; the SBB publishes booklets on special activities, for example, *Welkom bij de Rondeleidingen van het Staatsbosbeheer* and *Welkom op de Kamperterreinen van het Staatsbosbeheer*. These are updated each year.

poor soils available do not help, and 25 per cent of the forest yields 75 per cent of the timber.

Landscaping is also the responsibility of SBB. Development control is exercised in some areas, but a greater amount of time is spent on the landscaping of new projects such as motorways and the new lakes created by the Delta and IJsselmeer reclamation plans. The insertion of green belts and inter-urban buffer zones into provincial plans is also the task of SBB. Up to 1966 about Dfl 100 million had been spent on this work, resulting in the treatment of 0·25 million ha and the planting of 4500 km of roadsides. In addition, the SBB is the government agency for nature conservation, although supplemented by many private organizations. By 1966, eighty reserves totalling 15,533 ha were controlled by SBB on behalf of the Ministry of Culture, through which the necessary money came.

Increasingly, a major task of SBB is its work in recreation. It is involved directly through the use of its own forests and nature reserves, and indirectly through the advice it gives to other bodies who are planning developments for recreation. This latter work will be dealt with when discussing the appropriate organization.

The policy of SBB in its own forests is to provide as well as possible for rural recreation without detriment to landscape values or wildlife. Timber production is also part of the consideration but appears to be thought more expendable, although recreation is usually sited on the 75 per cent of the forest which only grows 25 per cent of the timber. Thus multiple use is an espoused concept and recreation may be made to fit in with dyke-building, water catchment and erosion control as well as the more obvious uses mentioned above. Access to roads and footpaths must be free although means of conveyance may be restricted; fees are charged only for special facilities such as campgrounds. Another cardinal point of management is zoning, especially where wildlife is concerned. The growth of recreation planning has been sudden and so the plans tend to deal with existing situations, i.e. they mostly ratify an already existing pattern of use but try to modify this pattern to avoid misuse of the resource. Only on 'new lands' can a plan be created *ab initio*.

In terms of development, SBB has placed some emphasis on swimming and camping. The former is especially popular in an informal setting and this is provided in some places by the presence of sand-pits in the forest. They may be long-standing, or new as in the case of the borrow-pits used in the construction of the motorway road

E35 from Amersfort to Zwolle. Old pits (an example can be seen in the hill-area east of Utrecht) tend to be over-used: heavy trampling results in soil erosion and the exposure of tree-roots, parking is un-controlled and sanitary facilities primitive or absent. The contrast with a recent pit is striking: here, parking is carefully controlled and screened as are toilet facilities, and picnic tables are placed around the lake; to take off some of the pressure marked trails lead off into the surrounding forest. The older pit, 'Henschotermeer', was en-larged in 1968–9 from 3 to 13 acres (1·2–5·3 ha) with the aid of a subsidy input of Dfl 2,500,000, which will also pay for sewerage, parking, kiosks and the reconstruction of the intersection with the main road to manage the 2500 cars expected on Sundays.

SBB owns fifty-eight campgrounds suitable for overnight family camping; some are for caravans as well, and there are also a few group camps. They are fairly evenly spread, with concentrations on the islands of Texel and Terschelling. A special SBB feature are the 'Kampeerpaspoortterreinen': more secluded and less developed campgrounds for those who have passed a simple examination in camping techniques and practices. The usual facilities of developed campgrounds are provided, in varying combinations, and a playing field is nearly always present. No fixed number of family sites is laid out and the picnic table/fireplace found in many North American sites is usually absent. The overnight fee in 1968 was Dfl 1·50 per per-son, plus Dfl 1·50 per car or caravan. There is as yet no policy for regional establishments or capacities. One of the major problems with the sites is their use as commuter-camps. Short-stay use for week-ends and vacations was intended but some people are coming in June and staying until September, with the breadwinner going to work each day as usual.

The most impressive contribution of SBB is probably in its day-use facilities. The swimming pools already mentioned form the foci of many of these but there are other areas where a complex of recreation sites has been developed. These usually involve a recreation-road leading off a public way. This road is narrow, winding and one-way. Off it are day-camping sites, games fields, conventional picnic sites and toilet facilities. Some special features may be included on the road or, more likely, led to by a number of colour-marked trails (for walkers and/or cyclists only) which lead off from various points and which are usually circular ('wandelrouten'). More specialized developments are also found as in a 1000-person picnic ground and playground, developed by SBB for the Utrecht Province, 'Doornse Gat'. Fourteen hectares of old sand-pits have been landscaped and prepared; another part of the pit will soon be abandoned by the extractors and all is ready to move in and bring this part speedily into use; in August 1968 the picnic tables were already stacked and the toilet foundations put in on one side.

Day-use complexes see the most impressive use of the zoning concepts of the SBB. Ample opportunity is given for the gregarious to congregate at a particular parking area, play-field or viewpoint, but the numerous trails encourage the solitude-seekers to find less-frequented places. The road and trail system is carefully planned so as to lead away from fragile areas or enclaves of private land and the whole is tied together by the large scale, coloured, 'Footprint' (Voetspoor) maps (1 cm : 200 m is a common scale) which are sold on the site for Dfl 1·00. Concentration areas are marked in bold colours and it is clear which areas are available for public use. Thus by means of this map and the signposts and map-boards, the zones are kept without any sense of compulsion, hectoring, or obvious exclusion, which is an avowed aim of SBB. Other interpretive services include nature walks ('rondleidingen') in summer, mostly free; visitor centres are beginning to be built, especially where the recreation element is in close association with a nature reserve, as in 'De Groote Peel', a mire area between Eindhoven and Venlo, and 'Savelsbos', an area of mixed deciduous woodland on chalk, with a prehistoric flint mine, in South Limburg, east of Maastricht.

The role of SBB in the Netherlands has been, and continues to be, crucial. Not only is it a big landowner with the opportunities to use a variety of resources but by means of its example and advice guides activity in other institutions. Its breadth of vision and integrated programmes make it an example well worthy of imitation in the sphere of user-oriented and intermediate types of rural recreation.

3.2 THE DELTA AND IJSSELMEER PROJECTS IN THE NETHERLANDS

Still at an early stage of development are the resources of the great reclamation schemes of the Delta Plan (in South Zeeland) and the IJsselmeer (Zuider Zee) projects.[10] Although their primary purpose is the reclamation of land, large areas of water are left between the new polders in the IJsselmeer and between the islands of South Zeeland. Thus are created long stretches of sandy beach fronting

[10] Most of this section is derived from observation in the field in 1968.

onto wide but shallow stretches of inland water, often of a relatively sheltered character. These conditions are excellent for recreation, especially sailing, and the plans include large numbers of yacht harbours (which are leased by the project authorities to private enterprise), picnic and day-camping grounds, and swimming zones. SBB has prepared landscape plans which usually involve large areas of planting. In the use of some of the South Zeeland areas, this is badly needed since the shores of the new lakes are very open and flat, and hence both exposed and monotonous. The Veersemeer, between Walcheren and the Bevelands, is an example of this. The small fishing villages cut off from the sea have been compensated by the great increase in recreational traffic, and small attractive towns such as Veere (Walcheren) are enjoying an unprecedented prosperity. In this area, also, the great seawall itself forms an attraction for recreation, partly because it is so high and thus forms a magnet for inhabitants of this flat land.

The shores of the Veluwe Meer, between the IJsselmeer polder of Oostelijk Flevoland and the mainland are intensively used for recreation. The water and beach are user-oriented areas for the Amsterdam-Utrecht-Arnhem region (South Zeeland tends to be intermediate for these areas). Camping sites are being developed inside the polders: tree planting has been done and the authority is now waiting for them to grow to a sufficient height before opening the campground fully, so that a maze-like structure of low bushes is in fact a campground *in utero*. Between Harderwijk and Elburg, similar developments are found, although the emphasis here is on picnics and day-camping since it is near the new motorway from Amersfoort to Zwolle. On the inland side of the road, north of Harderwijk, the upland forest and heath area of the Veluwe approaches the Veluwe Meer and here SBB have undertaken many of the developments for day-use described earlier. This combination of environments is especially useful in the uncertain climate of Western Europe: a day which becomes dull and windy is not lost if a retreat from the shore to sheltered forest recreation grounds can be made. The principle of full use of blocked-off arms of the sea is also seen in the Brielse Meer, on the southern periphery of Europoort. Here within sight (and smell) of the tank farms and refineries of the huge industrial developments is a sailing and beach area, with campground. A small nature reserve is also kept, as a partial compensation for the larger one destroyed in the building of Europoort.

89

Apart from the openness, which is being remedied as fast as alders, willows, and hazel can grow, the main disadvantage of the new beaches seems to be the relative ease of colonization by land plants so that sometimes only half a metre or so of bare sand remains between the water's edge and a more or less closed community of grasses and weedy species. It is clear that heavy use is essential to keep these beaches in useable condition; but there seems to be little danger of this not happening, even with the 162·5 miles (250 km) of public beach which the Netherlands enjoys.

3.3 JOINT BODIES IN THE NETHERLANDS

An outstanding feature of the Netherlands is the number of special bodies set up to manage a particular resource, or small region, especially for recreation or nature conservation. The Dutch words 'stichting' or '-schap' which are applied, do not translate easily into English but 'association' or 'foundation' are probably the best. The association may consist of representatives of the owners of the resource, the user-associations (for example, sailing clubs or walking clubs), the local Municipalities, the Province, the Municipalities from which users come, and probably also SBB and ANWB (the Automobile Association). This membership is variable but usually consists of whoever is appropriate, and the association is eligible for ORW money for development of recreation schemes. In this way quite complex areas such as heath-forest-agricultural land regions, with a multiplicity of ownerships can be given integrated management which will realize the recreational potential while inflicting the minimum damage on the other land or water uses.

(a) The 'Verenigen de Utrechtse Heuvelrug' (the Association for the Utrecht Hill Area) is one example.[11] This was set up in 1959 and consists of the landowners and interested parties of this area of forest and heath between Utrecht and Amersfoort. The Association does not itself own land but enters into 20-year leases with landowners.[12] Its location is critical for it is the first such environment met on the main roads west from the north wing of Randstadt Holland. The members are in two classes: the ordinary members (including the municipalities) who own at least 5 ha of land in the region, and the

[11] Verenigen de Utrechtse Heuvelrug, *A few information about the Utrechtse Heuvelrug Association* (mimeo, 1968).

[12] The work of the Utrechtse Heuvelrug Association, *Recreation News Supplement* 1 (1970), pp. 6–8.

co-operating members like the SBB, ANWB, Provincial Planning Office, the Association for the Preservation of Natural Beauty and a few others. The governing body has twenty-one members and is serviced by the Provincial Government.

The Association has encouraged the development of forest areas for day-recreation and linked these with an ANWB tourist route to draw traffic away from vulnerable areas such as nature reserves and 'quiet' zones for the solitary. Thus heavy use is hopefully diverted to the areas best fitted to receive it: a total of thirteen recreation sites has so far been developed and a regional recreation plan drawn up. About Dfl 1,500,000 had been invested by 1968 and a further Dfl 3,500,000 is planned in the next few years. The money comes almost totally from subsidies, and the landowners make their contribution through the solution of problems not the outlay of cash. The operating costs in 1968 were Dfl 140,000 and upkeep Dfl 48,500. The former are subsidized by the national and provincial governments, the latter only by provincial and municipal governments.

The actual developments include the SBB projects 'Henschotermeer' and 'Doornse Gat' already described, together with other picnic grounds, recreational parking areas and day-camping sites. Also very popular is the 'Belvedere Scesterberg', a hillside overlooking a large military airfield. A café, kiosk, and toilets, plus picnic tables, has been installed together with a car and 'bus park. The Association gets 4 per cent of the gross sales of the café owner. Since the government provided 50 per cent of the money, we may assume that security is not a particularly important consideration.

(b) The Plassenschap Loosdrecht en Omstreken (Loosdrecht Lakes Authority) was formed in 1957 to manage a large area of water formed from former peat diggings that were half land (the baulks) and half water (the flooded cuttings).[13] The members of this authority are the local municipalities (Loosdrecht, Brenkelen and Loenen), the three cities whose inhabitants contribute most to its use (Amsterdam, Utrecht and Hilversum), together with representatives of the province and the users. Again, investment can be channelled through governmental sources. This Authority has two main functions: development and management. Development has

[13] *Loosdrechtse Plassen*, AIT-Congress Info. Bull., (1966); *Plassenschap Loosdrecht en Omstreken* (mimeo, in English, n.d.); ANWB Waterkort Loosdrechtse Plassen, 1:15,000 (1966). (A splendid piece of cartography.)

included the clearing of peat baulks from large areas but their retention (and even revetment) in others and, most spectacular of all, the construction of islands in the main lake to provide variety and shelter. Camping and caravan sites and yacht harbours are also being developed, and the authority is trying to buy up the margins of the water bodies so as to regulate second home construction and irregular camping. Management functions are principally those of regulating house-boats, zoning the lake for different uses and controlling irregular building and camping.

The popularity of Loosdrecht has brought considerable prosperity to adjacent settlements like Oude and Nieuw Loosdrecht. Private harbours, boat sale and repair yards and a whole gamut of entertainment and refreshment facilities have sprung up.

Both the Utrechtse Heuvelrug and the Loosdrechtse Plassen suffer from the disadvantage that no government money is available for upkeep. For this user fees (not collected in the former case and for motorboats only in the latter) and municipal subsidies must be relied upon. The local authorities are somewhat reluctant to give money for maintaining facilities used by outsiders and so difficulties are arising; at the moment the problem is less acute in the Heuvelrug since the developments there are quite new.

(c) The term National Park in the Netherlands has no distinct meaning and is not used by governmental agencies for any of their developments. In one case it is applied to a Foundation of the type described above, the Stichting der National Park de Kennermerduinen, in which the State, the Province of North Holland and the municipalities of Amsterdam and Haarlem participate.[14] It is an area of 1200 ha of dunes on the coast between Bloemendahl and IJmuiden. Since this is an area of high population concentration, the twin purposes of protection of the dune ecosystem (including such rare plants as *Parnassia palustris*) and catering for mass rural recreation have to be reconciled. In addition, about 90 per cent of the dunes are used by water works which bring in river water and use the sand as a natural filter. Management of the dunes must not interfere with this use. The conservation of the area is facilitated by a boundary with five gates and the more or less complete authority of

[14] E. C. M. Roderkerk, *Recreatie, Recreatieverzorging en Natuurbescherming in de Kennermerduinen* (Delft 1961: English summary); Nationale Park '*De Kennermerduinen*', AIT-Congress Info. Bull. (1966).

the Director to manage recreation as he wishes. By skilful deployment of car parks, paths and signs, and the creation of swimming ponds, 90 per cent of visitors confine themselves (by choice not compulsion) to 155 ha of the Park, plus the beach. In 1969 there were 700,000 visitors,[15] and at any one time a maximum overall density of 100/130 persons per ha (20,000 visitors, achieved only on a few fine days each year) is reckoned as the carrying capacity. This can be regulated by closing car parks, since 75 per cent of the visitors come by this means. In the south-west of 'De Kennermerduinen' a 19-ha campsite has been laid out with a capacity of 900 caravans or tents with some segregation of each. About 200 of the pitches are reserved for short-stay visitors but the rest may be used on a long-stay basis during the holiday months. The peripheral location of the campsite helps to ensure the preservation of the character of the rest of the area and to keep people away from the most fragile parts.

Nature protection is carried out firstly by providing ample recreation opportunities, since most visitors who come want only to be in the open, secondly by persuading people not to walk on the dunes away from the numerous paths (this is done mainly by spreading branches near the pathside and has the additional virtue of stabilizing sand) and by a fence (more for psychological than physical effect) round the lake used by most of the birds. A notice here shows a bird saying 'this lake is for us—yours is down there'. Visitor fees are charged (Dfl 0·50 adults, 0·15 children, 1·00 cars in 1969, monthly and yearly tickets available) and a further income is gained from renting the pheasant shooting, charging Dfl 2500 p.a. for a club of eight people who are allowed eight shoots per year. The cull is one animal/ha/yr.

In spite of sophisticated and successful management, problems remain. The withdrawal of water is leading to die-off among pine and birch trees in the wooded interior of the dune system; rabbits are a deleterious influence and have to be shot at night, which is expensive and time-consuming; toilet facilities are almost inadequate at heavily used areas; there are no information or interpretation programmes. Above all there is the question of the ultimate carrying capacity for recreation. Visitor numbers tend to be more or less stable at the moment but should they rise steeply, how much sacrifice of nature will the Director and his board make to accommodate recreationists, and what criteria for decision will be used? In spite

[15] Het Nationale Park De Kennermerduinen, *Recreation News Supplement* 1 (1970), pp. 1–5.

of these difficulties, the writer feels that Kennermerduinen is one of the most successful recreation projects—in that type of context—that he has seen.

3.4 NATURE PARKS AND COASTAL USE IN DENMARK

The Nature Park is an idea put forward by the government's advisory secretariat on conservation, which attempts to satisfy some of the demands for landscape preservation and the protection of a desired milieu. The basis is an area of rural landscape in which the expected elements are found. It is unlikely to be natural or even necessarily wild, and a combination of woods, villages, water and ancient monuments would appear to form a satisfactory basis for a Nature Park. Eventually it is hoped that such parks will exist for every characteristic region of Denmark as well as encompassing features which are of national or even international significance. The conditions expected of a naturpark can be seen from the example of a 12,000 ha area in central Zealand, the Tystrup-Bavelse *naturpark*. Here the variety of landscape is very high: a lake is surrounded by woods, both coniferous and deciduous but in which old growth beech predominates, farmland separates the woodland areas, an eel-fisher's house (half-timbered) has been converted to a fish restaurant, and there are several small villages with typical rural churches, and some megalithic tombs. The whole forms a distinctly pleasing landscape, and in addition one to which public access is possible to a large degree. Most of the woodlands are open to the public and this is also permitted to parts of a large estate (Naesbyholm-Bavelse) that borders the lake. Agreements to safeguard the landscape, and other protection measures, apply to only 10 per cent of the area, and the rest is protected by the already existing general legislation which will be discussed later. Development for recreation is minimal, in keeping with the 'expected milieu' concept of landscape conservation; a small unsurfaced car park is provided about 1·5 km from the lake on one of the access roads. Since this area is within easy distance of Copenhagen, it seems likely that it will experience heavy recreational use in the future.

During the 1960s the Naturfrednings og Landskabsconsulet listed most of the potential Nature Park areas in Denmark, but until a government report[16] of 1967 finally resulted in the passage of the

[16] Denmark, Ministeriet for Kulturelle Anligger, *Betoekning om Naturfredning*, Statnings Trykningskontor Betoekning 461 (Copenhagen 1967).

1969 Conservation of Nature Act (Act No. 318 of 18 June 1969), little was done to acquire them. The 1969 Act recognizes the role of the state in actively acquiring recreational resources, and so a policy of buying or leasing such areas is being pursued as fast as funds for

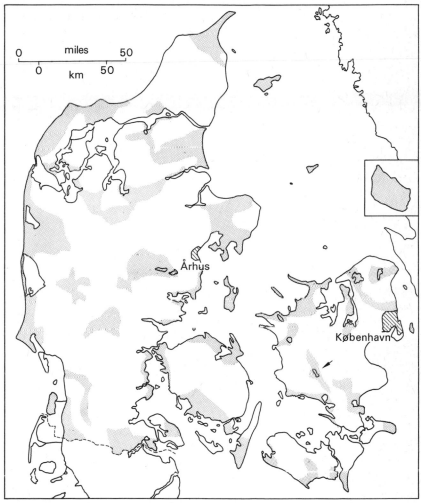

Figure 12   Proposed Nature Parks in Denmark (shaded areas). The Tystrup-Bavelse NP discussed in the text is indicated by an arrow.
Source: R. M. Newcomb, 'Has the past a future in Denmark? The preservation of landscape history within the Nature Park', *Geoforum* 9 (1972), p. 64.

purchase and compensation become available (Figure 12). There has also been a changed attitude towards management, it having been recognized that mere designation of an area was insufficient. Development for management purposes is now an active part of any naturpark plan, along the lines expected anywhere else in the West, but a special concern is evinced in Denmark for historical values, which are thought to be as good a reason for the designation of nature parks as those pertaining to the protection of flora, fauna, scenery, and the provision of rural recreation space.[17]

The provisions of the new Conservation of Nature Act also changed some aspects of shoreline recreation. Hitherto, individuals could own shoreline as far as 400 m seawards from their dwellings, usually summer cottages. Visitors could not be kept off the beach but legally had to keep moving along and not stop to bathe or picnic. Thus only as the coastline became truly urbanized, as for instance in the spread of Copenhagen northward along the Zealand coast, did access provisions improve. However the 1969 Act removed the 'keep moving' provision and beach use is now more normal, continuous movement being due to the bracing nature of Baltic and North Sea winds rather than the anachronisms of Danish law.

3.5 OTHER ASPECTS OF RURAL RECREATION IN DENMARK

As in many countries, a great deal of use of rural environments for recreation exists. Camping sites are plentiful in Denmark, being run by municipalities as well as private enterprise.[18] The Danish camping club records a rise of 150 per cent in the number of listed campsites between 1958 and 1967 (Table 2.1). The overall number in 1967 was 477 and Table 2.2 shows their distribution within the country. Nearly all of the sites are coastal and a disproportionate number of both the sites and their intensity of use as indicated by the number of overnight stays are on Zealand; again, the Copenhagen region claims a very large number of these. A comparison with the map of summerhouse distribution (see Figure 28) shows the distinct preference for similar areas and there can be no doubt that pressures on coastal resources from the former are reinforced by demands to develop camping sites in the same places. As with summerhouses, a national distribution policy would appear desirable.

[17] R. M. Newcomb, 'Has the past a future in Denmark? The preservation of landscape history within the nature park', *Geoforum* 9 (1972), pp. 61–7.

[18] A. Holst-Hansen, 'Danske campingpladser i 1967', *Kulturgeografi* 107 (1968), pp. 239–42.

Table 2.1　Denmark: camping club listed sites 1958–67

Year	Number of sites	Total overnights (thousands)
1958	149	1015
1959	189	1611
1960	217	1849
1961	271	2223
1962	290	2500
1963	321	3500
1964	331	3500
1965	391	3600
1966	418	4300
1967	443	5164

Source: A. Holst-Hansen, 'Danske Campingpladser i 1967'.

Table 2.2　Denmark: distribution of all camp sites 1967

Region	Number of sites	Total overnights (thousands)
Zealand	78	1543
Lolland-Falster and Møn	28	203
Bornholm	20	284
Funen and adjacent islands	61	591
Jutland	290	3021

Source: A. Holst-Hansen, 'Danske Campingpladser i 1967'.

The Danish idea of recreation as being outdoor in a characteristic milieu, leads to the use of many nature reserves for recreation, especially where these are woodlands, dunes and heaths. In the northern counties of Jutland, for example, (Hjørring, Thisted and Alberg amter), there were 109 protected areas in 1966.[19] Many of these are very small but others comprise large areas of dune and dune-heath, which may be flanked or transected by roads. Hulsig Klitter, totalling 1450 ha, has a main road through it and thus receives considerable recreational use. No developments, however, are made, in contrast to what would happen in the Netherlands, for example, so that although these areas are protected from urban and industrial development, some of them may be in danger of damage from recreationists. This is particularly so of habitats susceptible to fire and trampling. This is also true of the Hansted reserve in

[19] K. Dahl, *Naturfredninger i Nordjylland* (Copenhagen 1966).

97

northern Thy where 40 km of dunes and heath containing many species of considerable interest was threatened by recreational influx due to the building of a new road from Hanstholm to Klitmøller.

In such a maritime country as Denmark, the importance of water-oriented recreations such as sailing, motor-boating and water-skiing cannot be overlooked. No collections of statistics on numbers of users or on demand exist, but the Aarhus regional plan estimates an ownership rate which will produce a need for one mooring place per two hundred people, each boat-space needing 65 m of land for access, laying-up room, maintenance area, clubhouse and the like.[20] No fears have been expressed that there will be insufficient searoom for such a high rate of ownership and indeed it is hoped by many people that some of the smaller islands, whose agricultural economy is rapidly becoming unviable, may be re-vitalized by an influx of yacht traffic. 'Yacht trails' have been suggested as ways of channelling users towards places in need of this development but one of the major obstacles is likely to be the provision of fresh water on some of the smaller islands.

Roadside rests and picnic areas are present along a few main roads in Denmark, but otherwise no attempts at formalization have been made.

3.6 THE FORESTRY COMMISSION IN THE UK

Inaugurated under the Forestry Act of 1919, this Commission (which also extends to Scotland) is now the largest landowner in the country. Their estates are scattered over the whole country (Figure 13), there being at least 2500 separate parcels of forest, but there is a concentration on uplands and areas of poor soils in the lowlands, i.e. the areas where the Commission have been able to acquire land most easily. The job of the Commission has always been directed primarily at growing timber since it was created in order to build up a reserve of timber in a country largely depleted of forests: England and Wales have only 7 per cent of their land surface in woodland. To this end, it has afforested the poorer lands it has been able to buy and lease with fast-growing conifers, such as European and Japanese larch, Norway spruce and west coast trees like Sitka spruce (which accounts for the bulk of the Commission's plantings) and Lodgepole pine (Table 2.3). On this account, and because a heartlessly commercial approach to

[20] *Egnsplan for Arhusregen* (1966), pp. 283–4.

98

forestry practice was the order of the day, the Commission has for
many years been the object of severe criticism as a despoiler of landscapes and a ravager of amenity. Only where existing forest and heath

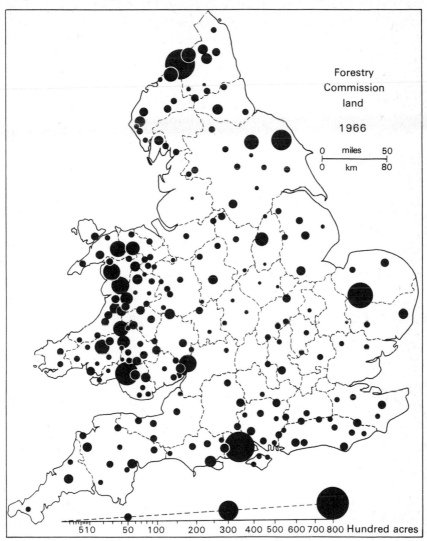

Figure 13   Distribution of Forestry Commission Land in England and
Wales, 1966. Apart from the New Forest and Breckland, the bulk of the
holdings are in the uplands, removed from centres of population (100
acres = 40·5 ha).
Source: J. A. Patmore, *Land and Leisure*, p. 140.

99

areas, such as the Forest of Dean and the New Forest, were taken over were the traditional hardwoods intended to be safeguarded and their perpetuation ensured. Nevertheless, in spite of being the anathema of the articulate, people began to use the new forests for recreation and as early as 1935 a National Forest Park was created in Scotland, to be followed during the next 20 years by six others, three of which are in England and Wales. Special attention to visual amenity is being given in these large areas, which comprise about one-fifth of the Commission's estate. They have also been areas of maximum recreation opportunity in the form of access to forest roads for walking, car-parking facilities, and rudimentary campgrounds.

Table 2.3   Forestry Commission: land use at 30 September 1969

	Ha		
	England	Scotland	Wales
Total area	304,072	676,696	153,531
Forest land	251,834	408,561	123,212
Agricultural land	11,801	107,437	4,746

Source: Forestry Commission, Annual Report 1966–7.

Other than in these National Forest Parks, public access for recreation was rarely encouraged but after a ministerial review of policy in 1963 the objective of creating a large reserve of standing timber was abandoned. The necessity of high timber production was emphasized because of its contribution to the balance of payments but the Commission was directed

. . . wherever possible, to provide public access and recreation, and to devote more attention to increasing the beauty of the landscape.[21]

The application of cost/benefit analysis to the Commission's operations has further emphasized their importance for recreation and visual amenity, although it concludes that the main justification for extra planting is the part it can play in sustaining the rural economy of regions undergoing rural depopulation. Thus since 1964, the development of recreation in the forests has increased rapidly and they are now rapidly becoming centres of attraction for recreation. Thus by 1972 the Commission had created for public use, for example,

[21] Forestry Commission, *Annual Report 1962–3* (London), p. 7.

100

11 camping and caravan sites with 3700 units, 36 organizational camping sites, 195 picnic places, 262 forest trails, 150 car parks and 9640 miles (15,424 km) of forest roads, including 4 scenic drives.[22] Some charges are made in the forests, for the use of facilities or on a per-car basis. The actual development programme appears to be decided at regional level so that to some extent the presence of foresters not well disposed to recreation could inhibit its growth. However, public pressure is probably now sufficient to force such a person into new attitudes. Examples of recreation-oriented developments in the forests include Grizedale Forest (7300 acres, 2956 ha), in the south of the Lake District National Park. This is a pioneer area for developing multiple use of the forests, with emphasis on wildlife and recreation. A campground is allied with a Deer Museum/Visitor Centre, nature trails, wildlife ponds and deer observation hides and is the centre for longer hiking trails into the surrounding forests and moorlands. Many of these forests are very large by British standards of land ownership: Snowdonia Forest Park is 23,800 acres (9639 ha), Forest of Dean Park, 35,000 acres (14,175 ha), and the Border Forest Park, 126,000 acres (51,030 ha). The 93,000 acres (37,665 ha) of the New Forest, in Hampshire, is largely under the control of the Forestry Commission, whose effect upon the 65,730 acres (26,474 ha) which they manage can be profound, particularly their attitude to the replacement of hardwoods and the control of the heavy recreation pressure, which according to one study would treble between 1965 and 1981.[23] In 1965, a Bank holiday Sunday brought 58,005 people with 20,002 cars to 145 sq miles (375 km²).[24] These were largely concentrated near the roads, making use of Forestry Commission and private woodlands, together with areas of open heathland and grassland to which access on foot is allowed. Unlike their other forests however the Commission has less managerial authority because of the traditional common rights of the New Forest and the interspersion of private land and National Nature Reserves.[25]

In many other forests, minor alterations have sufficed to cater well

---

[22] Forestry Commission, *Forestry Policy: a Consultative Document* (London 1972); and Annual Report 1971–2 (London 1972).

[23] Colin Buchanan and partners, *South Hampshire Study, Supplementary Volume 2; Methods and Policies* (London 1966), p. 143. Camping has been increasing at 15–20 per cent per annum, *Recreation News* 6 (1969), p. 2.

[24] *Ibid.*

[25] J. Tinker, 'Marrying wildlife to forestry', *New Sci.* 42 (1969), pp. 518–20.

for increased recreation demand. In Hamsterley Forest, Co. Durham, for example, a forest road has been constructed beside a stream so as to yield a number of streamside picnic places.

The use being made of the forests has been recently studied.[26] Ninety-three per cent of visitors came by car, and the mean distance of travel to the four forests studied was 25·2 miles (40·5 km) on the day of questioning. This latter statistic hides the fact that forests like Cannock Chase in Staffordshire receive a lot of day-use from local conurbations whereas Glen More in the Cairngorms has greater weekend and vacation use. A study in part of the Snowdonia NFP in North Wales showed that 43 per cent of visitors travelled more than 201 miles (323 km) to get to the campground they were using and that 50 per cent of them were on a 4–14-day vacation.[27]

A survey at 150 sites within the forests revealed a total of 4–8 million visits during the period 1 June–30 September 1968, about one-third of these being at weekends. But in holiday areas such as south-west England and parts of Scotland, weekday attendance was relatively high and may even exceed Saturdays and occasionally Sundays.[28] This shows that some forests are receiving resource-based type recreation, an indication of the drawbacks of this particular classification in small countries. The use of the forests on a national scale is quite clearly influenced by their proximity to large cities and although all of them report the main activities to be picnics, driving for pleasure and walking, the mix of these and the degree of development must reflect the intensity of demand at a given place, especially where forest roads are used for scenic drives (Table 2.4).

The demands for improvements quoted by Mutch[29] centre around improved sanitation and the provision of picnic tables. As far as access is concerned, round-walk footpaths of a stated duration were one of the chief requests, along with large-scale maps of the forest. If these changes are made, the move towards developments and management of the type practised by the Staatsbosbeheer in the Netherlands will be considerable and their experience will be very valuable.

[26] W. E. S. Mutch, *Public Recreation in National Forests: A Factual Survey*, Forestry Commission Booklet 21 (London 1968).
[27] J. A. and L. B. Sinden, 'A forest recreation survey: implications for future development', *Scottish Forestry* 18 (1964), pp. 120–27.
[28] R. M. Sideway, 'Estimation of day use recreation by the Forestry Commission', *Recreation News* 20 (1970), pp. 1–2.
[29] W. E. S. Mutch, *op. cit.*, pp. 85–6.

Table 2.4   Activities in British forests: per cent 1964

Activity	Cannock*	Allerston	Glen More	Loch Lomond*
Picnicking	29	19	9	17
Pleasure driving	28	42	23	34
Camping and caravanning	1	0	12	7
Walking and climbing	24	19	27	20
Photography	7	9	11	14

* Near to large population centres.
Source: W. E. S. Mutch, Public Recreation in National Forests: a Factual Survey.

Most visitors appear to want seclusion, quiet and the freedom to wander afoot, qualities difficult to come by in lowland England at any rate. The complete exclusion of the motor car is obviously impossible but its restriction and concentration appears to be a good solution.

3.7   RESOURCE DEVELOPMENT COORDINATED BY THE COUNTRYSIDE COMMISSION IN ENGLAND AND WALES

(a)   The National Parks[30]

Following the passage of the National Parks and Access to the Countryside Act 1949, ten National Parks were created in England and Wales between 1949 and 1955 (Figure 14). These areas cover about 8 per cent of the total area of the two countries and mainly comprise 'wild' land, although the valleys contain much agricultural land. Therefore, the Parks extend over a great deal of private land, as well as common land. Common land is obscure in its legal relations but it is certainly not public domain and except in Urban Districts, people have no legal right of access to it although a great deal of de facto use takes place. About 260,000 people live in the National Parks and a fair proportion of them earn their

[30] H. C. Darby, Britain's National Parks, Adv. Sci. 20 (1963), pp. 307–18; Annual Reports of the National Parks Commission (London 1950–68); Annual Reports of the Countryside Commission (London 1968–). At 30 August 1968, the National Parks comprised 5258 sq miles (13,612 km²); the first (the Peak District) was confirmed in 1951, the last (Brecon Beacons) in 1957. A useful map of protected areas of most kinds appeared in Geographical Magazine, October 1973 ('Geographical Magazine Map of Cherished Land').

103

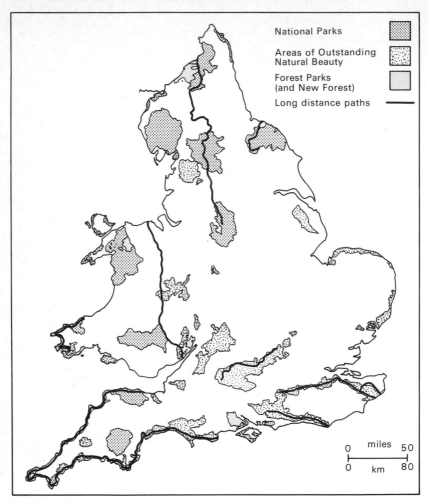

National Parks

Areas of Outstanding
Natural Beauty

Forest Parks
(and New Forest)

Long distance paths

miles 50
km 80

Figure 14   National Parks, and Areas of Outstanding Natural Beauty in
England and Wales in 1974.
Source: Dept of the Environment, *Report of the National Park Policies
Review Committee,* 1974.

living there, so that recreation has to come to terms immediately
with this central fact. The major ways in which conflicts then arise
are:

1   The road systems of these upland areas are unsuitable for heavy
    traffic. They are narrow, twisting and badly graded. Widening

them is very expensive, attracts little central finance, and is inimical to the values which the National Parks are supposed to protect. On many of them, there are few places other than grassy verges (often very soft) on which to pull off the road (Figure 15).

2 The predominant agricultural system of the uplands is the raising of sheep. Enclosed fields in the valleys give way to open fell or moorland beyond and the paths through the fields are often misused: gates left open, dogs allowed to worry animals, and litter scattered, some of which is edible by, but lethal to, stock.

3 On some moorlands, agricultural subsidies have made ploughing-up for arable crops profitable. Such areas are often near roads and thus badly-needed access land is reduced in area. The 1968 Countryside Act gave authorities the power to make an order requiring six months' notice of any intention on the part of a landowner to plough National Park moorland. This was first used in 1971–2 in the Exmoor park.[31] Authorities have been very loth to use their powers to make access agreements or acquire land by compulsory purchase, where moorland is concerned. Additionally, afforestation has reduced the extent of open land, and this has been stigmatized by open-air enthusiasts; but it seems likely that the forests when grown will have greater recreational potential than the open land, provided that they are in public ownership. In the interim, controversy over the informal arrangements about afforestation which exist between the Forestry Commission, private timber growers and the Countryside Commission still continues. The Ramblers' Association, the Standing Committee on National Parks and the Sandford Committee (see below) all called for forestry to be brought under planning control but a review of government policy in 1974 brought no change to the existing situation.

4 The extraction of minerals has been carried on for a long time in the areas which are now National Parks. Quarrying is the commonest form, although mining (for example, of potash) exists also. Planning consent usually involves strict conditions over lorry routes' screening and restoration, and firms are warned that their operations may cost more in the Parks. Indeed, some preservationists have suggested that mining of rocks such as limestone (consumption of which rose in the UK from 29 to 86

---

[31] *Fifth Report of the Countryside Commission* (London 1971–2), p. 5.

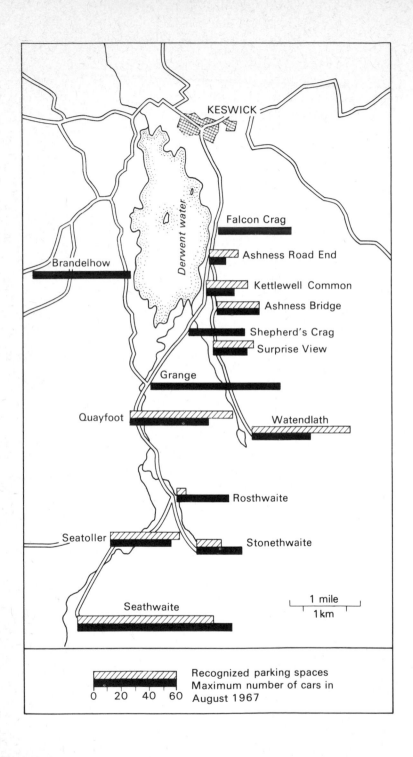

KESWICK

Derwent water

Falcon Crag

Ashness Road End

Brandelhow

Kettlewell Common

Ashness Bridge

Shepherd's Crag

Surprise View

Grange

Quayfoot

Watendlath

Rosthwaite

Seatoller

Stonethwaite

Seathwaite

1 mile

1km

Recognized parking spaces
Maximum number of cars in
August 1967

0   20   40   60

million tonnes 1955–72) may soon become little more expensive than quarrying, especially if a use for the excavated cavern can be found. Such a change, if feasible, would help to eliminate the many conflicts which mineral extraction creates but which seem mootable in view of the determination to secure cheap supplies and to continue to support the traditional economic bases of the Parks.

The recreation situation (Figure 16) has two main elements:

1 Informal use of open land such as moorland, heath, down and cliff, without any facilities for recreation other than, perhaps, a car park and toilets in a key village or a lay-by at a special view-point. Walking takes place along the network of public footpaths and across open land; picnics often take place on private land without permission. Land to which there is *de facto* access by the public is variable in quantity within the National Parks. Agreements (see below) negotiated with landowners may open up grouse moors, for example, except for a few days per year, and in parks such as Exmoor and the Lake District the contribution of the National Trust is considerable.

2 Use of *de jure* access land. This is confined to areas under Access Agreements negotiated by the National Park Planning Committees with landowners, who can be compensated for their loss of use; to land owned by a public body, usually small in area; to forest land belonging to the Forestry Commission; and to commons within the pre-1974 Urban Districts. (Most of the common land in the Lake District National Park is within the former Lakes Urban District, thus ensuring public access to the fells and mountains.)

National Parks are full of conflicts between 'economic' uses and recreation, apart from those between mass use of the areas and the amenity values which the Parks are supposed to protect. Increased visitor pressure is likely to bring the situation to some form of crisis point within a relatively short time. Part of the blame for this situation lay in the planning authorities for the Parks. It was intended that each Park should have its own Planning Board, but in the event

---

Figure 15   Parking overflows in August 1967 in Borrowdale, one of the most popular valleys in the Lake District National Park.
Source: J. A. Patmore, *Land and Leisure*, p. 140.

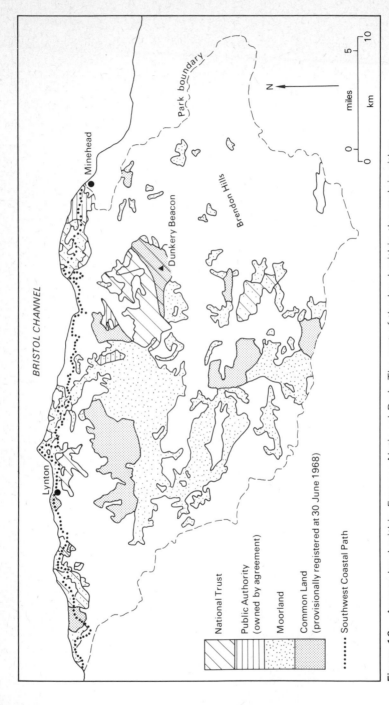

Figure 16 Access land within Exmoor National Park. The rest of the land within the park is either common land without *de jure* public access, or private land.
Source: J. A. Patmore, *Land and Leisure*, p. 198.

only two Parks (Lake District and Peak) acquired this form of management, the rest having delegated committees of the County Council or Councils. Each Committee has had two-thirds elected members of the County Council and one-third members nominated by the Minister of Housing and Local Government. One result has been a reluctance to spend money on recreation development, even though 75 per cent Government grants are available, and to concentrate instead on development control. This has saved many beautiful landscapes from spoilation but people want to do more than just look. The farmers are equally unhappy, for the term National Park brings many visitors who expect free access everywhere, and they chafe against the development control. This latter is little stricter than anywhere else, however, and agricultural land use changes and buildings are generally exempt.

With all their drawbacks, the National Parks receive a great deal of recreational use, though no nationally comparable and reliable documentation on the quantity of it exists. Most recreations are carried on in them: some legally, others not; some without detriment to economic activities, others much less so. Just looking is probably the most popular (often from inside a car since rainfall in upland Britain is normally above 40 inches (1000 mm) per annum), followed by roadside picnics and walking. There exists also a hardy band of walkers who seek the highest wildest places in the parks or who undertake the whole length of the Pennine Way as a holiday task (c. 1000 people in the summer of 1971, taking an average of 19 days[32]) or who endure the Lyke Wake Walk (40 miles (64 km) across the North York Moors National Park to be done at a stretch with only short halts allowed). These are emulated, regrettably, by others not so tough or well equipped, who get caught by changeable weather so that deaths from falling over mist-shrouded cliffs or from exposure occur every year in the hills, and every upland region has its rescue organization. But the great majority of visitors come by car and concentrate at favoured places so that crowding becomes a feature of the towns within the parks, along the roads and at particularly popular spots. The numbers of visitors and their vehicles impair the qualities they have come to enjoy and their presence produces demands for change which alter the character of the locality. Nowhere is this more apparent than in the Lake District National

[32] *Fifth Report of the Countryside Commission*, p. 10.

Park where demands for wider roads, more weekend chalets, caravan and campsites, more housing in the towns such as Windermere and Bowness and more facilities for water sport, are apparently inexorable. Added to these are the decision to allow one road through the park to be developed into a major highway, the pressure to widen another for use by heavy goods traffic, and the problems caused by slate quarrying. The responses of the planning board for the Park are varied and sensitive: visitor centres urge people to try different places, strict control of the quantity and quality of new building is enforced, and facilities erected where essential. That the Park remains essentially and recognizably 'The Lakes' is a tremendous tribute to the Board and its policies, but both their powers and the resources of land and water are limited so that halts will have to be called. The first of these must inevitably involve motor traffic, although experiments in 'tidal flow' traffic and the replacement of cars by minibuses in some of the narrow valleys have not been successful, usually due to opposition from local people catering to visitors; similar traffic control experiments in other parks have been better received.[33]

Most such problems are felt by the other National Parks: the Peak District is next in danger of what the London *Times* called death from ochlothanasia (overcrowding) and others on lesser but significant scales, all of which will be made worse by the extension of the country's motorway system. Expressions of dissatisfaction with the Parks led to the setting up of a National Park Policies Review Committee in 1971, which reported in 1974. This body (the Sandford Committee) reviewed[34] the inherent conflict between landscape protection and development for recreation and concluded that where conflict was acute, then the first purpose should prevail. Other important sections recommended the routing of all trunk roads outside the Parks, the inclusion of forestry and farm buildings under planning control, and firmer resistance to out-of-character development. Some American thinking perhaps permeates some of the members

[33] Countryside Commission, *Transport for Countryside Recreation* (London 1973); J. C. Miles, *The Goyt Valley Traffic Experiment* (Countryside Commission and Peak Park Planning Board 1972). A free bus service in the Hadrian's Wall section of the Northumberland National Park was run in the summer of 1974.

[34] Department of the Environment, *Report of the National Park Policies Review Committee* (London 1974). Estimates for 1974/5 reported in *The Guardian* 10 April 1974; proposals for the contents of new legislation by G. Haythornthwaite in July 1974, reported in *Recreation News* No. 64 (July 1974), pp. 2–3.

of the committee when they call for wilderness and similar places to be designated as 'National Heritage Areas', where the whole cost of their preservation would be borne by central government, and no damaging change or use or development would be allowed without reference to Parliament. Substantial reservations about this idea have been expressed since it is feared that such tight regulation could only be accompanied by relaxations of development control outside the Heritage Areas.

The Sandford Committee was hopeful that the new administrative arrangements which started in 1974 would ease some problems; each park has a National Park Officer with his own staff and he will have to produce a National Park plan by 1977 and review it regularly thereafter. The Exchequer is to pay some of the administration costs, and for 1974/5 the central government grant to the Parks is nearly doubled, coming to £1·43 million which is c. 3p/cap/yr. National Parks in England and Wales are therefore in some senses neither National nor Parks. Since 25 per cent of finance and a good deal of control is local, they are only partly National; since they contribute in limited ways and with conflicts to the recreation supply, they are only partly Parks. New legislation would be needed to produce any radical change in the situation: it would contain provisions for all development in National Parks to come under planning control, finance for public transport schemes which would make car-less zones feasible, and a statutory requirement that all developers public or private, should consider the environmental consequences of their activities before any planning consents are given.

Although their problems are many, the achievements of the Parks are very worthwhile and it is notable that their example is sometimes viewed with enthusiasm abroad, chiefly in nations with extensive publicly-owned resources but without much development control outside the government-managed areas.[35]

(b) Areas of Outstanding Natural Beauty (AONBs) (Figure 14, p. 104)

In 1974 there were 31 of these, covering 7·7 per cent of England and Wales. 'Natural' beauty is a misnomer, for they are man-made landscapes. They are areas in which development control is strict and where Treasury finance is available for removal of eyesores and

[35] W. A. Johnson, *Public Parks on Private Land in England and Wales* (Baltimore 1971).

111

derelict buildings. As far as recreation development is concerned, the County Council is the authority, and in the Cannock Chase AONB, for example, Staffordshire County Council have developed picnic areas and car parks.

(c) Long-Distance Footpaths (Figure 14, p. 104)

The instigation of these is the responsibility of the Countryside Commission; the negotiation for the rights of way is between them, the local authorities and the landowners. It is therefore a long time between the announcement of a proposal and the opening of the path. The longest is the Pennine Way, from Derbyshire to the Scottish Border, some 250 miles (400 km), and others include the Cleveland Way (93 miles, 150 km) around the North Yorks Moors National Park, the Pembrokeshire Coast path (167 miles, 210 km); seven had been opened by the autumn of 1974.

(d) The Countryside Commission

The Countryside Commission replaced the National Parks Commission following the enactment of the Countryside Act 1968. This keeps under review not only the National Parks but the provision of facilities for the enjoyment of the countryside, the conservation and enhancement of natural beauty (usually man-made in Britain, in fact), and the matter of access to open space and the development of recreation in rural areas. But the 1968 Act conferred no more executive power than its predecessor and the Commission can only inform, persuade and channel finance. The latter is generally inadequate in quantity, only pence per head per annum, and it is quickly cut in the recurring financial crises which appear with all the certainty of cyclonic rainfall over maritime upland. Within its remit, the Commission appears to be a very useful body, but the national refusal to recognize the realities of rural resource planning can only hinder it from providing the proper service to the people of Britain.

3.8 COUNTY COUNCILS IN ENGLAND AND WALES

At the present time, the County Councils are the main authorities responsible for rural planning. Until recently this has largely been confined to development control and the ensuring of village growth, for example, in an orderly way. The passing of the Countryside Act 1968 places firm responsibility on them for the provision of some rural recreation developments, and provides 75 per cent Treasury

112

finance to that end. Campsites and picnic sites are among the facilities which it is desired to provide, along with a class of rural recreation areas called Country Parks (Figure 17).

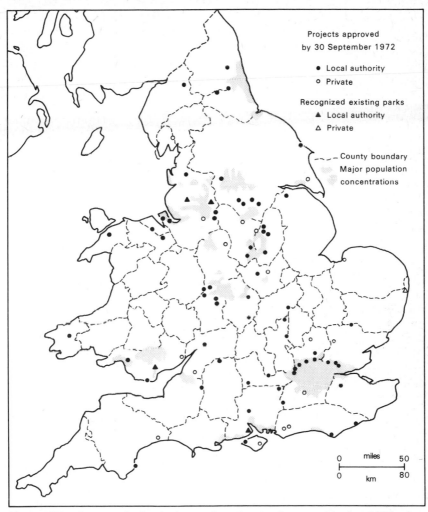

Figure 17 Country Parks designated under the Countryside Act 1968 of England and Wales. The general intent that they should be near urban population centres is apparently being carried out. (The county boundaries pre-date the changes of 1974.)
Source: J. A. Patmore, 'Recreation and resources II: Patterns of supply', *Geogr. J.* 139 (1973), p. 481.

113

Such areas are not closely defined in the Act, other than as intended to provide for the quiet enjoyment of the countryside[36] by the public and that they are to be sited with regard to catering for the population of large urban areas. Thus they are likely to be day-use and weekend-use areas with a variable degree of development and as such fall into Clawson's user-oriented and intermediate categories. The White Paper envisaged some as simple, with only basic works;[37] others with a restaurant and, 'perhaps some ornamental water'.[38] It appears that these Parks are to have two main functions:

1 To draw off some of the pressures from the National Parks, particularly those people who want access land rather than a particular scenic environment, and
2 To serve as focal points for countryside recreation, thus lessening aesthetic and physical damage in more vulnerable areas.

Many such Parks have now been designated,[39] some of which centre around historic houses and similar foci or 'rural rendez-vous' as Patmore calls them.[40] Counties which are in the vanguard of provision of such facilities have published studies either on a county-wide basis or of particular sub-regions with high recreation potential. The Countryside Commission, who channel the Treasury funds (available to individuals as well as local governments) suggest that the Parks should not be less than about 25 acres (10 ha) in size but recognize that their capacity to absorb high-intensity recreation or provide a variety of activities is of prime importance. Thus the priorities for grant aid reflect the need for more countryside access areas near large cities, the improvement of areas already in *de facto* use as country parks, and the transfer into recreational use of derelict or under-used public land.[41] By mid-1973, there were 99 country parks and over 100 picnic sites.[42]

Some County Councils have been running what are effectively

---

[36] Officially stated as, 'Recreation, the main aim of which is relaxation which requires little in the way of special skill or organization, which lacks any competitive element and which requires a countryside location for its full enjoyment'. See J. A. Zetter, *The Evolution of a Country Park Policy* (London 1971), p. 1.

[37] *Leisure in the Countryside: England and Wales*, Cmnd. 2928 (London HMSO 1966).

[38] *Ibid.*, p. 6.

[39] A list of new designations is published in *Recreation News* (London).

[40] J. A. Patmore, *Land and Leisure*, pp. 238–41.

[41] Countryside Commission, *Policy on Country Parks and Picnic Sites* (London 1969).

[42] *Sixth Report of the Countryside Commission 1972–3* (London 1973).

County Parks, although the designation has not been applied. An example is the Derwent Reservoir on the borders of Co. Durham and Northumberland. This water catchment development has been planned as a multiple-use facility by the Water Boards and County Councils concerned and recreation is an integral feature of the plan.[43] Picnic areas are found around the lake and a sailing club organizes the small-boat use. The cost of facilities for sailing was £75,000, of which £25,000 was paid by the Treasury, via the Department of Education and Science. Benefits have been estimated by Lewis and Whitby[44] at £7300 p.a. for trout fishing, and £1620 p.a. for sailing. Day visits on two Sundays were put at £160 per day, which are difficult to extrapolate to a yearly basis, the authors of the study giving a range of alternative multiplication factors of 10, 20 and 40. Part of the lake is designated for nature conservation and sailing is not allowed at that end. An interesting innovation is the management of the resource by a committee consisting of the owners, the planners and the users, which is analogous to the Foundations or Associations in the Netherlands referred to on pages 90–94. In this case there is no precepting power nor can the body independently apply for finance from the Treasury, but it is entrusted with the organization of the recreational use and the resolution of any conflicts which may arise.

There can be little doubt that the provision of user-oriented and some intermediate category facilities in rural areas will lie mainly with the County Councils and those which have poor recreation resources may well find themselves under strong public pressures to create them. A possible alternative will be the banding together of counties to form regional networks of facilities, although the new local government units created in 1974 will for some time be settling down to more basic issues. The larger of these new units that serve cities may be expected to pursue the most vigorous country park policies. Some counties have moved out from the consideration of recreation *per se*, to studies of rural resources in which rural recreation finds its place among other land and water uses. In the case of Dedham Vale, three counties joined to produce the study of this AONB; in south Hampshire a single county was responsible.[45]

[43] Anon., 'The use of reservoirs for sport', *Sports Development Bulletin* (January 1969), pp. ii–iii.

[44] R. C. Lewis and M. C. Whitby, *Recreation Benefits from a Reservoir*, Monograph 2 (University of Newcastle upon Tyne Agricultural Adjustment Unit 1972).

[45] *Recreation News Supplement* 2 (1970), pp. 27–9 and 37–42.

115

Integrated rural resource study teams led by the Countryside Commission have produced a study of the east Hampshire AONB[46] and a
similar study has been carried out in an upland area of the north
Pennines.

3.9 THE NATIONAL TRUST IN THE UK

This is a peculiarly British organization. It is a voluntary body
created in 1895, with members paying an annual subscription. But it
can acquire property, by gift or under covenant, since it is registered
under the Companies Act and property accepted by the Trust as part
of an estate is free from death duties. The particular *forte* of the
National Trust has been in historic houses and their gardens but its
properties now cover many types of terrain. Many of the high fells in
the Lake District, for instance, are National Trust property (Figure
18), some fine pieces of coastal scenery, and many woodlands.
Wicken Fen near Cambridge, a remnant of the original pre-drainage
condition of the Fenland, is owned by the Trust and managed
primarily for nature conservation.

There is no doubt that the Trust feels its main job to be the preservation of those landscapes over which it has control, and in the
case of its farmlands, for example, the tenants are restrained from
uprooting hedgerows and hedgerow trees as is happening on many
modern farms. Notwithstanding, there is tremendous recreation
pressure on some of its resources and the Trust is in a constant debate
about the extent to which development should be undertaken.
Covering about 1 per cent of England and Wales, the Trust owns
350,000 acres (41,645 ha), with protective covenants over a further
57,000 acres (23,067 ha). There are 250 miles (402 km) of coast and
2 million visitors paid to see its properties in 1966; many more visited
the open areas where no charge is made. Recreational development,
in spite of the debate about policy, is not totally lacking: there are 42
campsites, 9 caravan sites, 6 yacht-mooring sites, 32 dinghy parks,
22 boat launch places and 50 holiday cottages.[47] These are very
useful additions to the nation's stock of these facilities even though
the scale is not in keeping with the problem.

In the 1960s the Trust was especially concerned with the coastline

---

[46] Hampshire County Council, *East Hampshire Area of Outstanding Natural Beauty: A Study in
Countryside Conservation* (1968).

[47] The National Trust for Places of Historic Interest and Natural Beauty, *Annual Report
1966–7.*

and an appeal for funds to buy coastal properties, called Enterprise Neptune, was launched. Over £2 million was raised by public subscription and by 1974, 159 miles (255 km) of coast had been purchased, putting 340 miles (544 km) into the hands of the Trust.

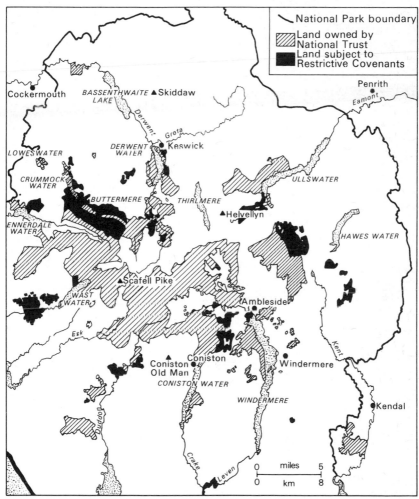

Figure 18   Land owned by the National Trust is of immense importance both in providing access and in protecting traditional landscapes in the English Lake District National Park. Land under restrictive covenant is similarly protected from certain types of development, notably afforestation. *Source:* J. A. Patmore, *Land and Leisure*, p. 188.

117

The National Trust (which covers England and Wales and has a Scottish equivalent) plays a major role in preserving visual amenity and in opening historic buildings; its contribution to rural recreation developments is currently small, and deliberately kept so except in places where the Trust has a concentration of properties and there is especially heavy demand, as in the Lake District National Park, where car parks and campsites have been developed by the Trust in order to try to accommodate the many visitors who would come anyway and otherwise scatter their cars and camping gear in promiscuous fashion all over the landscape both privately and publicly-owned. Whether this policy will stand up under the increasing pressures which will fall on the properties remains to be seen.

3.10 UK: THE COAST AND CARAVANS

The United Kingdom has about 900 miles (1448 km) of high quality coastline of which $\frac{1}{3}$ is in Ulster. The use of the coastal resource is subject to some pressures, especially since about 75 per cent of holidaymakers stay on the coast. If everybody in England and Wales went to the coast then there would be 4 inches (10 cm) each. The development of the coast for industry, housing, resorts and other economic purposes has proceeded to such a degree that the Ministry of Housing and Local Government issued a circular in 1963 calling on all relevant local authorities to make special studies of their coastal areas; and Circular 7/66 set up a series of regional conferences, from which a number of reports have issued.[48] These outline the main conflicts between use and scenic preservation of the British coastline (Figure 19).

So far as recreation is concerned, use has traditionally centred around the resort towns and, increasingly, sheltered mooring facilities for small boats, but increasing mobility brings people to the beaches in between. No particular developments are generally provided, although a few of the most popular rural beaches may have car parks laid out, for example, by a local authority anxious to stop motor access to fragile sand dunes. Recreation thus competes for space with industry, or industrial products (the County Durham beaches are largely fouled with coal from offshore dumping of waste); with nature conservation, for large numbers of visitors are inimical to

---

[48] Countryside Commission, The Coasts of . . .—a series covering the major coastal units of England and Wales (London 1968–9). A discussion of them is: E. W. Hodge, 'Whose coast?', Town and Country Planning 37 (1969), pp. 99–102.

bird life and plants; and with changes of an urban nature which although they may not affect the beach itself, may restrict access and change the milieu of that stretch of coastline.

Preservation has so far put 9 per cent of the coast of England and

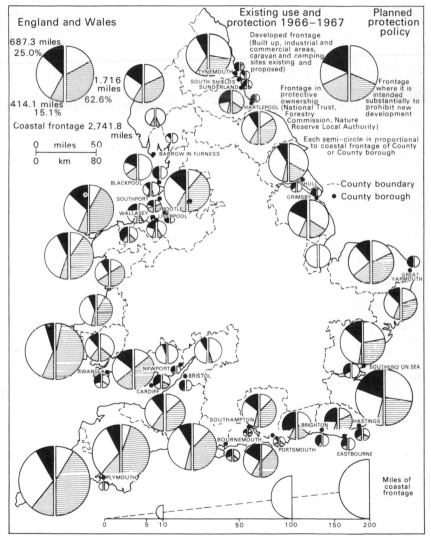

Figure 19 Coastal development and protection in England and Wales. *Source:* J. A. Patmore, *Land and Leisure*, p. 213.

119

Wales into National Parks, and 25 per cent into AONBs. The National Nature Reserves account for 75 miles (120 km) and Sites of Special Scientific Interest 678 miles (1091 km). The National Trust (whose 'Operation Neptune' was described earlier) controls another 340 miles (544 km),[49] much of which coast and immediate hinterland is subject to development pressures: protected status does not confer automatic immunity (Figure 19). Nature Reserves are threatened by atomic power stations and a natural gas landing terminal, and there is a tanker terminal in the Pembrokeshire Coast National Park; offshore from the North York Moors National Park will be dumped the waste from potash processing plants.

The major area of concern about coasts in Britain is not therefore, in the field of recreational development and access. It is about the restriction of development. A nationwide policy of coastal preservation is obviously under consideration and this will probably result in the scheduling of areas of coastline to be immune from the major sources of development pressure: housing, industry and caravans. The mass recreationist will probably gain from this policy even though it is not intended primarily for his benefit since it is unlikely that such scheduled areas would be 'locked up' but that access and recreation development would be permitted, probably in a zonal form. Occasionally, recreation will benefit from former industry. At Druridge Bay in Northumberland, for example, the County Council plan is reclaiming former open cast coal workings near the coast and making them into a Country Park which will have a seaside element and an inland sailing element.[50]

The possession of a second built home on the coast or in the countryside is not yet a very widespread characteristic. More usual is the possession or rental of a caravan (trailer) permanently stationed in a 'caravan park', near the coast or in a rural area. These parks vary in size but a significant number are quite large (Table 2.5). In Wales they provided in 1964 some 13 per cent of the accommodation for main holidays[51] and in 1965 182,960 beds out of a total of 353,666 beds for holiday accommodation were provided by caravans.[52] In

[49] G. Christian, *Tomorrow's Countryside* (London 1966), ch. 9, discusses the coast and its conservation.

[50] Countryside Commission, *The Coasts of North-East England* (London 1968).

[51] W. T. Rees Price, 'The location and growth of holiday caravan camps in Wales, 1956–65', *Trans. Inst. Brit. Geogr.* 42 (1967), pp. 127–52.

[52] *Ibid.*, p. 132. For examples of Consultation Drafts of plans for dealing with a coastal area heavily used for static caravans, see Lindsey County Council, *The Lindsey Coast, A Policy for*

Cornwall, for example, static caravans increased by 240 per cent in 1954–64 and nationwide 16 per cent of all main holidays were taken in them.[53] The growth of numbers and size of sites has been phenomenal in the period since 1945 but only in 1960 was the Caravan Sites and Control of Development Act passed which brought them under the scope of development control. With certain exceptions, planning permission has to be granted to sites and minimum levels of facilities are specified.

Table 2.5   Caravan sites in England and Wales: selected data

Characteristic	England	Wales
Total number of sites	1803	547
At or within 3 miles of the sea	1082	407
Inland	721	140
% sites with 25 caravans	38	45
% sites with 100 caravans	21	19
% sites with a density of 10 caravans/acre and over	43	54
% sites with a density of 40 caravans/acre and over	1	1

Source: T. L. Burton, Caravan sites for holidaymakers, *Town and Country Planning* 34, 1966, pp. 113–19.

Concentration on coastal regions (four fifths of the total number is within 3 miles (5 km) of the sea) has meant that a great number of coastal areas have become affected with these dwellings; and there is constant pressure for the establishment of more sites in scenic areas inland. The appearance of the caravans has led to a great deal of opposition from rural amenity bodies such as the Council for the Protection of Rural England and landscaping provisions are now generally part of planning permission. This is especially so when a development is allowed in a National Park or AONB; in some National Parks they are not permitted within sight of a road.

From an aesthetic viewpoint caravans are one of the worst intrusions upon the rural and coastal scene reaching urban proportions at places like Porthcawl and Skegness and there is no doubt that their control is necessary: this is one of the chief fields of conflict between recreation and landscape amenity in Britain and one from which there is unlikely to be any relief.

Conservation (Lincoln 1970); and *The Lindsey Coast, A Policy for Holiday Development* (Lincoln 1973).
    [53] J. A. Patmore, *Land and Leisure*, pp. 166–71.

3.11 INLAND WATER IN ENGLAND AND WALES

England and Wales together possess 108,000 acres (43,707 ha) of this resource. Little of it consists of large natural lakes except for the concentration amid the mountains of the Lake District and to a lesser extent in north Wales: a feature which emphasizes the spatial imbalance of water and people. Water-catchment reservoirs are common in almost every upland area and not a few relatively lowland areas too. Gravel and sand pits, now abandoned and filled with water, account for 5500 acres (2226 ha) in 27 counties and their total is being added to constantly although operators may be required to fill in wet pits after use. Rivers provide another important source of inland water, and canals are now being re-evaluated in recreational terms. The canal system, built for commercial purposes, is now largely unused by industrial traffic except for a few major arteries and many of the smaller canals have been falling into disrepair; attempts to revive them for recreational uses such as canoeing and sailing have been made under the aegis of the British Waterways Board[54] which has developed a network of 1400 miles (2240 km) of inland waterway[55] catering for some 16,000 craft.[56] The canals are also important for walking, fishing and informal play.[57] One unique resource is the Norfolk Broads: a series of reedswamp and fen-fringed meres connected by 120 miles (142 km) of winding river channels. They are artificial, being the flooded remains of medieval peat diggings,[58] and are very popular for recreation; especially sailing, motorboating and angling. As Patmore notes,[59] after the Lake District, the Norfolk Broads probably suffer the heaviest recreation pressure of any region in Britain. Erosion of banks, elimination of wildlife, conflicts between angling and boating, pollution by sewage and exhausts and noise are some of the problems afflicting this relatively fragile environment.

[54] For example, Publication 2, *The Great Western Canal* (Totnes, Devon, Dartington Amenity Research Trust 1968).

[55] Ministry of Transport, *British Waterways: Recreation and Amenity*, Cmnd. 3401 (London, HMSO 1967); British Waterways Board, *Leisure and the Waterways* (London 1967).

[56] F. Moon, 'Angling and pleasure boating on inland waterways', *Recreation News Supplement* 6 (1972), p. 27–9. This represented a growth rate of 10 per cent p.a. 1967–71.

[57] J. R. B. Lett, 'Notes on a survey of activity patterns associated with some canals in N.W. England', *Recreation News Supplement* 8 (1973), pp. 38–42; F. Pratt, 'Informal recreation on inland waterways in 1972', *Recreation News Supplement* 9 (1973), pp. 41–3.

[58] J. M. Lambert *et al.*, *The Making of the Broads*, Royal Geographical Society Research Monograph 3 (London 1960).

[59] J. A. Patmore, *Land and Leisure*, p. 257.

A very popular recreation on inland waters is ornithology. The major reservoirs and lakes are visited in winter by large numbers of wildfowl and waders[60] and the rapidly growing ranks of bird-watchers. This use carries the seeds of considerable conflict, actual and potential, with such other pursuits as sailing, motorboating and water-skiing. Angling is less inimical, though fishermen are prone to smash down the breeding habitats of smaller birds in order to get to the water's edge.

But none of these sources of supply (Figure 20) is keeping pace with the demand for water-based recreation. Most sailing and angling clubs now have waiting lists for membership, and since these groups often have exclusive use of a particular stretch of water, freelance individuals have a hard time. One hopeful change was the powers granted to River Boards (who managed the water resources of a whole basin or group of basins) by the Water Resources Act 1963, and which were passed to the 10 new Regional Water Authorities in 1974. They must manage their waters with regard to amenity, mainly visual, but can also undertake recreation development for which charges may be made. Little development has yet taken place, because of shortage of money, but the authority is there. Urban and industrial water supply is in the hands of Water Boards, who traditionally have excluded the public from their reservoirs (and where possible the catchment areas as well) because of the pollution threat. In 1963, most of the Boards reported that they would tolerate picnicking by the side of their reservoirs but only six permitted sailing on their supply waters.[61] Increasing pressures, and a change of attitude among resource managers, seems likely to bring about change, and as has been shown for the West Midlands,[62] use by a club usually means that sufficient control can be exercised to avoid pollution.[63] Even Manchester Corporation's reservoir in the Lake District, Thirlmere, which has long been the subject of execration (on account of public exclusion and the planting of a rather uniform blanket of conifers) is now being made more accessible with picnic spots and nature trails within the surrounding land, although access to the water surface is still denied.

[60] G. L. Atkinson-Willes (ed.), *Wildfowl in Great Britain*, Monog. Nat. Cons. 3 (London 1963).

[61] Institution of Water Engineers, *Recreational Use of Waterworks* (1963).

[62] Central Council of Physical Recreation, *Inland Waterways and Recreation* (1964).

[63] See also 'Focus on reservoirs', *Recreation News Supplement* 3 (1971), pp. 2–12.

Most user conflicts can be solved if there is sufficient space to zone the users or to separate them in time. But demand pressures frequently mean that conflicts are exacerbated and do not permit easy solution. Water-skiing arouses hostility from almost every other class

Figure 20 Inland water resources used for sailing in England and Wales. *Source:* M. F. Tanner, 'Recreation and Resources IV: The recreational use of inland waters', *Geogr. J.* 139 (1973), p. 489.

of water user: speed, noise, destructive wash are all cited. Nobody wants it anywhere near their living-places either, so that its growth will probably present more problems than most other users and is likely to be subject to considerable restriction.

Increasing urbanization means more demand for sand and gravel and this usually within 30 miles (48 km) of the construction site, because of transport costs. A tremendous resource is being created, some of which is passing more or less piecemeal into recreational use. In some places, planners have created an asset out of the dereliction, as in the Cotswold Water Park in the upper Thames valley. Since planning offices granting permission for mineral working have the power to impose restoration conditions on the extractors, it would seem worthwhile formulating long-term extraction plans so that some of the resulting lakes can pass into recreational use (possibly of different types) on a programmed basis, so that the water-skiers know they will get their lake in three years' time, and club x will be able to accept another 50 members the year after. Otherwise, another 10 years of growth at 80 per cent per decade (Table 1.13) will produce a chaotic situation.

3.12 'UNSTRUCTURED' RURAL RECREATION IN BRITAIN

The tradition in Britain, and one which probably accounts for a great deal of the current participation, is for the informal picnic or family ball game on an odd corner of land, by the wayside or on a beach. Thus none of the supply agencies so far described are involved and the estimation of the magnitude and locations of the activity are very difficult.[64]

(a) Common land

One of the principal sources of access land is common land. In the medieval system of agriculture, some land (usually woodland, heath or moorland) was held in common by all the villagers who used it for a variety of purposes, the chief of which was grazing for stock such as cattle or sheep. The land remained in the ownership of the lord of the manor. A lot of common persists and its legal status is generally unchanged, i.e. there is no right of public access except where the common land is in an Urban District or Metropolitan Borough. In 1956–8 a Royal Commission on common land took evidence and

[64] J. T. Coppock, 'The recreational use of land and water in rural Britain', *Tijd. Econ. Soc. Geog.* 57 (1966), pp. 81–96.

reported the existence of 1,505,002 acres (609,074 ha) of common land, in England and Wales.[65] In England, 1,047,608 acres (423,966 ha) fell into 2,073 parcels. The primary uses of the commons were for controlled ('stinted') grazing (33 per cent), uncontrolled grazing (46 per cent), woodland (1·9 per cent) and amenity/recreation (10·4 per cent). This last figure refers to primary use for that purpose and many more commons have recreation as one of the uses to which the land is put. This is particularly so in the uplands where open moorland may form attractive walking, picnicking and driving country, and frequently forms the open land core of a National Park. Before 1974, about 16·0 per cent of the land in the North Riding of Yorkshire, for example, was common, and this county had one National Park and half of another. The West Riding of Yorkshire had 22 per cent of its surface under common, and Westmorland 25 per cent which was about half the county's total of open moorland.

Some rural commons have been made available for recreation by the making of Deeds of Access by the relevant manorial lords, and some 118,500 acres (47,956 ha) constitute this category; a further 150,651 acres (60,968 ha) were within the UD and MB units mentioned earlier. The Commission, recognizing that these were insufficient, recommended that all commons should be open to the public as of right and that local authorities should have the power to make improvement schemes for recreation.[66] Registration of commons and common rights is now complete and when all are registered then legislation may be forthcoming. This should help local authorities to manage effectively those commons where recreational use is heavy (about 20 per cent of the total in England and Wales)[67] but where the legal situation at present inhibits them. Although the other uses of commons will be jealously safeguarded by commoners, there can be little doubt that one of their most essential future uses will be as open space, especially in heavily populated or intensively cultivated parts of the country.

The management practices evolved in medieval times are not capable of coping with contemporary conditions (40 per cent showed

[65] These and other statistical data on commons are from the *Report of the Royal Commission on Common Land 1955–58*, Cmnd. 462 (London, HMSO 1958).

[66] *Ibid.*, p. 131.

[67] D. R. Denman, R. A. Roberts and H. J. F. Smith, *Commons and Village Greens* (London 1967), p. 417.

'severe' or 'partial' general neglect)[68] and so any legislation must erect new mechanisms for reconciling old and new uses; Denman, Roberts and Smith,[69] for example, give instances of the possibilities of zoning commons so as to reduce conflict between components of a multiple use common; however they regard the Royal Commission's recommendation for a blanket right of access as misguided and think that local control by management committees, which found the best way of integrating public uses with other demands, would be a better use of the resource.

Since no definitive legislation on commons is likely for some time, the present pattern of recreational use[70] will probably intensify; until mandatory management committees are set up, voluntary bodies of users and owners might with advantage fill the gaps.

(b) Public footpaths and bridleways

A legacy of Britain's agricultural history is a dense network of footpaths and bridleways, mostly dating from days when they were an essential part of a rural communications network based on Shanks' pony. Nowadays, their use by the farming community is minimal and their main, and considerable, value is for recreation. They have been defined and now appear on the Ordnance Survey maps as Public Rights of Way. They may not be diverted nor blocked up without recourse to legal procedure, and the Countryside Act 1968 imposes upon the land owners through whose property the footpath passes the obligation to keep maintained features such as stiles and gates. If he does not do so then the County Council may carry out the work and reclaim the cost from him. The pasturing of bulls in fields through which footpaths run is also subject to restriction.

The main problems associated with the use of these paths as trails by walkers are those of trespass, when they stray from the path, and of litter, leaving gates open, and interfering with crops or stock. For these latter problems, no immediate solution is available but for the former, various experimental waymarkers are being tried, especially in National Parks. One trouble here is that some farmers then remove the markers, hoping that the paths will become 'lost'. Use of the

[68] *Ibid.*, p. 425.

[69] *Ibid.*, chs. 4–5. See also E. M. Yates, 'The management of heathlands for amenity purposes in south-east England', *Geographia Polonica* 24 (1972), pp. 227–40.

[70] J. Wager, 'Outdoor recreation on common land', *J. Town Planning Inst.* (November 1967), pp. 398–403.

footpaths seems bound to increase and ways of reducing conflict with agriculture would seem a desirable subject for investigation especially since the National Farmers' Union has claimed that the land devoted to footpaths could grow 750,000 tons of wheat.

(c) Roadsides

One of the commonest forms of rural recreation visible in Britain is the car pulled off onto the roadside with the occupants either having a picnic or sitting inside reading the (usually Sunday) newspapers. Until many more laybys and picnic sites are available this pattern will persist but two problems may be noted. Both pertain to popular areas, for light use creates few difficulties. Firstly there is the sanitation problem, which results in fouling of the area and very often of adjacent fields, access to which may be forced. The second problem is that of damage to vulnerable roadsides. This is especially common on uplands (such as Dartmoor) where poorer soils are found: damage to the top horizon of the soil allows wind and rain to attack the leached sandy A_2 horizon of the soil and erosion is widespread. (Similar phenomena can be seen at picnic sites on some of the heaths of the Netherlands.)

Hopefully, full use of the provisions of the 1968 Countryside Act by County Councils, may help to provide enough wayside halts and toilets to diminish the scale of this problem, although it is unlikely to be eradicated.

3.13 PARKS AND INTERMEDIATE-ZONE RECREATION IN JAPAN

A modern attitude to parks and recreation was crystallized in the National Parks Law of 1931, which added certain categories of protected area to the matrix of land to which there was public access for rural recreation. In general, the pattern of allocation of land and water resources has followed the practice of the USA in scheduling distinct areas as parks and expecting most rural recreation to be concentrated there, rather than the traditional European custom of partaking of informal recreation at suitable places throughout the countryside. In 1957 this legislation was replaced by the Natural Park Law and three categories of protected area resulted. National Parks represent the highest quality of scenery in the nation whether this be entirely natural or has a substantial element of cultural landscape, and are both designated and managed by the state through its Environment Agency. The second category, Quasi-National Parks come

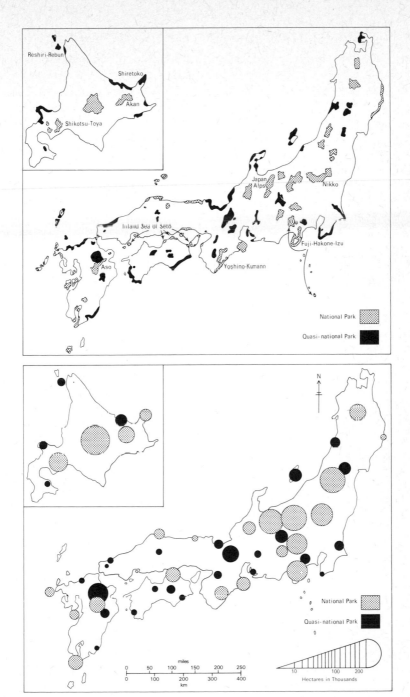

Figure 21   National Parks and Quasi-National Parks in Japan.
Source: National Parks Association of Japan.

next in terms of scenic beauty and indeed some have been upgraded to National Park status; others are located near to conurbations with the primary aim of providing space for rural recreation. These parks are designated by the environment minister at the request of prefectural governors but are managed by the prefectures, usually with a good deal of help from Tokyo (Figure 21). Thirdly, there are Prefectural Parks which are the entire concern of the prefecture. Other governmental activities in the field of protection include the attention paid to particular species of plant or animal which forbid their culling or allow the establishment of small isolated nature reserves, and the preservation of cultural monuments, especially shrine and temple buildings together with their associated lands. Table 2.6 summarizes

Table 2.6   Protected areas in Japan, 1972

	National Parks	Quasi-National Parks	Prefectural Parks
Number	26	46	279
Area (million ha)	1·99	0·99	2·02
% of national land surface	5·35	2·68	5·47
% State-owned	61·8	21·4	n.a.
Total visitors 1970 (million)	284·5	217·6	n.a.

Source: T. Senge, personal communication.

some basic statistics of the recent situation. As in England and Wales, the parks contain permanently inhabited terrain where the people expect to carry on with their economic activities. The National Parks and Quasi-National Parks are therefore zoned in order to facilitate the control of development and other management purposes (Figure 22). The threefold classification of the parklands adopted is given as Table 2.7.

Table 2.7   Zonation of parks, 1972

	Percentage of area		
	Specially-protected area	Special area	Ordinary area
National Parks	11·4	56·8	31·8
Quasi-National Parks	2·8	80·5	16·7

Data are not available for Prefectural Parks.
Source: T. Senge, personal communication.

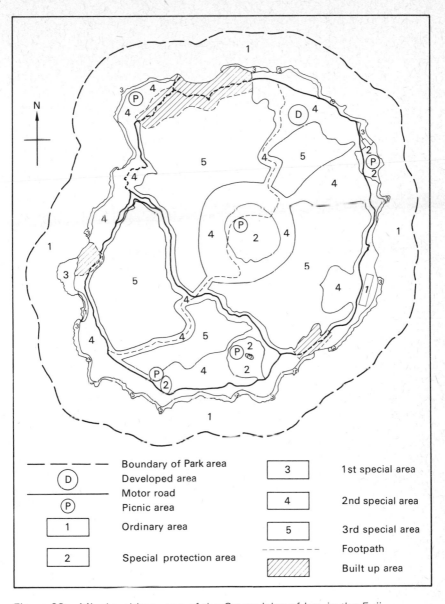

– – – –	Boundary of Park area	
(D)	Developed area	
——	Motor road	
(P)	Picnic area	
1	Ordinary area	
2	Special protection area	

3	1st special area	
4	2nd special area	
5	3rd special area	
– – – – –	Footpath	
/////	Built up area	

Figure 22   Miyake-shima, one of the Seven Isles of Izu, in the Fuji-Hakone-Izu National Park, Japan. This map shows the application of the zoning scheme to a small area. (The original map has no scale; the diameter of the island is approximately 10 km.)
Source: Environment Ministry of Japan, planning map for Seven Isles of Izu.

1 *Special Protection Areas.* These are kept strictly free from development and include floral and faunal phenomena of particular interest, topographical and geological features of especial scientific interest, together with historical and archaeological sites of particular significance. Special Protection Areas comprise 8·8 per cent of National Parks and 2·4 per cent of Quasi-National Parks.

2 *Special Areas.* There are three possible sub-classes, of which the first confers almost as much protection as a Special Protection Area. The other two contain areas of slightly lesser value and are administered so as to allow certain kinds of development (including industry) while protecting the natural scenery and ecosystems. The Special Areas encompass 59·2 per cent of National Parks and 59·9 per cent of Quasi-National Parks.

3 *Ordinary Areas.* Practically any land or resource use is allowed in this area subject only to prior consultation with the park authority. Some restrictions can be enforced, for example on height of buildings. In National Parks 32 per cent, and Quasi-National Parks 37·7 per cent, of the areas fall into this category.

The criteria for selection of these protected areas are dominated by the quality of the natural scenery so that like the National Parks of England and Wales, development control is considered more important than the provision of recreational facilities. Additionally, the scenic criterion means that they are usually at some distance from the cities and hence more readily available for weekend and vacation trips. For shorter excursions, other resources are brought into the array of choice.

One of the rationales for Quasi-National Parks is to act as recreation areas for the inhabitants of large urban areas, but their numbers and distribution again reflect the primary criterion of scenic quality rather than urban proximity. Some however, fulfill their intended role, such as the Lake Biwa Quasi-National Park. This is 90,674 ha, of which most is water surface but including a strip of shoreline and adjacent hills of variable width; most of the Quasi-National Park is zoned as Ordinary Area, with some Special Area designations around cultural features such as the Ishiyamadera Temple. Reached from Kyoto in 15 minutes by tramway to Otsu, the lake offers boat trips, seaplane rides and urban resort features, as well as providing space for some marinas at which sailing boats are kept and which are also the venues for motor-boat racing. Angling is practised along in-coming rivers but is subsidiary to commercial fishing. The shores of the lake where undeveloped are either rocky or artificially protected with riprap. The whole presents therefore an appearance which does not apparently reflect either protected status nor especially good facilities for rural recreation; its Quasi-National Park status how-ever means that consultation with the prefecture must take place before private development occurs along the shores.

Since many mountainous and forested areas surround large cities of Japan and because much of the forest is State-owned, National Forests have become perceived as possible areas for recreation. Until recently these were considered largely as timber producers (where have we heard that before?) and as protectors of watersheds, but the Forest Agency is now planning recreation as one of its secondary aims. To this end, 'authorized recreation forests' have been designated since 1967. Twenty-five scenic areas, totalling 36,000 ha, have been set aside primarily for recreation, and facilities con-structed; it is planned to expand the system to 100 areas. Ski areas and camping sites have also been constructed, and the aesthetic qualities of the forest lands safeguarded by the strict pro-tection afforded by categorization as Special Forest Reserve.[71] National Forests also form important links in long-distance walking trails currently being developed by the Environment Agency; the first of these stretches through the mountains to the west of the country's major megalopolis, linking the outskirts of Tokyo and Osaka; others are planned.

Several National Parks are close to major cities, and so they attract not only visitors from other parts of Japan and overseas but day-use or weekend-use recreationists from their immediate periphery. The outstanding example is the Fuji-Hakone-Izu National Park, which contains natural attractions such as Izu Seven Isles, cultural drawing-points like the Twelve Spas, and the combined natural and cultural focus of Fujiyama (3776 m). This park claims the highest number of visitors (c. 76 million/yr) in the system. Most of these are confined to the roads and many are parties conveyed by chartered bus, so that their direct impact upon the environment is small. Nevertheless, the erection of facilities to cater for them in the Ordinary zone and parts of the Special zones of the park means an

[71] Ministry of Agriculture and Forestry, Forestry Agency, *Forest Management in Natural Park Area upon the Multiple Use Basis* (Tokyo 1971).

increasingly urbanized appearance. Where possible, the parks authorities are negotiating zoning plans for the developed areas of National Parks, in order to prevent sprawl of visitor facilities; in general this means the clustering of most types of accommodation and camping sites in the same locality.

Such developments are paralleled on a smaller scale at Lake Toya in the Shikotsu-Toya National Park in Hokkaido, easily reached from Sapporo. The caldera lake (formed by the collapse of a volcanic cone) is surrounded mostly by private land and so there has been little check on the development of a resort town along the lake-shore, and the foot of the recently erupted (1943) volcanic cone Showashinzan has a considerable rash of commercial establishments.

The size of Japan and the rapidity of transport makes National Parks such as Nikko available for day use by Tokyo residents and visitors, since it can be reached in 1 hour 45 minutes by limited express train, thus attracting 14 million visitors/yr. The cultural attraction of the Toshugu shrines in Nikko City drains off many visitors, but large numbers of cars and buses drive up the precipitous road to the Kegon Fall, Lake Chuzenji and several small hot spas. Because of the focalizing effect of Nikko City, and because much of the upland is National Forest, undue urbanization has been avoided.

3.14 DEVELOPMENTS AT PROVINCIAL AND REGIONAL LEVEL IN CANADA

(a) General

The recognition by the provinces of their responsibility to provide rural recreation facilities, especially Intermediate-type areas, is relatively recent: in the urbanized parts of Ontario in 1954 there were only three provincial parks, in 1961 this had risen to 28 and is now still higher. British Columbia started in 1911 and rose to a 6·5 million acre (26,300 km²) system by 1940 since the depression years were good for emparking; by 1960, 155 areas comprised 8·5 million acres (84,400 km²). Saskatchewan only started after 1957,[72] so the picture is uneven but is principally of a response to the boom of the 1950s especially by these provinces with a dense urban population. The relevant statistics for camper nights are given below (Table 2.8); they show a considerable rise which reflects their

[72] E. Hardy and F. J. McGilly, 'The hierarchy of government and public agencies in Park development', in *Resources for Tomorrow* (Ottawa 1962), vol. 2, pp. 1037–46.

Table 2.8   Provincial parks: camping use 1965–70 (thousands of camper nights)

	1965	1966	1967	1968	1969	1970
Canada	4,483	4,826	5,907	5,496	6,480	7,743
Newfoundland	62	60	83	103	121	148
P.E.I.	22	75	75	107	94	121
Nova Scotia	68	76	70	110	121	131
New Brunswick	113	141	145	172	158	170
Quebec	110	n.a.	492	401	485	722
Ontario	2,495	2,653	2,805	2,485	2,956	3,524
Manitoba	214	249	316	325	419	503
Saskatchewan	99	110	146	180	254	314
Alberta	202	290	400	360	482	527
B.C.	1,098	1,172	1,375	1,280	1,390	1,583
Day use						
Canada	20,447	20,678	25,241	25,910	29,336	34,154

Source: Statistics Canada, Travel, Tourism and Outdoor Recreation: a statistical digest, 1972, Table 8.4.

popularity, especially for the weekend usage of the intermediate zone, where the rate of use has risen rather more rapidly than in the day-use zone.

(b) Ontario

Since it contains the most heavily urbanized part of Canada, and has perhaps least variety of resources within easy reach of the cities, it will be instructive to examine the situation in that Province. As Pleva has pointed out, it is a 'fragmented and multi-layered system'.[73] He identifies the major interested levels as Federal: (not particularly important in Ontario although a large National Park has been designated north of Superior and just before the October 1972 election the Federal government announced it was to fund a water-front park adjacent to downtown Toronto. The ruling Liberals proceeded to lose most of their seats in Ontario.) Provincial: important, with an extensive system in both urbanized southern Ontario and in the wilder north. Regional: with several important constituent units; and Local: cities, townships, towns and villages. Individual layers may themselves be highly fragmented: at least fifteen Provincial

[73] E. C. Pleva, 'Ontario's Parks', in J. G. Nelson and R. C. Scace (eds.), *The Canadian National Parks: Today and Tomorrow* (University of Calgary Studies in Land Use History and Landscape Change, National Park Series 3, 1969), vol. 1, pp. 439–52.

departments and agencies are engaged in parks and open space programmes.

The context of the discussion is a province of 412,562 sq miles (1,088,535 km²) (land 80 per cent) which is half as large again as Texas and five times the size of Great Britain. It houses one third of Canada's population, yet 88 per cent live in the southern 29,000 sq miles (75,110 km²) (*c.* 7 per cent of the province's area), which is an area of sand and clay plains and rolling hills and is nearly all privately owned. About 80 per cent of the population live in urban agglomerations of more than 5000 population.[74] It is this area of Ontario, and not the other 93 per cent, which experiences the greatest demands for rural recreation, although the north is becoming more accessible as roads are built; nevertheless the demand for day-use facilities, for example, are not likely to be great there.

(i) *Provincial parks.* In 1972 the Department of Lands and Forests administered a system of 104 units which was started in 1893 but which by 1944 had only six elements (Figure 23). These vary in size from a 5-acre (2 ha) picnic site to the 7000 sq miles (18,130 km²) of Polar Bear Provincial Park, a wilderness area on James Bay. The majority of them are in southern Ontario, where they cater largely to the intermediate and user-oriented demands of the urban population. The demands upon the system are symbolized by the increases in visitor numbers to the expanding park system. In 1957 there were 55 parks which had a visitation of 2·1 million people and 396,132 camper days. The equivalents in 1970 were 108 parks, 12·1 million visitations and 3·5 million camper days. The average length of stay has remained at *c.* 2·4 days throughout this time.[75] The terrains represented in the system are varied including lakes and rivers, although it may be noted that the shores of Lake Ontario and Lake Erie are rather lacking in parks, due to the difficulties of land acquisition.

The variety of parkland and the different types of use has led the Department of Lands and Forests to classify their parks, and to adopt zoning within them.[76] The classes are:

1 Primitive parks: wilderness areas for wildland recreation, for geological research and, interestingly, the 'psychological need,

[74] E. C. Pleva, 'Multiple use land and water districts in Ontario', in H. Jarrett (ed.), *Comparisons in Resource Management* (Lincoln, Nebraska 1961), 189–207.

[75] Ontario Dept of Lands and Forests, *Provincial Parks of Ontario Statistical Report 1970*, Table I.

[76] Ontario Dept of Lands and Forests, *Classification of Provincial Parks in Ontario* (Toronto 1967).

of many people, to know that unspoiled wilderness areas exist '.[77]
Development is confined to trails, portages and designated
campsites.

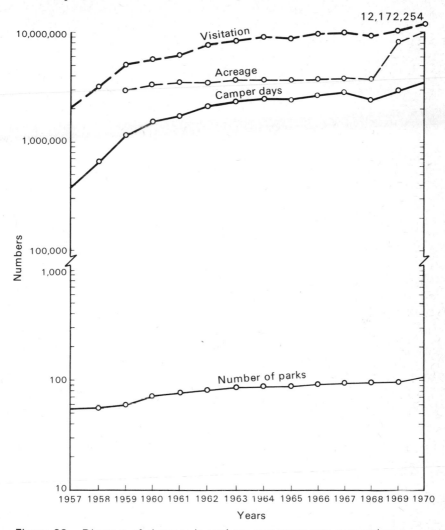

Figure 23   Diagram of changes in various measurements concerning
Provincial Parks in Ontario, 1957–60. The vertical axis is logarithmic.
Source: Ontario Dept of Lands and Forests, *Provincial Parks of
Ontario Statistical Report 1970*, p. 1.

[77] *Ibid.*, p. 3.

2   Wild River parks: sections of rivers not less than one-day's upstream travel by canoe in length, with a minimum shoreline depth of 400 feet (122 m) on public lands. Some recreation development at access points and logging will be allowed subject to any restrictions needed to preserve the aesthetic quality of the environment. Motor-powered boats may be restricted or prohibited.

3   Natural Environment park: areas for medium and low intensity rural recreation in a natural environment, together with some wilderness or semi-wilderness areas. The management will be on a multiple use principle, recognizing recreation as the primary use on all lands and the exclusive use on some. Complete interpretive services are among the facilities provided.

4   Recreation park: these are user-oriented with two sub-classes, Recreation areas, in which day use activities tend to dominate and indeed may be the only use; and Campgrounds, providing for intensive camping and associated uses. The Recreation areas will include many good beaches. This category comprised the largest number of units (64) in the system in 1972. These parks are also available for winter use, when heated washrooms are maintained, and activities such as ice-fishing, snowshoeing, skiing, skating, and tobogganing are followed. In all but a few of the parks, snowmobile trails are laid out.

5   Nature Reserve: Areas for the preservation of unique natural areas where the presence of the public is not significantly detrimental to the natural value of the area. Only two such parks exist in Ontario. One of them is Polar Bear Provincial Park, an area of forest and tundra on James Bay, with no road access; the other is intended to bring wilderness recreation nearer to the major population centres of Ontario, in an area of quartzite hills and deep lakes which is unsuitable for more intensive forms of recreation.[78] This latter is Killarney Provincial Park, an area of 84,990 acres (34,420 ha) of the La Cloche Mountains on the north shore of Georgian Bay, buffered to some extent by a more intensively used provincial recreation area in the same region.

Within these classes of park, zoning is to be employed in the drawing up of a master plan for the park. The purposes of the zones coincide closely with some of the park classificatory ones.

[78] Ontario Dept of Lands and Forests, Division of Parks and Recreation, *Killarney Provincial Park: Options for the Future* (Toronto 1972).

1 Primitive zone: for the preservation of natural landscapes and their scientific study.
2 Natural zone: for public enjoyment and recreation at unique natural areas such as lookout points and biological phenomena. No development except where absolutely necessary, and in connection with the interpretive programme.
3 Historic zone: self-explanatory.
4 Multiple Use zone: low intensity recreation use is managed in consort with the use of other resources. This other use is usually logging.
5 Recreation zone: this zone is for intensive recreational use and will be confined to areas with high capability for this purpose. A twenty-year period of use is envisaged.

Since the province has the most funds, and since 90 per cent of Ontario is Crown Land, it is the leader in the field of park provision for rural recreation and has more flexibility than other agencies in deciding how to manage its areas. Acquisition of more parks and the enlargement of existing ones is planned. The chief source of conflict is in the multiple-use zone, where recreationists are often annoyed by logging operations. The ecological damage done by them, the closing of areas to public access and the opening of wilderness areas, via logging roads, for intensive or noisy recreation uses are all regarded by some as undesirable effects. These conflicts have been most marked in the case of two large and very popular provincial parks: Algonquin Provincial Park and Quetico Provincial Park. The former provides both intensive use areas and virtual wilderness, the latter a very wild area mostly used by canoeists and other water-borne recreationists. In both cases, the impact of logging upon the perceptions of the users of the primitive parks has been the subject of considerable controversy. In the case of Algonquin Park the recreation values have been in direct conflict with economic uses since an economic impact study of the park shows the pre-eminence of the timber industry in bringing money to both the local area and the province: the local impact in 1968 was \$17·3 million of which three-quarters was generated by forestry; the provincial impact was \$52 million, of which four-fifths came from timber extraction.[79] Nevertheless, after citizen pressure, the provincial government has agreed to diminish the impact of the industry. In the Quetico Pro-

[79] Ontario Dept of Lands and Forests, *Algonquin Provincial Park: Economic Impact Study* (Toronto 1969).

139

vincial Park, the basic purpose of the park as a wilderness area has been recently affirmed and commercial cutting is to be phased out, cutover land rehabilitated, and mining terminated. Additionally, buffer zones are to be established in which land use controls are to be implemented and watershed management carefully watched; within the park, only the native peoples will be allowed to hunt in perpetuity; whites' traplines will cease to be transferable. Recreation restrictions include areas zoned for boats with no more than 10 hp engines and, most significantly, a visitor quota is recommended[80] (although the method of establishing carrying capacity is not established), a theme to be mentioned in connection with wilderness use in resource-based areas.

The vulnerability of parks to influences outside their boundaries is shown by the controversy over the quarrying of sand from property adjacent to Sandbanks Provincial Park in Prince Edward County on Lake Ontario, where it has been argued that the park dune system will be degraded. Although a consultant report recommends the rapid termination of the extractive lease, it also says that the public probably misunderstands the dynamics of dune formation and is mistaken in thinking that high dunes are permanent features of the landscape anyway, quarrying or no.[81]

The Department of Lands and Forests also assists in certain ways outside its parks. It has marked out and published guides to a series of canoe trails through the waterways of central and northern Ontario, with information on portages, supply points and features of interest; and has constructed water access points to lakes and rivers even where these are outside park management. They are fully serviced with roads, docks, landing ramps and parking areas.

(ii) *Conservation authorities.* An act of 1946 enabled the setting up of multiple-use land and water conservation districts, along the lines of soil conservation districts in the US.[82] The success of these districts has brought about continual revision of the legislation and their flood control powers have been augmented, especially after Hurricane Hazel in 1954; they now operate under the Conservation

[80] Ontario, Quetico Provincial Park Advisory Committee Report, *Quetico Park* (Toronto 1972).

[81] W. M. Tovell, *The Sandbanks, Hallowell Township, Prince Edward County* (Toronto 1972).

[82] There are considerable differences in administration and operation. See E. C. Pleva, 'Multiple purpose land and water districts in Ontario', in H. Jarrett (ed.), *op. cit.*, pp. 189–207, and Ayers Brinser, 'What the US can learn', in the same volume, pp. 208–18.

Authorities Act 1968. The aim of the area is nothing less than total watershed management but recreation is a frequent spin-off product, especially on water impoundments created for flood-control purposes and watersheds where more intensive uses are thought inappropriate. Sailing and swimming are important activities, as are nature conservation and wildfowl hunting, scenery preservation, a pioneer village reconstruction, and a ski area purchased from a private operator.[83] In the thirty-two Conservation areas of Ontario, over 150 areas are now (1972) open for public recreation of these kinds, and their use is heavy. In the Metropolitan Toronto and Region Conservation area, problems are especially acute. At present these are being contained by an aggressive programme of land acquisition and development with the aim of providing a wide range of recreation facilities within the Metro Conservation Authority area. In 1972 the MTRCA owned 18,500 acres (7492 ha) of land, of which 7250 acres (3046 ha) was developed for recreation, at fifteen 'Conservation Areas'. Some areas are intensively used such as Cold Creek CA where city shooting clubs are given space to practice, and Albion Hills CA where a children's residential centre is attached to a working farm; on the other there are areas as yet undeveloped at all which will be used for conservation education or kept as wild areas. The Metro CA has also taken over responsibility for the amenity aspects of the Toronto waterfront plan. Its task may be to some extent alleviated by the decision to stop the outward growth of Toronto and leave a 'green belt' between it and other cities of South Ontario.[84] Apart from the pressures for day-use facilities near the conurbation (c. 2 million), there is the particular problem of river and lake pollution. A long-term programme for tertiary treatment of sewage has been designed since it is estimated that recreational use of water will have necessitated investments totalling $40 million by 1980, and the cost of pools to substitute for the swimming alone, if pollution were allowed to continue, would be another $15 million. Thus treatment plants and river flow control must be planned together since minimum flow above Toronto is about 80 cubic feet per second at present, and by 1980 it is estimated that 50 cfs of effluent will be delivered to these streams.[85]

[83] G. D. Boggs, 'Recreation', *Watersheds* 2 (1967), pp. 8–10.

[84] Govt of Ontario, *Design for Development: The Toronto-Centered Region* (Toronto 1970).

[85] Metropolitan Toronto and Region Conservation Authority, *Pollution Control and Recreation in the Metropolitan Toronto Region* (Toronto 1963).

Conservation areas are linked to the provincial schemes because the province pays 75 per cent of the maintenance costs of flood control schemes, and 50 per cent of the capital costs of all other schemes together with 50 per cent of the administrative costs. Because of their total environment nature, the CA authorities have rather more flexibility in planning than in provincial parks but their location and resource type has placed them firmly in the user-oriented class.

(iii) *Other authorities at sub-provincial level.* A number of other authorities exist to plan recreation for particular areas, either specifically or as part of multiple purposes schemes. The Metropolitan Toronto Planning Board has produced a Metropolitan Toronto Waterfront Plan which extends for 50 miles (80·5 km) along the lakeshore which is multiple-purpose but in which seven of the thirteen objectives are recreational in character; although they will doubtless not account for seven-thirteenths of the investment. In the area of the plan 30 out of 50 miles (48/80·5 km) of shoreline will be made accessible via a scenic park drive, public beach increased from 4 to 17 miles (5·6 to 27·3 km) and lakefront swimming pools from 2 to 12 miles (3·2 to 19·3 km). The 7 miles (11·2 km) of protected waterway for small boats will be doubled and more harbours will be built.[86] The implementation of the plan has been handed over to the Metro Toronto and Region Conservation Authority.

The theme of access to a lakefront is a key issue to the Niagara Regional Development Council. Here, private ownership of access to the lakefront has prevented park development and very few areas are open to the public; furthermore Lake Erie is extremely heavily polluted. Cottage development and quarrying have also used up shoreline land. A study proposes that extensive acquisition by a public body is essential if the recreational demands of the area are to be satisfied.[87]

Other bodies involved include the Niagara Parks Commission (concerned primarily with parks and scenery preservation), the Ontario-St Lawrence Development Commission, and the Hydro Electric Power Commission (concerned only secondarily with recreation) all of which contribute to the pattern, which now has an

[86] Metropolitan Toronto Planning Board, *Metropolitan Toronto Waterfront Plan* (Toronto 1968—fold-out brochure).

[87] J. N. Jackson, *Recreation Development and the Lake Erie Shore* (Niagara Regional Development Council, n.d.—1957 or 8).

overseeing, bureaucratic, body, The Ontario Parks Integration Board, to try and bring co-ordination of the efforts of all the public authorities.

Of all parts of Canada, Ontario experiences the heaviest demands for intermediate and resource-based recreation, not only because of its urban situation but also due to its proximity to part of the US Middle West. In coping with the problem, the multiplicity of agency response confers the advantages of flexibility, but on the other hand may lead to unnecessary duplication and a failure to consider the system as a whole. Research being carried out on recreational travel and demand may eventually point to new ideas in the integration of provision.[88]

In a province like Alberta which is more evenly settled (with the exception of its northern areas) but relatively little urbanized, the province dominates park provision outside the National Park system. This latter (4·5 million acres, 1·8 million ha) dominates, but there are 1·7 million acres (688,500 ha) of provincial parks plus 5000 acres (2025 ha) in municipal ownership and a small private enterprise sector, chiefly campsites provided by the forestry industries. The province's parks are classified by type according to their long-term purpose: park, recreational area, historic site, natural area, wilderness area and roadside campsite, are the categories used, and different management policies pertain for each, relating to the nature and purpose of the area and the degree of protection given to it.[89] Here, the lower pressure upon rural resources allows the agency to have oversight of the general direction of recreational provision, in contrast to the multi-layered system in Ontario. Even in the less densely populated provinces like Alberta and Saskatchewan, public pressure is in favour of as little development as possible in provincial parks.

3.15 INDIVIDUAL STATES OF THE USA

(a) The role of State governments

In some ways the State resembles the Federal government in microcosm. This is particularly so in the field of natural resources where all

[88] R. I. Wolfe, *A Use-classification of Parks by Analysis of Extremes* (Ontario, Dept of Highways, Report RR 134, 1969), and *A Theory of Recreational Highway Traffic* (Ontario, Dept of Highways, Report RR 128, 1967).

[89] C. H. Harvie, 'The provincial parks of Alberta', in J. G. Nelson and R. C. Scace (eds.), *op. cit.*, pp. 461–72.

States have agencies which correspond to most of those discussed in the Federal departments of Agriculture and Interior. (See pp. 174–7.) Thus there is usually a State department of water resources, of forestry, of wildlife management, and of recreation. These departments operate on a smaller scale and are less complex in their ramifications than the Federal departments but it should be remembered that many of the States, in size or population, are bigger than the European countries discussed in this work.

The States are also important in co-ordinating the work of smaller political subdivisions such as cities and counties, and supra-county agglomerations such as special purpose districts (for example, soil and water conservation districts, grassland districts, regional park associations). The States, and through them these smaller units, qualify for matching grants under the Land and Water Conservation Fund Act of 1965 if a comprehensive Statewide plan for rural recreation is presented to, and approved by, the Bureau of Outdoor Recreation. (See pp. 175–6.)

(b) State resource management

(i) *State Park systems.* All the States have an agency or branch which is concerned with the designation and running of State Parks. In a sense they are miniatures of the Federal system: some are primarily general-purpose outdoor recreation areas, some mainly scenic and in others historic features are the main attraction. In a few cases an area primarily of significance to nature protection may come within the SP system as at Point Lobos Reserve, California. The differences from the Federal system are generally those of size since the State units are usually much smaller than National Parks, although some, like Baxter SP in Maine and Anza-Borrego Desert SP, California, are large by any standards. They do not usually represent the finest outdoor areas, which are likely to have been appropriated for the Federal system, and they most often fulfil user-oriented and intermediate recreation needs rather than resource-based recreation demands.

The number and complexity of these Parks, which are nearly all single-use areas with recreation as the prime aim, is tremendous and in most States both bond issues and Federal grants are being used to acquire new areas and to round out existing holdings. A report published in 1965 totalled 4800 'existing nonurban Park and related areas',[90] and most of these will be State-agency areas. It suggests that another 2297 areas (totalling 7·3 million acres (29,543 km²) and 62,000 miles (10,142 km) of linear-type recreation areas) are of significance at State scale and should be added to the State systems.[91] In suggesting criteria for selection, a differentiation is made between State Parks and State Recreation Areas, which parallels a Federal distinction (pp. 180–88). The Parks are for 'inspirational landscape and wilderness values',[92] whereas the Recreation Areas are on the basis of 'providing non-urban recreation opportunities accessible to the people'.[93] Though such operational distinctions may exist, the majority of States continue to designate one major unit, the State Park. Of interest are the standards suggested for provision, on a rule-of-thumb basis (Table 2.9), gathered from a variety of studies; their

Table 2.9   Provision of Parks: USA suggested standards of provision

Type of Area	Acreage/ 1000 pop.	Location features
(1) Areas of state signif.:		Within 50 miles or $1\frac{1}{4}$ hours
Parks and natural areas	30	travel time of urban centres.
Recreation areas	15	Within 25 miles or 1 hour.
(2) Non-urban local areas:		
Park and natural areas	15	Within 25 miles or 1 hour.
Recreation areas	5	Within 15 miles or $\frac{1}{2}$ hour.

(30 acres = 12 ha; 50 miles = 84·5 km)
Source. NPS, Parks for America, 1965, p. 485.

basis, however, is probably empirical. Changing attitudes towards environmental matters, combined with increasing development, have nevertheless made possible more comprehensive planning for large areas in which recreation has a significant use. In Upper New York State, an Adirondack Park of nearly 9000 sq miles (23310 km²) was created in 1973.[94] Within it are wilderness areas, primitive areas, a canoe area and wild forest areas, as well as intensive use areas and private land. A comprehensive land-use and development plan forms part of the legislation, and this restricts many forms of change even in the privately-owned parts which comprise over half the Park's

[90] NPS, *Parks for America* (Washington, DC 1965), p. vii.
[91] *Ibid.*, p. viii.
[92] *Ibid.*, p. 482.
[93] *Ibid.*, p. 483.
[94] G. Crosette and P. H. Oehser, 'The Adirondacks', *American Forests* 79 (1973), pp. 25–40.

145

area. This type of comprehensive planning, paralleled, for example, by the land-use controls introduced in Hawaii in 1961, is probably a model for the future and will very likely enhance public recreational opportunities.

(ii) *Other State agencies.* Where appropriate, other branches of State resource-managing units participate in the provision of rural recreation areas. The contribution of each of these varies from State to State according to the importance of particular types of terrain and the exact constitution of the institutional infra-structure. The State Forestry department may well manage its forests on a multiple use basis that includes recreation, but on the whole such forests are not very large: larger forests are likely to be National Forests. Texas for example has about 6000 acres (2428 ha) of State Forest compared with ten times as much National Forest; Massachusetts on the other hand has no National Forests, and 25,000 acres (10,117 ha) of State Forests. The water resources agency may also be important, where impoundments provide a supply of water for aquatic activities— in New England the 'ponds' which were power sources for early industry are now very important for recreation. Similarly, the State fish and wildlife agencies may administer tracts of lands impor- tant not only for hunting and fishing (and their role in stocking other waters is often crucial) but for less specialized forms of activity as well. But in the east, for example, where public land is less frequent than privately owned property a most important function of such a department is the provision of access points to fishable waters. Table 2.10 gives some statistics for a few states to indicate the activities of some of these agencies.

In most States, the prevalence of automobile travel for recreation has ensured a response by the Highways Department to the need for small rest stops, sometimes with picnic tables and toilets, small over- night campsites for travellers, and laybys at scenic places. On free- ways in California, these are designed to be 30 minutes driving time apart.

(c) California: an example

(i) *The State.* Although California is perhaps hardly typical of present-day America, its trends tend to be those experienced by the rest of the nation at some future time and so it is a useful example of

Table 2.10   State agency administrations: USA selected states only, 1960

State	Agencies	Number of areas	Acreage 1000 ac. = 4 km²	Comments
R.I.	Parks and Recreation Division	19	8,071	Attendance 1960, 2·7 million. R.I. has highest av. pop. density in US.
	Division of Forests	9	14,404	
	Division of Fish and Game	11	5,943	27 fishing access areas.
Neb.	Game, Forestation and Parks Commission	3 44 16 6	2,428 48,169 15,022 100	State Parks. Recreation areas. Wildlife management areas. Waysides
Ore.	Parks and Recreation Division	153	59,991	1960 attendance 11,538,000.
	Game Commission	16	73,313	104 fishing access sites.
	State Forestry Board	1	71,644	
	Highway Department	67		Highway rest stops, scenic overlooks, small picnic areas.
Miss.	Park Commission	14	13,405	1960 attendance 920,000.
	Forestry Commission	1	1,760	
	Game and Fish Commission	n.a.	1,307,000	Mostly leased.
	Highway Department	84		Roadside parks.

Source: NPS, Parks for America, 1965.

what other less 'advanced' places may expect. The population of the State is now about 20 million (86 per cent of which is urbanized), and projected to rise to 23·5 million by 1975. A highly developed system of freeways gives access to the manifold diversity of the State's terrains: a varied coastline, deserts, high mountain ranges with lakes and streams, coastal boating areas like San Francisco Bay and the Sacramento Delta. Winter sports are also important, yet at lower elevations picnics and camping can be enjoyed all year (Figure 24).

(ii) *Demand.*   The information collected in the State's Park and Recreation Information Systems (PARIS) shows that in California,

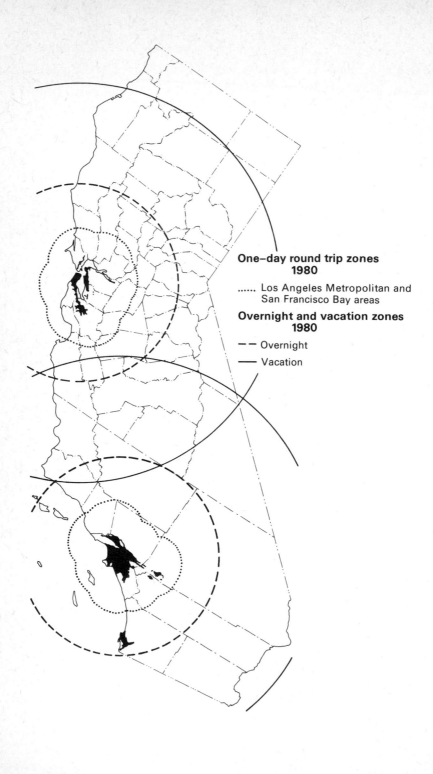

**One–day round trip zones
1980**

...... Los Angeles Metropolitan and
San Francisco Bay areas

**Overnight and vacation zones
1980**

– – Overnight

—— Vacation

rural recreation is inescapably tied to the private car and passenger car mileage for social and recreational purposes rose from 6600 million miles (11,155 million km) in 1940 to 17,600 million (19,749 million km) in 1960, with a projected rise to 47,900 (80,965 million km) by 1980.[95] Present participation rates in rural recreation are higher than the rest of the nation and demand studies suggest that they will continue to rise because of more free time (39,012 million hours of leisure in 1960 is expected to become 71,815 million in 1980).[96] Since income and mobility will rise too, with 1 mile in every 3 travelled being for pleasure by 1980,[97] then between 1960 and 1980 total potential demand for all rural recreation activities in California is expected to double.[98] Because much of the extra leisure time will come in small parcels, user-oriented and intermediate type facilities will be especially demanded. In spite of the climate about 35 per cent of total demand is in June, July and August (because of school holidays, largely), but there is more fluctuation in northern than southern California.[99] (Figures 25 & 26). 'Overflow' camping occurs during the peak periods and during August of 1963, 201 thousand people were turned away from the State Parks; during the entire year 1·5 million would-be campers were not permitted entrance.[100] One result of this is the imposition of a camping time limit at some State Parks: 7 days at the 9 most popular (all coastal), 10 days at another 9 and 15 days at a further large group. An overall limit of 30 days prevails in the summer months, and a campsite reservation system has been introduced. None of these developments is expected to cater for all the projected demands; in the demand area of the Bay Area cities, and especially in the inner zones there will persist a

[95] California Public Outdoor Recreation Plan Committee, *California Public Outdoor Recreation Plan* (Sacramento 1960), part I, p. 27.

[96] L. J. Crampon, *Recreation and Parks Study*, part I (South Pasadena 1965), p. 3. (A report prepared by Stanford Research Institute for the State of California Dept of Parks and Recreation.)

[97] *Ibid.*, p. 4.

[98] California Dept of Parks and Recreation, *California Outdoor Recreation Resources Plan* (Sacramento 1972), p. 25.

[99] L. J. Crampon, *op. cit.*, chs. II and III.

[100] California Dept of Parks and Recreation, *Accelerated Development Program, Projecting through 1980* (Sacramento 1965), p. 10.

Figure 24   The projected zones of rural recreation demand in California in 1980, based on the assumptions of the early 1960s. Experience suggests that the boundaries of the zones are somewhat conservative.
Source: California Public Outdoor Recreation Plan, part II, pp. 86–7.

149

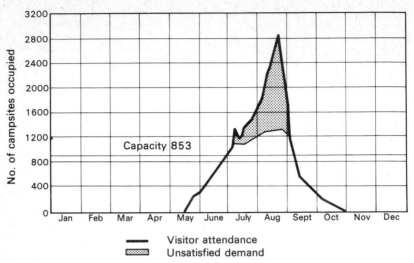

Figure 25 Camper attendance and overflow at the Northern Redwoods State Parks in California during 1963. The coolness of these environments makes them attractive during the height of summer but the season is relatively short.
Source: California Dept of Parks and Recreation.

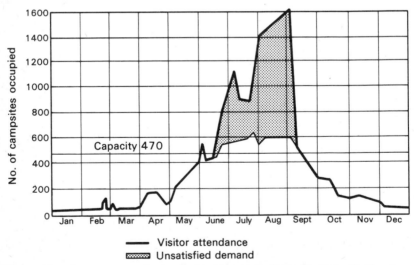

Figure 26 Camper attendance at the Mountain State Parks in California during 1963. A very sharp and high overload was experienced in the summer months but all year demand is present. These parks are not in the High Sierra but rather in the foothills.
Source: California Dept of Parks and Recreation.

deficiency of resources (notably camping facilities) which is likely to get worse. Only in the further travel zones is it expected that demand can be met.[101]

(iii) *The State Parks*.[102]   The system in 1970 comprised 202 units, with 813,527 acres (329,234 ha) of land and water. Of these areas, 52 were Parks, 73 Beaches, 25 Recreation Areas, 34 Historic parks, 3 Wayside campgrounds and 15 Reserves. Over 43 million visitor days per annum are currently being recorded, the 1960–70 increase being 80 per cent. The Parks cover a wide variety of terrains from the desert of the south of the State to the northern Redwood parks which are often considered to be the finest elements in the system. The Redwoods are, in fact, inspirational rather than recreational; the dark forests are not suitable for many activities. The beaches and recreational areas carry the heaviest load, and this is especially so in the southern part of the State, where population is densest. Thus the Recreation Areas within the system are expected to absorb many of the heaviest impacts of the next decade, when, according to one official estimate, 44,800 new camping units, 56,800 new picnic places, 30,400 new boat access parking spaces and 2700 extra miles of riding and hiking trails will be needed.[103] Although California has a long and varied coastline, very little of it is in public hands, so that there is a shortage of public beaches, especially in and near the two largest urban agglomerations. New developments in coastal protection and recreation development are described below in section (d). Other popular recreation areas are Lake Tahoe[104] in the Sierra Nevada, and the various reservoirs and lakes which provide boating and swimming. The Historic parks are concerned with preservation and interpretive programmes and offer other forms of recreation only as ancillary activities.

The overall purpose of the system is to keep in public lands some of the unique resources of California, and to supplement the Federal system in the intermediate and user-oriented fields. Management

[101] California Dept of Parks and Recreation, *California Outdoor Recreation Resources Plan*, p. 23.
[102] *Parks Are Forever*, a yearly guide to the California State Park System (Sacramento, Dept of Parks and Recreation).
[103] *Idem, Report on a Decade* (Sacramento 1970), p. 4.
[104] This lake is situated on the California-Nevada border, and the balance between public and private land acquisition and development, the influx of sewage, water consumption and soil erosion have posed special problems. See BOR, *Lake Tahoe. A Special Place* (Washington, DC 1973).

policies consist of complete preservation of some areas, especially those in the Reserve category, limited development in others, and extensive construction in beaches and parks where recreation use is intensive. Camping sites are designed to be away from traffic noise, a task made more difficult by the determination of highway construction engineers to drive freeways through or close to State Parks. Californian innovations include a trail for the blind in the Redwoods, an aerial interpretive trail across the desert for private flyers, and a computerized campsite reservation system.

Extensive though the system is, and great though the sums spent on acquisition and development are,[105] it can scarcely be said to be adequate. As discussed above, use is very heavy and overcrowding the usual situation, to the point of closure at summer weekends. Over use results in heavy trampling of vegetation, destruction of vegetation in overflow and unauthorized campsites, overloading of toilet facilities and many other ills, besides the undesirable atmosphere of 'campurbia' produced by a high density of campers. This latter is exacerbated by the affluent Californians' habit of giving up tent camping in favour of either a trailer (caravan) or a 'camper'—a caravan-type unit mounted on a pickup truck body or even larger chassis. Also, the small size of most of the State Parks makes them very vulnerable to crowding, and the feeling of being in wild country is soon lost.

It is obvious that the State Park system requires considerable development, but the high costs of land and the general reluctance of taxpayers to contribute more to the State's purse[106] (for any purpose) mean that a vastly expanded acquisition programme is not possible. Reviews of resources have suggested that demands are most likely to be met by investing in increased development of the existing units; it is suggested that hitherto, development has not kept pace with acquisition,[107] and plans are being drawn up to expand considerably the number of camp units, picnic units, parking spaces and boat ramps. Table 2.11 compares the 1964 availability of these facilities

[105] Acquisition costs since 1927 (when the system was started): total c. $60 million; development costs $25 million. The 1969–70 total expenditure on the system was $40·8 million and revenue was 45 per cent of the operating costs. See California Dept of Parks and Recreation, *Report on a Decade*, p. 28.

[106] There was a $150 million State bond issue on the 1964 ballot which was voted on positively by the electorate, but fiscal attitudes in the State have changed since then.

[107] California Dept of Parks and Recreation, *Accelerated Development Program, Projecting through 1980*, p. 13.

A wilderness area in the Wind River Range of Wyoming. Although very remote and lacking developed facilities, such areas are attracting increasing numbers of walkers and riders. Their carrying capacity is, however, very low in both ecological and perceptual terms and for these reasons the majority of rural recreationists will be unable to take advantage of them. (*Grant Heilman, Lititz, Pa*)

The picnic (*see also opposite*) can be enjoyed in a variety of situations. Reasonably typical of many European countries is the roadside picnic tea requiring no installed equipment, merely space for pulling the car off the road, preferably in a rural area. The presence of nearby traffic is rarely a deterrent. (*John Topham Picture Library*)

Opposite

North American picnickers prefer an installed table and benches and some shade is usually a necessary accompaniment to the summer climate. This roadside picnic area in Georgia lacks the fireplace which larger parks would possess. (*Barnaby's Picture Library*)

The escalation of camping technology produces quite orderly but distinctly suburban conditions, as here in Lake of Ozarks SP, Missouri. The advent of the hard-top integral chassis camper has meant heavier demands upon space and facilities in campgrounds, since power hookups and holding-tank flushing are often provided. The expectations of such campers regarding toilets, showers and the like are also high. (*Alan Pitcairn*)

Opposite

The latest product is the 'mobile home', to which the term 'camping' is virtually an insult. These are extensively used for recreation and are equipped with all comforts. The price and availability of gasoline may slow down their penetration of some markets.

Even where camping gear is mostly dominated by tents, overcrowding of popular places is often found during peak periods. This part of Yosemite National Park in California resembles a 'campurbia', and indeed the density of living and parking makes the environmental quality inferior to most North American suburbs. Regeneration of the forest is possible only by 'resting' the campground for some years. (*United States Department of the Interior*)

Sailing small boats is frequently subject to crowding because of the concentration of suitable water and of launch facilities. Here in Lyme Regis, UK, the preparation of boats has to be interspersed with family-group use of the sands. (*Peter Baker*)

Opposite

Simple water-based recreation involves relatively inexpensive equipment and may have very little environmental impact. However, high quality surroundings are often required by the purists, and National Scenic Waterways in the USA are designed to cater for such people, amongst others. These areas are virtually linear parks, protected against incompatible uses. (*National Park Service, United States Department of the Interior*)

An increase in the popularity of skiing has meant its spread into areas formerly considered climatically marginal, like the Cairngorms of Scotland. The tow facilities form a node on the run system, especially when snow cover is incomplete. The rather obvious environmental impact of these installations can be seen in the background. Cross-country skiing has also experienced a resurgence, probably as a reaction to crowded slopes and tows. (*Popperfoto*)

The snowmobile is potentially a very disadvantageous piece of recreation equipment with high social and environmental impacts. Here, in Maine, snowmobiles are enjoying a trail specially for their use and thus not interfering with wildlife or other recreationists, nor endangering themselves. (*United States Department of the Interior*)

Another piece of recreation equipment which can penetrate into remote areas and fragile habitats is this 6-wheel drive, amphibious 'Amphicat', seen here in use at a 'scramble'. They are often used by hunters and fishermen to seek out game in areas previously difficult of access. (Betton Industries Ltd, Canada)

Serious walking or hiking is another weekend activity and some are prepared to carry large amounts of gear in order to be independent of man-made facilities even in England, where settlements and accommodation are rarely spaced at long intervals.

Opposite

The Amsterdam Forest. The rowing course is the most obvious feature, but beyond it are the numerous paths and cycle tracks which connect and intersect the areas of planted woodland and of open grass. The interior is free from motor traffic. (*KLM Aerocarto*)

A part of the coast of the Netherlands near Bloemendaal. The facilities for visitors have to be concentrated in order to save the sand dunes from the degree of pressure which would allow them to blow out. The degree of pressure can be gauged from the numbers of people and cars. (*KLM Aerocarto*)

In small nations, the presence of wild country forms a magnet for car-drivers at weekends and vacation times. The presence of a lay-by in wild country such as this, overlooking the Kyle of Lochalsh in Scotland, concentrates traffic, which in unforested terrain easily becomes the dominant element of the landscape. (*Barnaby's Picture Library*)

Opposite

Weekend cottages may be placed in environmentally and aesthetically unsuitable places, as near Dungeness in southern England. Once established, their removal is difficult even in countries with strict land-use planning controls. (*John Topham Picture Library*)

The weekend cottage is here typified by an island near Parry Sound, Ontario. While the nature of the terrain makes it generally highly suitable for recreational use, it can also present problems. On such rocky areas, sewage must generally be discharged into the lake. Given a small lake and many cottages, pollution results. (*The Photographic Survey Corporation Ltd, Toronto*)

Walking for pleasure is one of the most popular outdoor recreation activities. It is often helped by the use of waymarked trails, and a small group in Wales is about to use one leading from a picnic area which is also a leaflet-guided nature trail. (*Ron Chapman*)

One of the world's most famous scenic and recreation areas: the Yosemite Valley of Yosemite NP in California. Although here screened by the trees, a great deal of development had taken place to accommodate visitors. This is now to be removed, to allow the valley to be mostly natural habitat. (*Alan Pitcairn*)

Wilderness areas in Europe are hard to find but the harsh terrain of Iceland (here near Lake Myvatn) is one of the outstanding examples: however, all the Nordic countries have large areas of very wild terrain. (*Barnaby's Picture Library*)

Table 2.11   Actual and potential numbers of selected facilities
in California: 1964 onwards

Facility	1964	Additional potential
Camp units	5,892	22,919
Picnic units	5,091	29,882
Parking spaces	18,263	54,512
Launching ramps	50	211

Source: California Dept of Parks and Recreation, *Accelerated Development Program, projecting through 1980,* 1965, pp. 18, 41.

with the potential development of lands already acquired. Nevertheless, twenty-eight new units were added to the system in the period 1960–70, totalling 52·49 thousand acres (21,242 ha).[108]

A method of assigning priorities for capital inputs on construction projects has been evolved. This consists of allocation of points (or ranking numbers) to various categories, for example 'protection of irreplaceable resources', 'protection and repair of facilities', and 'initial development'. These have subdivisions. Totals are then multiplied by the region in which they occur, with higher values being given to certain activities in the more crowded regions such as the coast of southern California.

Changing tastes and attitudes probably surface more readily in California than other regions of the USA, and current trends show emerging problems and opportunities. The State cannot but be involved in demands for wilderness, both large-scale and smaller-scale, near-city wildernesses. Underwater parks and reserves are also needed, as are facilities for long-distance cycling in the form of trails and hostels. Activities such as rockhounding, cross-country skiing and off-road recreational vehicle use must be recognized as legitimate and facilities provided, all of which involves the recognition of the carrying capacities of various types of terrain and the scheduling of visitation so as to avoid over-use.

The State Parks system is moving inexorably in the direction of greater development, i.e. more and more towards user-oriented recreation and away from resource-based and even intermediate categories. Incomes and mobility in California, of course, are such that the user-oriented zone is probably rather wider than in many States; time is the limiting factor. Nevertheless the trend towards priority for developed facilities within easy reach of conurbations in

[108] *Ibid.,* p. 18.

California is reflective of the nation's movement as a whole. It must be remembered that the State Parks of California are only one public system catering to the demand for intermediate zone facilities. Because of the highway system, some Federal units are available for weekend use, such as Yosemite National Park, which is *c.* 5 hours' drive from the State's major population centres. Similarly, county parks such as those on the coasts of Marin and Mendocino Counties are much used for weekend recreation, as are other county parks. The whole set of parks from Federal through State and Regional to much smaller jurisdictions forms one system, and public awareness of the usefulness of the various units is very high.

(d) The coast of California[109]

The State has 1037 miles (1659 km) of shoreline, of which nearly 58 per cent is in private ownership, but only 24 per cent is available for public recreational use, 54 per cent being undeveloped in any form. Thus for a highly mobile but mostly coastal dwelling population, there have been insufficient recreational opportunities (Orange County alone provided 3·5 million out of the State's 23·5 million recreation days in 1969) caused by lack of public access, both visual and physical; pollution, as in 1970 when Monterey Bay was unusable because of poor sewage treatment; the destruction of historic and cultural sites; commercial development; and severe erosion. The comprehensive plan for the coast, approved and funded by a Proposition on the November ballot of 1972, proposes a comprehensive land-use plan for coastal zones which, rather radically, suggests State acquisition of all land seaward of highways over 300 feet (91·5 m) from the coast. The next major priority is to enhance the recreation opportunities of the 85 per cent of day-users of the coast who live in Metropolitan areas. To this end, the immediate steps are to enlarge ten State Parks, purchase inholdings of another nine, purchase other parks, especially those which are suitable for specialized activities, like the Santa Monica dunes for beach-buggy riding. Financing will mean an outlay of $1 billion up until 1980, raised from State bonds, tax sharing, the Land and Water Conservation Fund (a Federal source), a gasoline tax and toll roads along the coast.

[109] The major documents are: US Army Corps of Engineers, *National Shoreline Study: California Regional Inventory* (San Francisco 1971); and California Dept of Parks and Recreation. *California Coastline Preservation and Recreation Plan* (Sacramento 1971).

154

(e) The role of the States

A cursory analysis of the concerns of the States in rural recreation suggests that they are engaged mainly in the planning, administration and development of user-oriented and intermediate category areas near cities. Even though large sums. of money are available under Federal grant programmes, it appears to be felt that the large resource-based areas (whether they be primarily natural areas or recreational places) are mostly the concern of the Federal government. This power can co-ordinate its acquisitions on a much larger scale than the States, naturally enough, but the main reason is financial. Land costs are so high that only Uncle Sam can afford to pick up the tab for new areas of National Park or NRA quality.

3.16 PRIVATE ENTERPRISE

Most of the examples so far quoted are of the supply of recreational resources by governmental agencies. In the intermediate zone, however, the concentration of recreationists is such that commercial provision may become profitable, especially if government aid is forthcoming in the form of know-how and capital. The types of enterprise which can yield a living are, however, limited and it has to be acknowledged that in the more extensive recreations, governmental agencies are best equipped to provide the necessary facilities.

In the Netherlands, no complete study of the role of this economic sector has been made, and its contribution has to be deduced. The most obvious part played is in the concessionary operation of yacht harbours and refreshment facilities at developments which are government-built and controlled.

Less noticeable in the landscape, but equally important, is the opening of private woodlands to walkers by their owners. This is done under the authority of the Scenery Act of 1928 and operates in two stages. Firstly the owner of a large estate, castle with grounds or forest-heath-agriculture complex may apply for registration as a scenic estate. If he agrees to keep the landscape unaltered for twenty-five years, then the value of the estate for taxation is reduced to 10–25 per cent below the marked price. Secondly, if the estate is made available to the public (who may be required to pay a small fee) then an extra reduction of 50 per cent on property and legacy tax is granted. Because of the impossibility of collecting fees for some woodlands, for instance, free public access to many areas has been

155

assured. Walking is the main activity and damage appears not to be a serious problem. About six hundred estates are now open to the public on this basis and two hundred are managed for their amenity value under the Scenery Act of 1928. Since 1966 funds are available to assist private landowners in management and maintenance costs of estates which are open to the public. The net result is the opening to the public of a great deal of land which otherwise they would, given the current pressures, have used illegally and no doubt improperly in some places.

In North America, service clubs donate equipment and facilities for camps and parks, often providing what the public purse cannot or will not bear. Organizations of people on behalf of rural recreation provision assist park planners to make their work and aims more widely known and bring political pressure for more and, hopefully, better, provision.

The private sector of the economy is involved at most stages of the total rural recreation experience (i.e. from anticipation to memory) but its part in the supply of on-site resources is of three major types. These are the provision of facilities (lodging, food, campsites, marinas, etc.) for profit; the public-service opening up of private lands by, for example, lumber companies; and the provision of facilities as part of another rural enterprise such as farming, especially in marginal areas where profit from the main enterprise is low.

The operation of resorts, lodges, ski-lifts, restaurants, private camp grounds and associated facilities has always accompanied rural recreation. In the National Parks and similar areas, the policy of the government until recently has often been to encourage concessionaire development of visitor-oriented facilities, so that nearly everywhere that recreation takes place, private enterprise is on the lookout for a profit opportunity, from roadside stands selling worms to fishermen, through luxury ski resorts in the Rockies. The contribution is so large and diverse that adequate description of it is practically impossible: the ORRRC investigation of this sector was by mail questionnaire sampling,[110] and the main activities identified were resorts, dude ranches, camp grounds, commercial beaches, yacht clubs, boat clubs, ski areas, shooting preserves, vacation farms and resort hotels. Many of these areas are small: 23 per cent were 9·9 acres (4 ha) or less; 18 per cent (the second largest group) how-

[110] ORRRC Report 11, *Private Outdoor Recreation Facilities* (Washington, DC 1962).

ever were 200–499 acres (81–201 ha) in size. Seventy per cent of the acreage in the survey was used for recreation purposes, and most of it, indeed, had recreation for its primary use, with farming and forestry most frequently mentioned as associated functions. As with publicly-owned facilities, water is very popular and 48 per cent of the choice listings placed water-oriented activities (swimming, fishing and boating, in that rank order) first. Hunting, picnicking and skiing account for another 41 per cent.[111] Something of an agglomeration effect is shown by the finding that 90 per cent of the facilities were near public lands and water used for recreation and nearly half were near other privately owned facilities.[112]

Some of the largest privately-owned areas which come into use by the public are forests belonging to large lumber companies. One western company has 1·5 million acres (6000 km²) of 'tree farm', on which hunting is the major recreation activity and campsites, etc., are developed primarily for the hunters' use. On another part of their holdings, the company has developed larger picnic areas and trails, and made available logging roads for recreational travel. Although these programmes cost the company money, they are willing to bear the costs in the causes of public relations, of concentrating people so as to reduce fire hazard and to help the economic growth of nearby communities. Similar rationales have been developed by power companies on their watersheds and impoundments.[113]

The role of family farms in rural recreation provision has come under quite close scrutiny whether for the development of some extra income as an addition to the farm enterprise, or using the farm resources solely for recreation.[114] The activities encompass almost everything, but with a trend to an emphasis on swimming, fishing and picnics. Small impoundments, especially if kept well stocked with fish or surrounded by picnic-site and swimming facilities, are especially popular.

The success of such ventures, from the commercial point of view, has been distinctly limited. There has been a considerable amount of difficulty in raising the capital for initial developments, often because

[111] *Ibid.*, pp. 132–4. These findings were confirmed by BOR's *1965 Survey of Outdoor Recreation Activities* (Washington, DC 1970), Tables 2B-1 and 2B-2.

[112] ORRRC Report 11, *op. cit.*, p. xv.

[113] *Ibid.*, pp. 116–21.

[114] US Dept of Agriculture, *Rural Recreation. A New Family-farm Business* (Washington, DC 1962), and *Farmers Home Administration. Handbook of Outdoor Recreation Enterprises in Rural Areas* (Washington, DC 1966).

potential loan sources regard rural recreation as a capricious activity.[115] Again, there have been many cases of poor management, partly because the marginal farmers who are most tempted to try this source of income are sometimes the least suited for the new resource- and people-management attitudes which are required. In the period 1960–70 in New Hampshire, the failure rate of camp-grounds was 2·6 per cent in the northern part of the State, but only 1 per cent in the southern half,[116] emphasizing that many operators have not realized the critical nature of the accessibility factor. Because of competition from within the private sector and from the whole of the public sector, a farmer has to be situated within the right distance from a large population agglomeration com-mensurate with the type of recreation he is offering. Although put forward by many advisory services as an aid to farmers, it must be admitted that small-scale private farm recreation is scarcely likely to form a significant element in recreation provision except in very limited zones around major urban centres.[117] In such places, re-creation has other competitors which are just as likely to be suc-cessful unless prevented by environmental constraints. Table 2.12

Table 2.12   USA: distribution of private rural recreation facilities relative to cities

Activity	In primary SMSA* county	In other counties in metro area	Non-metro counties contiguous to metro area	Counties separated by other counties from metro area (numbers)		
				1	2	3
Hunting	2	2	15	62	14	5
Water-skiing	6	6	33	39	15	1
Fishing	6	8	28	35	15	8
Camping	11	8	34	35	10	2
Riding	18	11	28	26	14	3

* Standard Metropolitan Statistical Area: i.e. this county is the historical heart of the city.
Source: BOR, The 1965 Survey of Outdoor Recreation Activities, 1970, Table 26.4, p. 109.

[115] BOR, Financing of Private Outdoor Recreation (Washington, DC 1967).

[116] W. F. La Page, P. L. Cormier and S. C. Maurice, The Commercial Campground Industry in New Hampshire, US Dept of Agriculture Forest Service Research Paper NE-255 (1972).

[117] For example, US Dept of Agriculture, Economic Research Service, Farm Vacation Enter-prises in Ohio, ERS-164 (1964); Opportunities for Improving Rural-Family Income through Recreation Enterprises, Bull. 673 (1963); and Opportunities and Limitations in Private Recreation Development (H. A. Johnson, mimeo, 1966); W. F. Le Page, Successful Private Campgrounds, USFS Res. Pap. NE-58 (1967). The leaflet advertising a private camping park ('a division of Hedonics

emphasizes this importance of location: really close to the city, land is not available for such activities, and three counties and over away is too far to tap the market. So that only within a relatively narrow band contiguous with the metropolitan area (but usually beyond the city fringe and its associated belt of speculation land) and into the next county is most private enterprise in recreation likely to be a success.

As with the public sector, problems centre around fire and vandalism, with the added uncertainty of public liability laws which may put the owner at risk for accidents which happen on his land. Although optimistic views about the likelihood of success for the private operator in 'the recreation business' can be found, more sanguine and low-key appraisal is perhaps more common. The seasonal nature of recreational enterprises, the ease with which recreation can be trimmed from the family budget, the high labour input and the capriciousness of public taste (the national survey reported that 62 per cent of all facilities were under-used at weekends),[118] all combine to render the realization of capital for such enterprises difficult.[119] Money is most likely to be made in particular and specialized fields such as ski resorts in the absence of competition from publicly-owned developments,[120] intensive-recreation oriented resorts, the making of money on land values peripheral to a recreation facility which may not itself be profitable (for example, housing around a golf course or chalets around a ski area), the provision of supplemental facilities such as accommodations outside a National Park, and concessions on publicly owned land.[121] There is in the USA a role for private initiative but it is not a dominant role.

Incorporated') near Peterborough, Ontario, some 90 miles (145 km) from Toronto, significantly gives directions to the park only from Toronto.

[118] BOR, *The 1965 Outdoor Recreation Survey* (Washington, DC 1970), Table 2B-13, p. 115.

[119] Capital costs for a 12 acre/60-unit camping site in Alabama have been estimated at $85,000 (A. B. Sherling and E. W. McCoy, *Considerations in Establishing Camping Facilities in Alabama*, Auburn University Agricultural Experimental Station Circular 193 (January 1972), p. 14).

[120] In a 1966 survey of Wisconsin recreation enterprises, only medium and large size resorts brought in returns to family labour and management of over $20,000/yr. Most profitable enterprises yielded less than $2000, and one loss of $2688 (on 'miscellaneous field sports') was reported. See College of Agricultural and Life Sciences, University of Wisconsin, *Some Organizational and Income-Determining Features of the Wisconsin Outdoor Recreation Industry* (Madison 1972), p. 14.

[121] H. L. Diamond, 'The private role in the provision of large-scale outdoor recreation', in B. L. Driver (ed.), *Elements of Outdoor Recreation Planning* (University of Michigan School of Natural Resources 1970), pp. 171–6.

In the absence of any concrete information beyond that of casual information, it is not possible to assess the contribution of private individuals and companies to rural recreation in Britain. A number of activities may be noted:

(i) *Camping sites.* This is usually rather informal, and a farmer typically allows campers to use one or two fields with access to a water supply and an outside lavatory. In wet weather the poor access and soft surface frequently lead to him providing towing services as well.

(ii) *Bed and Breakfast.* In many rural areas, people will let off a spare bedroom and provide 'bed and breakfast' at a relatively low cost. This is a valuable addition to the stock of accommodation in rural areas and also supplements incomes without much capital outlay. In recent years, surveys have shown that 13 per cent of farms in upland Denbighshire, 18 per cent in Cornwall and 30 per cent in the Lake District engaged in this enterprise.[122] Since 'B & B' is relatively cheap, it probably increases the demand for weekend recreation by bringing out for that period a group of users who otherwise could afford only day trips.

(iii) *Refreshment facilities.* In some scenic laybays, for example on the North York Moors National Park, converted caravans or delivery vans dispense light refreshments, especially tea. They are unlandscaped, since temporary, and not subject to control by the Park Planning authority. However hideous they may be (and however ridiculous the situation that at such places there can be satisfaction of input but no output), they obviously fulfil a demand which cannot be catered to in any other way.

3.17 SECOND HOMES

The desirability of the possession of a second home varies with affluence and opportunity. It is nowhere more marked than in Scandinavia where both factors are favourable, and continues to be a dominant theme in parts of North America, particularly California and the States along the Canadian border, as well as in metropolitan Canada. The supply of these cottages is often a sole prerogative of the private sector of the economy, where individually or

---

[122] 'Review of farms and tourism in upland Denbighshire', *Recreation News* 52 (1973), p. 1.

corporately-owned farms and forests are turned over to recreation, and the subsequent structure results in work for private enterprise as well. Occasionally, government bodies release land for cottage building, as with some Crown Land in Ontario and Federal land in, for example, National Forests of the USA, but public pressure has in effect put an end to the latter instances. Two major patterns of cottage development are found: those where an old settlement has provided the structures, with possibly a few new houses, so that a change of function is dominant over a change in structure: this is evident in parts of Sweden and Britain. Elsewhere the cottages are new buildings and arrayed in response to access by road: parts of the Muskoka and Haliburton areas of Ontario demonstrate this feature as does Denmark. This latter pattern can of course be superimposed upon the former, older layout.

For most Danes, the summerhouse comes practically at the top of discretionary spending desires. This has led to an enormous—and continuing—expansion of areas given over to summerhouses, especially by the sea. The movement of land into summerhouse use has been piecemeal and unplanned and many aesthetically un-pleasing areas have grown up, as has happened with caravan (trailer) parks in Britain. Near Aarhus, for example, a road separates one group of summerhouses from the beach, another example of poor planning and layout (Figure 27). Other colonies are clearly very well landscaped and carefully laid out so that all the cottages have easy access to the sea.

The number and location of summerhouses have been studied[123] and the rates of growth between 1959 and 1965 is given in Table 2.13 and Figure 28. In 1971 the total number of summerhouses increased to 145,000 so that since 1959, when the great expansion began, there has been an increase of c. 10 per cent per annum. This rate clearly cannot be projected for long into the future, otherwise the whole of Denmark will be covered in nothing but summerhouses. The greatest demand is quite near to urban centres, with the apparent exception of the east coast of Jutland. For weekend use, however, these repre-sent easily accessible areas in a rural setting and can be reached by numerous ferries from Zealand. On a local and regional scale, attempts are being made to control the number and location of summerhouses but it is apparent that their distribution really needs

[123] Landsplanudvalgets Sekretariat, *op. cit.*

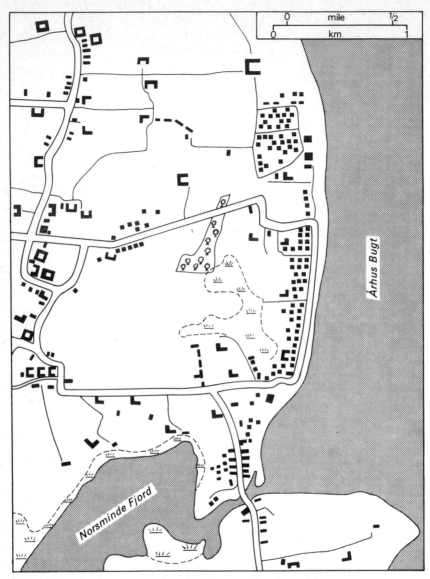

Figure 27 A map extract showing the proliferation of summer cottages along the coast of Denmark near Århus. (The cottages appear as blank squares whereas other buildings are typically open squares or [-shaped.) Note the interposition of a road between one major development and the sea.
Source: Danmarks Geodetisk Institut 1:100,000 series sheet 1314 Århus, rev. 1962.

considering at a national level and in the context of a national physical plan.

The most typical and traditional feature of rural recreation in Sweden is the vacation house and the total number in the country is probably about 490,000, with every fifth house in the urban areas of the country having access to a cottage. The elongated nature of the

Table 2.13 Summerhouses in Denmark

Area	1959	1965
Zealand	21,700	43,700
Bornholm	1,100	1,400
Maribo	2,000	4,300
Funen	4,000	6,100
Jutland	17,400	31,300
Total	46,200	86,800

Source: Landsplanudvalgets Sekretariat: Strandkvalitet og Fritidsbebyggelse, 1966.

country means that the areas nearest the population centres of the south and east are the most popular sites for cottages, especially near to the numerous lakes. The generally forested nature of much of Sweden, together with its rocky coast, provides an abundance of suitable habitats for the weekend and vacation cottages. Some areas are pre-eminent by virtue of their location or their particular features. Such an area is the Stockholm archipelago where a retreat from the city is easily reached and where water-based recreation is immediately available. Inland, the country of Dalarna, centred on Lake Siljan, is a very popular cottage region both for summer residence and as a base for cross-country and downhill skiing in winter. Here, the pattern of cottages is dominated by the take-over of summer grazing farms (*fabod*) now no longer thus used, with some newer additions by lakeshores and along access roads. The result is a total in 1965 of 3278 vacation houses[124] in an area of approximately 3250 km². In the richer and more urbanized parts of Canada such as Ontario, Wolfe has noted that,

[124] H. Aldskogius, *Studier i Siljansomradets Fritidsbebyggelse* (Uppsala University Studies in Regional Geography 4, 1968), p. 29; see also his 'Vacation house settlement in the Siljan region', *Geografiska Annaler* 49 (1967), pp. 250–61.

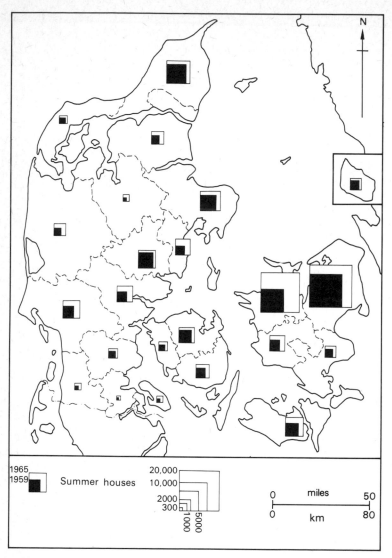

Figure 28   The growth of the numbers of summer houses in Denmark 1959–65. Demand near Copenhagen and in the remote north of Jylland is emphasized.
Source: Landsplanudvalgets Sekretariat, *Datakort Danmark*.

the summer cottage remains . . . the single most characteristic and desired place of recreation for the people of Ontario and for the vacationing visitors from beyond its borders.[125]

The result has been the development of parts of Ontario as 'cottage country' where all lakes and most roads are lined with summer dwellings (increasingly these are 'winterized' for year-round use since cross-country skiing and snowmobiling are popular and since the taxes paid by the cottager entitle him to request that his access road be snow-ploughed) with small resort centres at intervals to act as supply foci. The large amount of Crown Land in Ontario has helped supply the demand for some time but in the areas most accessible to Toronto and to the US border, there is now none left for this purpose and cottages change hands for high prices. Only in the further districts, perhaps half a day or more driving time from the urban centres, is any Crown Land still available. The situation has reached such levels that many lakeside cottages are now badly polluting the lakes on which they stand and into which they discharge their sewage. Studies of the carrying capacity of the lakes to absorb sewage and of methods of identifying problem areas are now being produced,[126] and citizen groups such as Pollution Probe in Toronto have issued guides to cottagers showing them how to wreak the least environmental damage.

Since the area of publicly owned parks is relatively small in Ontario, and since the second home is so popular, it is not surprising that private enterprise in the form of entrepreneurs who supply cottage land (and the building which has to be erected within 2 years of purchase to a minimum value of $1800 and at least 320 sq feet in size in 1969),[127] and who operate summer and winter resorts both inland and on the lakes should appear to dominate the rural recreation scene in Ontario in the intermediate zone. This emphasis was implicit in Wolfe's[128] provincial survey of 1954 and intensified by more recent developments.

[125] R. I. Wolfe, 'The changing pattern of tourism in Ontario', in Ontario Historical Society, *Profile of a Province* (Toronto 1968).
[126] Ontario Dept of Lands and Forests/Hough Stansbury Associates Ltd, *Lake Alert Phase 1: Data Analysis*; Ontario Ministry of Natural Resources/Hough Stansbury Associates Ltd, *Lake Alert Phase 2: Methodology* (Toronto 1972).
[127] Ontario Dept of Lands and Forests, *Summer Cottage Lands in Ontario* (leaflet, Toronto ?1969).
[128] R. I. Wolfe, *Recreation Land Use in Ontario* (Ph.D. thesis, University of Toronto 1954).

Private enterprise dominates the provision of second homes in the USA. The expectation of the luxury of a vacation cottage, though not as high as in Scandinavia, is becoming more frequent and concerted efforts are made to buy up and sell off suitable (and not-so-suitable) hill, shore and mountain properties for cabins, the luxury of which tends to amaze non-Americans. The weekend newspapers, in particular, have large advertisements devoted to sites for and sales of second homes, and sometimes the amount of development can be so high as to produce a kind of sylvan suburbia. A total of 1·55 million vacation homes was estimated for 1967, with the north-east containing some 38 per cent of the total, and the north central states, 30 per cent. Thus the popularity of New England's forests, lakes and ski facilities, and of the woods, lakes, fishing and hunting of Minnesota, Michigan and Wisconsin are confirmed, as is their presence close to large urban centres since 80 per cent of vacation homes were found to be within 100 miles (160 km) of the primary residence[129]— in certain areas of Minnesota (where a 1967 survey estimated 63,000 in that state) and Wisconsin, for example, and the foothills of the Sierra Nevada of California. The presence of Federal land tends to inhibit such developments but inholdings in, for example, National Forests, are especially popular (and expensive) because the presence of surrounding government land more or less completely precludes further development.

In the absence of economic depression, there can be no doubt that the demand for second homes is going to increase very rapidly and that the private enterprise sector of the economy is going to be the major agent of supply. Probably the major areas to move into this use will be cut-over forest or forests whose commercial value is low; and other wooded communities (such as oak-pine-chaparall of the Coast Range and Foothill country of California) where cabins are a more profitable crop than cattle. Also in California, there are large recreational subdivisions upon which little or no building has taken place: often the land is bought largely for speculation or as a hedge against inflation.[130] Considerable

[129] United States Dept of Commerce, *Second Homes in the United States*, Current Housing Reports, Series H-21, no. 16 (Washington, DC 1969); R. L. Ragatz, 'Vacation homes in the North-eastern United States: seasonality in population distribution', *Ann. Assoc. Amer. Geogr.* 60 (1970), pp. 447–55; see also L. W. Tombaugh, 'Factors influencing vacation home locations', *J. Leisure Res.* 2 (1970), pp. 54–63. University of Minnesota, Minnesota Lakeshore Development Study, *Minnesota's Lakeshore*, Part I (Minneapolis 1970), p. 12.

[130] J. J. Parsons, 'Slicing up the open space: subdivisions without homes in northern California', *Erdkunde* 36 (1972), pp. 1–8.

problems of servicing exist and it is doubtful if many of the owners pay the true costs of their isolation. One group that probably does are the owners of the 'jack-rabbit' shacks in the Mohave Desert. Although street lines are laid out, these areas (bought from the public domain under the Small Tract Act, 1938) have no services: water is brought round by tanker. Needless to say, the desert wind and diurnal temperature changes make their appearance unsightly in a very short time.

The role of the second home in Britain has until recent years been limited but demand now far exceeds supply, hence the popularity of the standing caravan. The cottage is usually a small dwelling either in a village or isolated, often a former farm worker's or miner's house; in Scotland the crofts of the Western Highlands are a target for this purpose. The demand is such that even ruined structures with perhaps only the walls standing are eagerly sought after in desirable areas such as the Yorkshire Dales or Lake District. In National Parks few new private dwellings are permitted, putting great pressure upon the price of extant structures, to the point where, if a house or cottage is for sale, no local agricultural worker for example, can possibly afford it. Only the very well off can hence afford country cottages in National Parks. The impact of second homes can be quite large even in Britain: in Wales an estimated 8700 vacation cottages generate £4·7 million/yr and 1500 rural jobs. In one county, Denbighshire, they represent 7 per cent of total dwellings, increasing to 1 in 5 in one parish; their owners spend almost £300,000/yr in the county and subsidize the local taxes to a significant extent since they do not use the schools, for instance.[131] Their role is therefore economically favourable although of course resented by some local people: especially in the case of English property owners in Wales. In a national context, only about 2 per cent of households own a second home, but growth has been forecast at 15–18,000/yr, reaching a total stock of over one million by 2000 AD.[132] Long before this time, all the old property will have been taken up and demand for new buildings will become strong, presenting a considerable planning challenge.

In North America and Britain, private enterprise also dominates the fast-growing sector of winter sports. Common to both of them is

---

[131] Denbighshire County Planning Dept, *Second Homes in Denbighshire* (Ruthin 1972).

[132] P. Downing and M. Dower, *Second Homes in England and Wales*, a report prepared for the Countryside Commission (London 1973). See also C. L. Bielckus *et al.*, *Second Homes in England and Wales* (Wye College Studies in Rural Land Use 11, 1972).

the pre-eminence of downhill skiing, and commercially-provided equipment and social facilities dominate developments in Canada, the northern USA, California and Scotland. In Ontario, for example, out of 116 ski facilities listed[133] in 1972, only four are in publicly owned parks. In Scandinavia, cross-country skiing is more popular but even so a number of ski lifts in, for example, the Lake Siljan area find it profitable to stay open throughout the year, transporting summer tourists to high points. Such economies are even more binding in Scotland where the climatic marginality forces summer use of ski lifts thus transporting large numbers of people to considerable altitudes and on to fragile ecological systems.

3.18 OFF-ROAD RECREATIONAL VEHICLES (ORRVs)

Canada invented the snowmobile or skidoo, and here it flourishes most as a recreational vehicle (Table 2.14). Its initial impact was

Table 2.14   Households owning snowmobiles, 1971

	Canada	Nfdld.	P.E.I.	N.S.	N.B.	Que.	Ont.	Man.	Sask.	Alta.	B.C.
No. of households (000)	423	5	*	28	14	150	163	14	22	25	9
% of households	7·3	4·8	*	3·7	9·5	9·8	7·5	5·2	8·7	5·6	1·4

* Sampling variability places the estimate of total number of households at <4000.
Source: Statistics Canada, *Travel, Tourism and Outdoor Recreation: a statistical digest*, 1972, Tables 9.3 and 9.4.

considerable since deep snow enabled the driver to transgress property boundaries; chopping off the tips of young trees and chasing deer were improprieties also laid at the snowmobiler's feet. Organization of snowmobile trails has been the response, and the tourist literature lists 111 areas where the sport can be pursued; at some centres a snowmobile can be rented, in the manner of ski equipment, at 1972–3 prices in the order of $8·00/hr or $30·00/day. Inevitably, there has been pressure to open up public parks to snowmobiles and so a limited number of them have snowmobile trails through areas of the parks which are thought not to suffer from this form of activity. In Ontario, Georgian Bay Island National Park has 15 miles (24 km) of skidoo trails, and other Provincial Parks and Conservation authorities have established facilities. In addition, the Ontario Department of Lands and Forests has designated two 6000-acre

[133] Ontario Dept of Tourism and Information, *Ontario Winter Facilities* (Toronto 1972).

(2428 ha) snowmobile areas on varied terrain near Coldwater, south of Georgian Bay.[134]

The outdoor purists are greatly offended by the snowmobile, largely on account of the noise it creates from an air-cooled 2-stroke engine (82 decibels at 15 feet is common), and because of the behaviour of some of its *aficionados*, who transgress property boundaries, run down wild animals and fish out hitherto isolated lakes. Death rates are unusually high: a Canadian total of 58 accidental deaths of snowmobilers in 1969–70 rose to 118 in 1970–71, and was 116 in 1971–2. In Ontario, for example, snowmobilers are now allowed on provincial highways (a major site of accidents, along with lakes where ice is insufficiently thick), but its share of deaths (34 in 1969–1970, 48 in 1970–71, 27 in 1971–2 and 31 by mid-February of 1973) reflects the high proportion of recreational users.[135] (It is said that in parts of Ontario all the doctors go away on winter weekends because they are tired of treating the spinal injuries of snowmobilers.) There is some possibility that the packing of snow caused by the passage of skidoos reduces the insulation provided by the snow to the soil beneath and so change in fauna and flora may result. If this is so, then the discovery of the carrying capacity of different types of terrain for these vehicles is an urgent priority. The concern caused by snowmobiles has been such that in 1973 at least three Provinces were holding inquiries or considering legislation to control snowmobiles. The banning of these vehicles on roads, of their use at night, their exclusion from isolated and depleted lakes and from wilderness areas, and reform of Trespass Acts are all being sought. But strong opposition is to be expected from user groups and inhabitants of towns such as Espanola, Ontario, with 1600 households and 1400 registered snowmobiles.[136]

Other types of ORRV present problems in particular areas. In remote country where only narrow trails exist, the trail bike may be used. This stripped-down motorcycle has a specially strengthened suspension and the energy of its engine appears to be transformed mostly into noise. Apart from the disturbance to the peace of areas where it is used, it also allows hunters to penetrate further into wild country: a blessing in the areas where, for example, deer present problems of over-population, and a curse where rarer species are concerned.

[134] *Ibid.*
[136] *Ibid.*

[135] *Toronto Star* (13 January 1973).

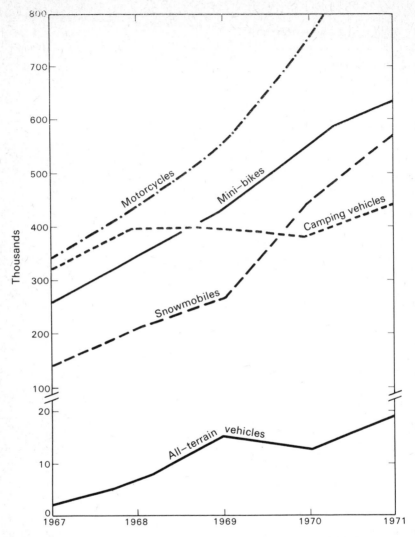

Figure 29 Growth in ORRVs manufactured in the USA, 1967–71.
Source: BOR, *Off-Road Recreation Vehicles*, 1972, p. 19.

Sandy areas such as dunes of both coasts and desert attract ORRVs, including trail bikes. More popular in these habitats, however, are dune buggies: basic autos with wide tyres. Apart from noise and smell, their potential for erosion of desert landscapes or partially fixed dunes is very high, and their access to most public lands is restricted. Except on Bureau of Land Management areas, the US Department of the Interior affirmed in 1973 that all its lands were to be considered closed to such vehicles unless specifically opened to them. This has led to an opening for private enterprise where an operator has control over a sandy area and can hire out buggies for short periods: examples can be seen along the coastal dune zone of northern Oregon, where there are gaps in the publicly owned Oregon Dunes National Seashore and Oregon State Parks. The ultimate in ORRVs seems to be the 'go-anywhere' vehicle which can cope with all kinds of terrain, including open water. One such vehicle is the 'Amphicat' developed in Canada. Costing in 1973 approximately $1600, this can carry two adults and has a 16-hp single-cylinder engine driving all six wheels through a two-speed and reverse transmission. On land it can achieve 40 mph, and in the water 2 mph (an outboard motor can also be fitted) and can thus penetrate very varied terrain such as muskeg.

Data on the total number of ORRVs are recognized as unreliable, but Figure 29 gives a good estimate of the number of vehicles manufactured up to 1971. The in-use stock is even more difficult to assess: probably about 5 million vehicles in the USA has been suggested.[137] The US Bureau of Land Management, a Federal agency (see pp. 188–9) has estimated that 39 million visits/yr are made to its terrain by ORRV users: 1 million motorcyclists, 700,000 pickup truck drivers, 600,000 four-wheel drive vehicles, 80,000 snowmobiles and 50,000 dune buggy users.[138]

It is generally accepted that legislation to control such vehicles is inadequate, and a series of recommendations have been put forward[139] which recognize their use as a legitimate use of recreational land and water but one which needs strict regulation because of the conflicts created. Such control will be even more necessary if, as industry spokesmen predicted in 1971, North American sales were likely to rise from 1·8 million units/yr to 2·5 million units/yr by

---

[137] BOR, *Off-Road Recreation Vehicles* (Washington, DC 1972), p. 11.
[138] *Ibid.*, p. 20.
[139] *Ibid.*, pp. 70–73.

1980.[140] By the winter of 1973, however, some modifications of that prediction were being countenanced.[141]

[140] Anon., 'Men, machines and the land', *News Highlights* 6 (Dept of Park and Recreation Resources, Michigan State University 1971), p. 1.

[141] The general opinion seemed to be that future growth in ORRV numbers is uncertain. This, and much other material, can be found in D. F. Holecek (ed.), *Proceedings of the 1973 Snowmobile and Off The Road Vehicle Research Symposium*, Michigan State University Department of Park and Recreation Resources Recreation Research and Planning Unit Technical Report 9 (East Lansing 1974).

Part 3
Resource-Based Recreation

1 Introduction

1.1 THE RELEVANCE OF SIZE

The relatively small size and rapid communications of Europe and Japan make it difficult to apply a user-resource classification based upon North American conditions, for although its apparent relevance can be easily perceived there exists a considerable overlap between resource-based and intermediate areas. A mountain area like Snowdonia in Wales, for example, receives many of its visitors at weekends from the conurbations of Lancashire and the west Midlands, but there is an additional group for whom it is the goal of a summer holiday. The same is true of the Stockholm archipelago in summer; or a seasonal contrast can be drawn, for example the use of some mountainous National Parks in Japan for weekend skiing in winter and for family vacations in summer. Access may change a situation rapidly: the extension of the motorway system of Britain to Devon will mean that the Dartmoor and Exmoor National Parks will fall even more securely into the weekend ambit of the residents of Birmingham and Wolverhampton, but they will presumably also continue to attract people for annual visits. Overlap exists in North America too: the famous National Parks of the Sierra Nevada of California such as Sequoia-King's Canyon and Yosemite are filled with San Franciscans and Angelinos at weekends, and Mt Rainier National Park is practically in the back yard of Seattle-Tacoma. Not unnaturally, the perceptions of weekend locals and long vacation off-comers about degrees of development may differ, as in the case of the use, development and protection of the parts of the Banff National Park which are nearest to Calgary.[1] So while the areas described under the heading of resource-based are predominantly

---

[1] L. Hamill, 'Outdoor recreation in the Calgary region: problems and potentials', in J. G. Nelson and R. C. Scace (eds.), *op. cit.*, pp. 473–522; see also in the same volume papers (untitled) submitted by G. A. Leroy, pp. 798–805, and F. Scott, pp. 806–16.

used thus, they may also have an identifiable component of inter-mediate-type use.

1.2 DEMANDS AND ACCEPTABILITIES

In the cool temperate lands which are the major locale of these descriptions, climate and social customs combine to produce a heavy demand in the summer months: in the USA, for example, between Memorial Day and Labor Day. In Britain, the pressure is even more concentrated, since 62 per cent of all main holidays begin in July and August and 91 per cent between June and September. School holidays are thus the key factor in determining recreation demand at resource-based areas in the West. Compared with summer, the use in winter is small and a growing number of people prefer to have another 'summer' holiday by flying to warmer places.

The outstanding characteristic of the whole resource-based complex is the paramount importance of the environment, to which everything is, or should be, subject. Recreation should therefore consist of those activities especially suited to a particular resource and is probably dominated by the experience of being in the milieu of some outstanding part of the nation's heritage: the most obvious example is the Grand Canyon of the Colorado River in Arizona, where everything must be subordinate to the sight of the chasm itself. Interestingly, vocal and articulate public opinion is leading managers of such resources further in the direction of ecological pristinity, and demands for less human impact upon such areas are strong. Whenever public opinion is sought on the future of resource-based recreation areas, a loud call for emphasis on the wilderness elements rather than the developed areas is always made. In this part of the book, the USA and Canada are examined first, with particular emphasis upon the contribution of their Federal governments to the supply of the wilder type of recreation resources. These well-endowed lands are then compared with the more crowded conditions of Europe and Japan, especially with regard to the least-developed type of recreation area, the wilderness.

2 Resource-based recreation in the USA

2.1 THE CONTRIBUTION OF THE FEDERAL GOVERNMENT

Our present purpose can divide the function of this area of government into resource management versus other functions. Although the management function is very important (Uncle Sam owns about 34 per cent of the forty-eight contiguous States, which means a very high proportion of some of the Western States; in Alaska the Federal ownership is very high indeed), the other functions cannot be ignored since they strongly affect provision at other levels.

Taken together, the Federal contribution to the nation's rural recreation comprises ten categories, each with a number of programmes (Table 3.1). These programmes are divided among the

Table 3.1   USA: federal programmes in 1967

Type	Number of Programmes
Resource management	16
Grant programmes	61
Credit programmes	18
Technical assistance	32
Regulatory	11
Co-ordination	11
Information	20
Training	13
Research	52
Miscellaneous	19

Source: Dept of the Interior, Bureau of Outdoor Recreation, Federal Outdoor Recreation Programs, 1967.

government's many departments, with their constituting agencies and bureaux, along with some independent agencies like the TVA.

Although this account will be devoted mainly to the resource management functions, the others cannot be overlooked. Principal among them is the Bureau of Outdoor Recreation in the Department of the Interior. This was set up in 1962 following the recommendations of the Outdoor Recreation Resources Commission. Its functions are the nationwide co-ordination of rural recreation and amenity preservation programmes at the Federal level; to assist all other efforts 'to reclaim and protect the outdoor environment, and provide outdoor recreation opportunities';[2] long-term planning, which is to result in a Nationwide Outdoor Recreation Plan. The Bureau is very important because it administers the Land and Water Conservation Fund[3] (which has had a minimum guaranteed income

[2] BOR, *Federal Outdoor Recreation Programs* (1967), p. 27. For the pre-BOR situation, see ORRRC Report 13, *Federal Agencies and Outdoor Recreation* (Washington, DC 1962).

[3] I. G. Simmons, 'Americans for open space', *Town and Country Planning* 33 (1965), pp. 255–9; and 'The Ninetieth's fall special', *Town and Country Planning* 37 (1969), pp. 127–8.

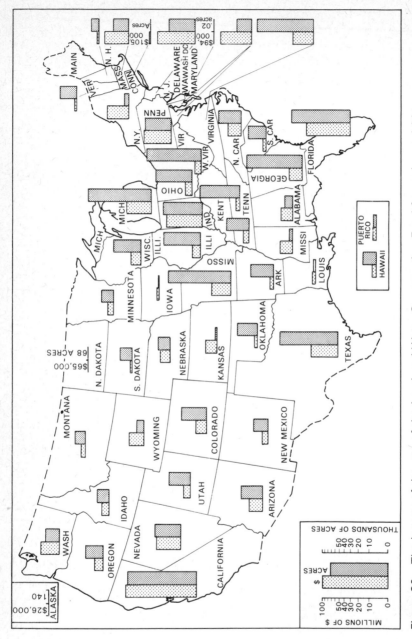

Figure 30 The legacy of the use of the Land and Water Conservation Fund for park acquisition 1968–72. The relative heights of the two columns may well provide an interesting commentary on land prices in different regions of the USA.
Source: BOR Press Release, 30 June 1972.

of $200 million p.a. and whose funds can since 1968 be obligated to purchase land in advance of price rises, to a maximum of $30 million/yr), which provides financial assistance to States (and via them to counties and other local divisions) for rural recreation planning, land acquisition and development. By late 1972, over 1 million acres (4047 km²) of Federal recreation areas had been acquired through this Fund, at a cost of nearly $500 million (Figure 30). BOR can also provide money to other Federal agencies for rural recreation provision.

Of the Departments and their subdivisions, the Departments of the Interior and Agriculture are outstanding. Agriculture contains the Forest Service which owns and manages the National Forests; Interior has the vital National Parks Service, the increasingly needed Bureau of Land Management which looks after all the residual Federal lands, and the Bureau of Reclamation whose Western dams and impoundments are a focus for water-based recreation. Most of these Agencies participated in the other nine types of programmes, but to facilitate description the land/water managing bodies will be described first and given the fullest treatment; the non-managing bodies must of necessity be less emphasized since their study is more political economy than geography.

2.2 FEDERAL RESOURCE MANAGEMENT PROGRAMMES

(a) General

There are seventeen of these but eight are singled out for special attention since they are spatially more important and have features of interest for comparative purposes; some details for all of them are summarized in Table 3.2. The treatment will be by resource management programme rather than by agency, so Table 3.3 identifies the Department(s) responsible for each programme. The main features of each programme will be identified, together with current trends and a discussion of any special problems that arise, as in the case of the National Parks, for example.

The nine programmes not accorded more extended discussion (those without an asterisk in Table 3.2) are not irrelevant but may be thought of as having secondary importance. This is principally because they are either specific in location, such as the AEC's Washington and South Carolina management areas, highly specialized in nature such as the fish hatcheries, or even unique as in the case of FDR's summer home.

177

Table 3.2   USA Federal government OR resource management programmes

	Selected details		
Programme	Area (acres) 1967 (1 million acres = 4047 km²)	Single or Multiple use	Remarks
Atomic Energy Commission Lands	2·7 million	M	Security and health prevent much public use but 5000 acres of wildfowl management on Columbia River; 201,000 acres of deer hunting in South Carolina.
Bureau of Indian Affairs: Federal land management	970,000 4 million in Alaska	M	Distinct from Indian Reservations. Very little recreation except hunting especially Alaska. May conflict with natives' use of land.
Bureau of Public Roads	n.a.		Plans and builds roads on Federal lands: roadside recreation facilities important.
* Military Reservations: Department of Defence	23 million	M	Military use not always exclusive: 230/459 installations allow fishing, hunting and other recreation-integrational conservation plans set up.
* US Army Corps of Engineers	8 million of water 28,000 miles shore	M	Multipurpose water resource development—350 reservoirs. Rapid increase in public use of recreational facilities.
Fish hatcheries: Bureau of Sport Fisheries and Wild-life	18,200	S	97 hatcheries attract large numbers of visitors—most have picnic sites, some have campgrounds.
*National Forests	186·3 million	M	81% is west of 100° meridian. Sustained yield multiple use. Recreation not confined to developed areas.
*National Park System	14·4 million of National Parks	S	232 areas, including Historic Sites.
*National Recreation Areas	3·5 million	S	17 units, managed by NPS or FS. Must be certain minimum size and within 250 miles of urban population centres.

Table 3.2 (continued)

Programme	Area (acres) 1967 (1 million acres = 4047 km²)	Single or Multiple use	Remarks
*National Wilderness Preservation System	10 million	S	Many in NF's but NP's and BLM lands also eligible. 1964 onwards— classification still proceeding.
National Wildlife Refuges: Bureau of Sport Fisheries and Wildlife	28 million	S	304 units, 65% of area is in Alaska. Recreational development on some to cater for visitors, for example, 920 acres of campsites.
*Public Domain Lands: Bureau of Land Management	487 million	M	Mainly in western states and Alaska. Recreation a relatively new development.
*Reclamation projects	4·0 million	M	Multi-purpose water development in western states mainly large dams and reservoirs. Planned development of recreation.
Roosevelt Campobello International Park	11 acres	S	FDR's summer home on NB/Me. border.
TVA Waterfowl production areas	600,000 acres water, 10,000 miles shore-line	M	1933 onwards: multiple purpose scheme. Wetlands in four prairie states for waterfowl nesting/ migration.

* Given more extended treatment in text.

Source: BOR, *Federal Outdoor Recreation Programs,* 1967, with later additions.

The National Wildlife Refuges are on a nationwide scale, however, and although their primary purpose is nature conservation, they do provide recreations of a varying character under the aegis of the National Conservation Recreation Areas Act of 1962. In the conterminous States there are 9·7 million acres (39,256 km²) of refuges and ranges, and 18·6 million acres (75,274 km²) in Alaska. Because of the variation in the biota conserved, the recreation opportunities vary and this activity is always secondary. Observing the wildlife, and where appropriate hunting it, are most commonly found, but picnicking, swimming and boating also occur. Camping and water-skiing are restricted. Against the totals (except Alaska) of 236 waterfowl refuges, 36 general bird refuges, 10 big game

179

Table 3.3 USA Federal government major OR resource management programmes

Programme	Dept/Agency Responsible
Military Reservations Natural Resource Management	Department of Defence (Army, Navy, Air Force and other Defence Agencies).
Multiple-Purpose Water Resource Development	Department of Defence (US Army Corps of Engineers).
National Forest System	Department of Agriculture (Forest Service).
National Parks System	Department of Interior (National Park Service).
National Recreation Areas	Department of Interior (National Park Service) Department of Agriculture (Forest Service).
National Wilderness Preservation System	Department of Agriculture (Forest Service) Department of Interior (National Park Service, Bureau of Land Management).
Public Domain Lands Administration	Department of Interior (Bureau of Land Management).
Reclamation Projects Management	Department of Interior (Bureau of Reclamation).

Special Case	
Indian Reservations Recreation Development	Technically the property is Indian Trust Lands (50·3 million acres) which are run by the Indians assisted by the Bureau of Indian Affairs.

refuges and 5 game ranges, the development of 32 camp-grounds, 90 picnic sites, 308 boat launching ramps and 40 swimming areas, reflects this primary purpose of nature conservation. No charges are made unless there has been substantial investment in development.[4]

(b) National Parks system

The first National Park in the world was Yellowstone, founded in 1872. Since then the US system has grown substantially, and new parks are still being added; for example Canyonlands (Utah) in 1964 and the Redwoods and North Cascades in 1968. It was desired to complete the acquisition of National Parks by 1972, 100 years after

[4] BOR, *Federal Outdoor Recreation Programs*, pp. 77–8.

180

Yellowstone. The National Parks Service was founded in 1916, in order to:

> promote and regulate the use of . . . national parks . . . to conserve the scenery and the natural and historical objects and the wildlife therein and to provide for the enjoyment of the same in such manner and by such means as will leave them unimpaired for the enjoyment of future generations.

The numerous categories of resource specified in that Act have meant that as the system has grown it has diversified in order to conserve not only the wild country but also places and sites of historic significance. Table 3.4 shows the kinds of areas currently managed by the National Parks Service. The National Recreation Areas are dealt with separately.

Although certainly not insignificant in area, the various historic sites usually provide recreation of a sight-seeing character; restoration is usually undertaken. Some selected activities such as picnics and hiking may be allowed provided there is no interference with the integrity of sites and structures. Of more interest at present are the recreational areas administered by the National Parks Service, some of which are considered later under National Recreational Areas, and the so-called 'natural area' category. This includes the National Parks and Monuments that are the highlights of the system and of course the features for which, in this context, the USA is primarily known, and which exhibit land and water areas so outstanding in quality that their preservation by the Federal Government is imperative. They should also be adaptable to a management programme which will provide a wide range of outdoor recreation opportunities provided these are consistent with the preservation of the natural setting.[5]

In 1972, there were 38 National Parks covering 14·7 million acres (59,086 km²) and 82 National Monuments, totalling 9·6 million acres[6] (Table 3.4). The National Monuments are usually smaller than the National Parks and preserve resources which have a primarily scientific significance; recreation activities consistent with the preservation of these features are permitted but the broad range

---

[5] NPS, *Criteria for Selection of National Parklands and National Landmarks* (Washington, DC 1971), p. 11.

[6] NPS, *Areas Administered by the National Park Service and Related Properties as of 1 January 1970* (Washington, DC 1970).

of visitor activities generally found in National Parks is not to be expected.[7] Some of the monuments have historical rather than 'natural' interest and others have occasionally to share the resource with another use, like borax mining at Death Valley, California. Others are indistinguishable from National Parks except that they are not so large nor so splendidly scenic and preserve a single outstanding feature of the landscape rather than an assemblage. White Sands, New Mexico, is an example of this type.

Table 3.4   USA: National Parks and Monuments
(*1 January 1970*)

	Total acreage	Number
National Parks	14,770,856 (3650 km²)	38
National Monuments	9,665,531 (2388 km²)	82

Source: *Areas Administered by the National Parks Service and Related Properties as of 1 January 1972, 1972.*

The National Parks are found from coast to coast but with considerable emphasis on the western third of the country. They preserve examples of the native environments and wildlife in accordance with the organic Act of 1916. The types of terrain are extremely varied and no capsulated description can easily be given except that most are 'natural' areas except where park-related development has taken place. A few are extremely specialized, like Hot Springs, Arkansas, which is more or less a resort, and Carlsbad Caverns, New Mexico, which is a fine set of limestone caves. But mostly, the Parks are pieces of outstanding terrain such as Yellowstone, the Olympic NP, Yosemite, the Grand Canyon and the Great Smokey Mountains, the largest eastern National Park. The scenery is incomparable and the wildlife generally abundant since there is complete protection, except for fish.

Hunting excepted, almost every rural activity is practised in one or other of the Parks, although uses such as water skiing are generally frowned upon as being incompatible with the National Park concept. The most popular recreations like driving, walking and swimming find considerable outlet here, and the campgrounds are always full in summer. Winter use is allowed as well, with an emphasis on cross-country skiing but six NPs have downhill skiing developments as at

[7] NPS, *Criteria for Selection of National Parklands and National Landmarks*, pp. 10–11.

the Hidden Valley ski area in Rocky Mountain NP, which has T-bars and rope tows. Even snowmobiling is permitted in twelve NPs but it is strictly regulated and generally confined to roads which are unploughed: Acadia NP has thus about 40 miles (68 km) of snow-mobile trails for example.[8]

The visitor numbers to the NPs have soared along with other recreation demands and they continue to rise[9] from 1 million visits in 1920 to 200 million in 1971, representing an annual growth rate of *c.* 10 per cent. Forecasts for the near future suggest a continued rise in the number of visitors to all elements of the National Parks System, which includes heavily-used NRAs and Historic Sites as well as the National Parks and Monuments. For the entire system a rise from 202·6 million visits in 1971 to 241·0 million in 1975 and 288·8 million in 1980 has been predicted.[10] One result of the large number of visitors has been the overcrowding of facilities, especially camping sites. In 1956 a 10-year programme called Mission 66 was launched to expand visitor facilities but this proved inadequate before the period was two-thirds complete.

The tremendous visitor pressure upon the National Parks has meant the expansion of the man-made at the expense of the natural.[11] More roads have been built, many planned but not executed because of public opposition, more campgrounds, trails, visitor centres and the like have all been necessary. In Yosemite Valley there is a village catering for all the visitors,[12] and the valley has its own sewage treatment plant and garbage incinerator. This pressure upon the resource has exacerbated some of the tensions inherent in National Park management, for they are in fact multi-purpose areas and some of the uses are scarcely compatible. The rural recreation aspect of them has been mentioned already but others can be listed: scenery preservation, wilderness preservation, wildlife conservation, resort areas, watershed protection areas. Conflicts can be readily espied. The

[8] NPS, *Winter Activities in the National Park System* (Washington, DC 1971).

[9] NPS, *Public Use of the National Parks December 1971* (Washington, DC 1972).

[10] NPS, *Forecast of Visits to the National Park System 1971–1975 and 1980* (Washington, DC 1971), table 1. The figures given in this source are not comparable with those from before 1970, owing to differences in the method of collection.

[11] R. Cahn, *Will Success Spoil the National Parks?* Christian Science Monitor Reprint (Boston 1968); A. S. Leopold *et al.*, *Wildlife Management in the National Parks* (Washington, DC, US Dept of Interior Advisory Board on Wildlife Management 1963).

[12] The first travel count for Yosemite was for 1906 and totalled 5414 persons. By 1923 this rose to 130,000, topped 1 million in 1954, 2 million in 1967, and was 2,416,380 in 1971 (National Park Service, Yosemite statistics).

developments needed for rural recreation may not be compatible with remaining natural scenery, and the demands for more roads to spread the visitor load intrudes upon the wilderness function and may of course interfere with some of the biota. The presence of large numbers of people disturbs the ecosystems so that forest areas may not regenerate and some animals (bears especially) become scavengers that lose the ability to forage naturally or because of their uncertain behaviour become a danger to humans. The resort function results in golf courses, the artificial stocking of lakes and at Yosemite the famous firefall, now discontinued as inconsistent with the parks' values. These contradictions, exemplified in many conflicts between park managers and citizen groups, were the subject of a special advisory committee to the Secretary of the Interior, of which the Chairman was A. S. Leopold. It was especially concerned with wildlife and presented the view that the ecology of the parks was more important than their management for the benefit of visitors. The conclusion of the Leopold report was that the goal of managing the National Parks and Monuments should be: 'to preserve or where necessary to recreate, the ecologic scene as viewed by the first European visitors',[13] and that habitat manipulation and animal population control programmes should be defined to that end, in order to 'enhance the esthetic, historical and scientific values of the parks to the American public, vis-à-vis the mass recreational values'.[14]

Beginning in 1964, the NPS began to rethink their attitudes towards park management,[15] and particularly towards the confusions over purpose that had arisen. The results are becoming apparent in the definition of three major areas of the National Parks System— natural, recreational and historic—in which the NPs and NMs are the leading elements in the first, and important in the third. New administrative policies for the 'natural areas' of the system have been evolved, which emerge as:

1 Safeguarding forests, wildlife, and natural features against impairment or destruction.
2 The application of ecological management techniques to neutralize the unnatural influences of man, thus permitting

[13] A. S. Leopold, *op. cit.*, p. 21.
[14] A. S. Leopold, Letter of Transmittal (4 March 1963).
[15] Memorandum from Secretary Stewart L. Udall to Director George B. Harzog Jr (10 July 1964).

184

the natural environment to be maintained essentially by nature.

3 Master planning for the appropriate allocation of lands to various purposes in a park and location of use areas as needed for developments.[16]

This control of biota, for example, is permitted in order to keep say a large ungulate population from over-browsing its range; where wildlife has to be supressed, prescribed burning may replace it as an ecological management tool.

Recreation activities 'that can be accommodated without material alteration or disturbance of environmental characteristics or the introduction of undue artificiality into a natural environment are to be encouraged. . . .'[17] This means that many NPs where a great deal of undue artificiality has accumulated are, gradually, to be reorganized so that the developed areas for visitor's needs are to be at the edge of or outside the park; the possibility of banning cars and using shuttle minibuses or other public transport has also been studied under a policy given emphasis by the first Secretary of the Interior in the Nixon Administration.[18] In Yosemite, Everglades and Mt McKinley free bus services are now provided in areas of the park formerly subject to congestion, and cars are banned from such zones. In King's Canyon and Rocky Mountain and Great Smokey Mountains the number of back country visitors has been limited. Master plans for Yellowstone and Grand Teton parks envisage all facilities being concentrated outside the parks, and visitors entering them only without benefit of their cars. Further such 'de-development' is anticipated in the next few years.[19]

The future role of the National Parks is not yet clear. It seems that they hold a special place in the minds of the American people and that, although attempts are being made to relieve pressure on them by developing systems of State Parks, National Recreation Areas and similar resources, either the net growth in demand is so large or the attraction of them is so great that they continue to be magnets for

[16] NPS, *Administrative Policies for Natural Areas of the National Park System* (Washington, DC 1968), pp. 16–17.

[17] *Ibid.*, p. 48.

[18] Memorandum from Secretary Walter D. Hickel to Director George B. Harzog Jr (18 June 1969).

[19] R. Cahn, 'People, traffic, noise: can parks survive?' *Christian Science Monitor* (18 September 1972).

immense numbers of people. Many of these probably do not appreciate the special values which the National Parks enshrine and an expansion of interpretive services has been an important feature of recent years. The new aims of the Parks Service will include a desire to create a more 'significant' use of the Park by visitors and to preserve more rigidly the values for which it was established. Even the concessionaires should relate to the individual Park by providing low-impact recreations such as cross-country skiing, and by developing interpretive services. To these ends, management policies will centre around the formulation of the master-plan for each Park. This will almost certainly require most visitor facilities to be moved outside the Park, and the acquisition of all inholdings. The use of the private car as the dominant mode of transport in the Parks is likely to be diminished, and the likelihood that users will have to reserve facilities and services will be increased.[20] When this type of management has been in operation for a few years, there will be an opportunity to observe the tenacity of the image of the National Parks and Monuments as all-purpose rural areas.

(c) Reclamation projects management

The main function of the Bureau of Reclamation of the Department of the Interior is to provide irrigation water for the arid west and it operates only in the seventeen western States, where over 8 million acres (32,376 km²) of irrigated land have been treated. In order to achieve water control, dams are built and the ensuing reservoirs provide recreation foci. Thus by 1967,[21] a total of 219 public recreation areas had been developed at a cost of $77·3 million. The area involved was 3·7 million acres (14,974 km²) of land, 1·6 million acres (6475 km²) of water surface and 11,000 miles (17,669 km) of shoreline. Four hundred and fifty campgrounds, concession facilities providing 6500 beds and parking space for 93,500 cars also formed part of the attractions that resulted in a visitor-day total of 44·9 million in 1967. The most popular appeared to be Jackson Lake Reservoir, Wyoming, with 2·4 million visitor-days, and Lake Havasu, Arizona, with 2·1 million. The biggest lake is Lake Powell,

[20] The Conservation Foundation, *National Parks for the Future* (Washington, DC 1972). The authors of one section of this volume (at p. 54) even suggest that the NPS should develop a whole new layer of regional, urban-oriented Parks, citing the Federal experience in Washington, DC as evidence of the Service's ability to operate strictly urban Parks.

[21] Bureau of Reclamation, *Reclamation's Recreational Opportunities* (Washington, DC 1968).

filling the former Glen Canyon of Utah, which has a shoreline of 1960 miles (3146 km).

Not surprisingly, these facilities are primarily oriented towards water-based recreation and devotees of most of these activities can find places to go. Reclamation facilities tend to be intermediate in character, especially with regard to location, although some are remote enough to be classified as resource-based. Development tends to be intensive and the solitary back-country recreationist is seldom found here; these areas are for the gregarious.

Because some very wild country is often drowned when the dams are built and because the economic reasoning behind them appears suspect to some, there has often been fierce controversy over reclamation projects: Glen Canyon was one instance of this. The opponents contend that irreplaceable wildlands are being destroyed: the Bureau says that now hundreds of thousands of people can enjoy recreation where before only a dozen or two hardy types could venture. When, however, the Bureau decided it wanted to build dams at Marble Canyon and Flaming Gorge, in and near the Grand Canyon, the opposition was such that the projects were withdrawn.

In spite of its detractors, the Bureau (along with the Corps of Engineers, see below) obviously provides a necessary supply of water for sailing, power boating, water skiing and the like (the lakes are generally too large for smaller craft such as canoes), in attractive situations with a dry sunny climate. The chief difficulty is the weighing of the terrain lost against the benefits gained from the dam and reservoir (which of course increases total water loss because of its evaporative surface) both recreational and otherwise, and this argument is not yet settled.

(d) National recreation areas

Seventeen units, totalling 3·5 million acres (14,164 km²) comprised this system in 1971, the components of which are mostly administered by the National Park Service, although four are managed by the Forest Service.[22] It was developed in the years following 1963 in order to provide intermediate and resource-based areas which were primarily recreational, as distinct from the historical and natural values of the National Parks. At the same time, the areas concerned should be

[22] BOR, *Federal Outdoor Recreation Programs* (1971).

. . . well above the ordinary in quality and recreational appeal . . . affording a quality of recreational experience which transcends that normally associated with areas provided by State and local governments.[23]

The selection criteria involve consideration of size of an area, its ability to withstand a high recreation carrying capacity and location —usually not more than 250 miles or 400 km ('within easy driving distance') from urban population centres.[24] A natural environment is not required and most of the areas are primarily for water-based recreation along artificial impoundments, such as the Shasta Dam and Lake in Northern California which is part of the Central Valley Project.

The management of the areas is predominantly in favour of recreation; if there is any additional natural resource utilization, such use must be compatible with the primary aim and it must not be significantly detrimental to it. Secondary criteria involve the consideration of the relationship between carrying capacity and estimated cost, their management to provide compatibility with the recreation potential of adjacent rural areas in private ownership, and a preference for areas thought to be significant in the economic improvement of a Redevelopment Area as designated by the Department of Commerce.[25] The NRAs are clearly intended to provide a substitute for the recreational attractions of a National Park and draw away those people who do not desire the other values of the National Parks. One possibility is that they may merely create additional demand by adding a new source of supply.

(e) Public domain lands administration

The immense areas of land owned by the Federal government were once managed only with the thought of ultimate disposal to private or corporate bodies, but this approach has been modified to the point where the government realizes that it is probably a more effective manager than smaller units could ever be.[26] The Bureau of Land Management of the Department of the Interior is the authority for

[23] NPS, *Administrative Policies for Recreation Areas of the National Park System* (Washington, DC 1968), p. 69.

[24] *Ibid.*, p. 71.

[25] *Idem, Criteria for Selection of National Parklands and National Landmarks*, p. 19.

[26] M. Clawson and R. Burnell Held, *The Federal Lands, Their Use and Management* (Baltimore 1957) and M. Clawson, *The Federal Lands since 1956* (Washington, DC 1967).

the 490 million acres (1,983,030 km²), mainly in the western States and Alaska, which are now managed under a Classification and Multiple Use Act of 1964, which puts recreation as one of the primary uses of this land. (The lands are mainly mountain, desert and forests and some are highly suitable for recreation.)[27] To this end, BLM has undertaken recreation development itself and also sells or leases land to cities, counties and other governmental agencies who wish to provide recreation space. The prices are very low and so cities, for example, can acquire parks outside their boundaries at very low cost. Since BLM lands are extensive, unfenced and mostly un-attended, the level of their use is not calculable, although in 1965 some 700 areas (totalling 195 million acres) (789,165 km²) were designated as public recreation areas in the USA. These were pre-dominantly in the mountains of the western Cordillera.[28] One of the main recreations is hunting, and this is little susceptible to the orderly collection of statistics. This also applies to ORRV use (see pp. 168–172), which is more likely to be acceptable on BLM lands rather than on most other lands, private or public. As demand increases, the role of this immense amount of 'residual' land is bound to increase in importance.

(f) Military reservation natural resource management

Where Defence Department needs do not preclude other uses, the development of resources for rural recreation, natural beauty, fish, wildlife and forestry is encouraged. The authority in development is delegated to individual base commanders, and where installations (such as camp and picnic areas, trails, marinas or fishing piers) exist, they can decide whether these are for service personnel only or whether they can be opened to the public. Either way these develop-ments are important, for even if they are only available to service families, they represent an alternative to use of the public system. No statistics on their use, are however, available, other than that 230 out of 459 installations participate (Table 3.2).

(g) Multiple-purpose water resource development

The Corps of Engineers of the Department of the Army is nationally responsible for public works for navigation, flood control, major

[27] BLM, *Room to Roam, A Recreation Guide to the Public Lands* (Washington, DC 1968).
[28] BOR, *The 1965 Nationwide Inventory of Publicly Owned Recreation Areas and an Assessment of Private Recreation Enterprises* (Washington, DC 1973), table 2A-3, p. 50.

drainage and related water resource schemes. They are authorized to plan on a multiple-purpose basis and so their projects may also include HEP, water quality and quantity control, nature conservation, and recreation. The scale of operation is large: the Corps administers over 8 million acres (32,376 km²) of land and 28,000 miles (45,060 km) of inland and intracoastal waterways.[29] The 350 reservoirs in 44 states have a variety of water-oriented developments which include 1051 public campgrounds, 4035 public boat-launching ramps, and 256,063 car parking spaces.[30] The use of them has had a very high rate of increase in recent years—in 1957, 85 million visits were recorded; 1960—106 million; 1963—147 million; and 1966—194 million.[31] The most popular area appears to be Lake Sidney Laurier on the Chattahoochee River of Georgia, whose 540 miles (869 km) of shoreline attracted 8,803,300 visits in 1966. The peak daily high was experienced by Mosquito Creek Reservoir, Ohio, with a figure of 1,309,600.[32] It can be seen that the Engineers' projects have broadly the same appeal and effects as those of the Bureau of Reclamation but they are spread over the whole country. The criticisms levelled at the Bureau of Reclamation about its dam-building policies have been equally applied to the Corps, if anything with more vigour, since their only response to flooding problems appears to have been the building of dams.

(h) The National Forests

The major responsibility of the Forest Service of the Department of Agriculture is the management of the 186 million acres (752,742 km²) of National Forests and National Grasslands. Of the 173 operating units, 154 are in fact National Forests.[33] Approximately 81 per cent of the area of National Forests is west of 100° but NFs are also important in the Lake States, Appalachia and the South. In the mountains of the West they reach their greatest extent, and the large Federal land holdings in some States are primarily due to the presence of National Forests. The National Grasslands are mainly on the Great Plains.

Over such a large country the terrain and vegetation types included in the system are very diverse. Coniferous forests predominate,

[29] BOR, *Federal Outdoor Recreation Programs*, p. 15.
[30] *Ibid.*, p. 70.
[31] US Army Corps of Engineers, *Recreation* (Washington, DC 1967).
[32] *Ibid.*
[33] BOR, *Federal Outdoor Recreation Programs*, p. 72. In 1971 the figure had not altered.

and in the West, altitude often includes alpine scenery beyond the tree-line within the Forest holdings. Deciduous woodlands are mostly found in the north-east (but here the higher altitudes of the NFs ensure that mixed woods are frequent) and Appalachia.

The management of the NFs is specifically directed by a policy of multiple use, enshrined in the Multiple Use-Sustained Yield Act of 1960. The major elements of management schemes are timber, watershed management, wildlife, grazing and recreation, and the planning of road and trails systems and fire protection for example are directed to the realization of sustained use of those resources. Recreation is an equal partner in those uses and the Forest Service spends a great deal of time and money on recreation research and information. One particular feature of the NFs is that access for recreation is virtually unlimited unless there are special reasons such as fire risk or scientific research which make necessary the exclusion of the public. Otherwise the whole area, with 103,000 miles (165,757 km) of trails and 188,000 miles (293,804 km) of roads is open to them.

In such a vast area, the recreation uses are manifold and almost every kind of recreation is practised (Table 3.5), from large resort-type developments at popular lakes for example, to solitary hiking in the back country. A major use that should be stressed is the use of the NFs for hunting, which is subject to State regulations even on the Federal territory.

In order to differentiate the use of different areas, the Forest Service has classified some of its lands as special use areas. These include resort-type developments where concessionaires are allowed to undertake provision of user services and the other extreme of Wilderness Areas (see next section) and also 34 Primitive Areas totalling 5·5 million acres (22,258 km²) and 95 scenic-type areas of virgin forest or special scenic, geological or archaeological areas, adding up to 726,000 acres (2998 km²).[34] These can be managed primarily for the value of the special features and the other uses demoted either to secondary positions or not allowed at all. The relative popularity of some of these types of area is shown in Table 3.6.

The adoption of multiple use as a management aim is bound to raise problems, especially since the recreation users are now as vocal and organized as the grazers, lumbermen and miners who formerly

[34] *Ibid.*

Table 3.5   USA: recreational use of National Forests 1972

Activity		Public use	
		Visitor-days*	%
Camping		50,062,500	27·3
Picnicking		7,411,200	4·0
Recreation travel (mechanized):		42,274,700	23·0
automobile	(36,231,500)	(19·7%)	
scooter and motorcycle	(2,910,200)	(1·6%)	
ice and snowcraft	(2,862,600)	(1·6%)	
other	(270,400)	(0·1%)	
Boating:		5,423,200	3·0
power boats	(3,365,900)	(1·9%)	
self-propelled boats	(2,057,300)	(1·1%)	
Games and team sports		771,000	0·4
Waterskiing and other water sports		573,200	0·5
Swimming and scuba diving		3,666,200	2·0
Winter sports:		6,964,400	3·8
skiing	(5,812,800)	(3·2%)	
other	(1,151,600)	(0·6%)	
Fishing		15,457,100	8·4
Hunting		13,739,700	7·5
Hiking and mountain climbing		6,862,100	3·7
Horseback riding		2,616,000	1·4
Resort use		3,525,200	1·9
Organizational camp use		4,122,400	2·5
Recreation residence use		7,839,500	4·3
Gathering forest products		1,250,600	0·7
Nature study		924,100	0·5
Viewing scenery, sports, environment		7,073,900	3·9
Visitor information (exhibits, talks, etc.)		3,101,300	1·8
Total		183,958,300	100

* Recreational use of NF land and water which aggregates 12 person-hours. May entail 1 person for 12 hours, 12 persons for 1 hour, or any equivalent combination of individual or group use, either continuous or intermittent.
Source: US Forest Service, *National Forest Recreation Calendar Year 1972*, mimeo.

dominated the lobbying of the Forest Service. The resort-type development managed by a concessionaire now comes in for frequent criticism from the summer recreationists who are in favour of keeping as much undeveloped land (except for campgrounds) as possible; the skiers are less worried. The proposed development of Mineral King in the Sierra Nevada of California as an alpine village by Walt Disney Enterprises is a particularly controversial example of this difference of opinion of the use of the forests.

Recreation itself may well create difficulties in the management of

Table 3.6   USA: recreational use of National Forests 1972 by kind of site and area

Kind of site and area	Estimated visitor-days of use*		
	National recreation areas	Wilderness and primitive areas	Special-interest areas†
Observation sites	25,800	1,900	50,300
Playground, park, sports sites	—	—	—
Boating sites	178,700	—	5,400
Swimming sites	20,000	—	—
Campgrounds	999,500	31,800	394,100
Picnic grounds	12,400	9,600	83,500
Hotels, lodges, resorts	89,100	—	120,200
Organization sites	40,500	—	—
Other concession sites	11,300	—	1,000
Recreation residence sites	39,400	—	24,000
Winter sports sites	—	—	22,400
Visitor centres, recreation-oriented	800	—	—
Roads, recreation	589,700	—	344,900
Trails, recreation	42,200	1,382,900	644,700
Waters, recreation	1,254,600	1,427,200	325,300
General undeveloped areas	366,300	3,602,900	651,100
Interpretive sites	15,700	700	129,800
Total, all components	3,686,200	6,457,000	2,796,700

* Recreation use of NF land and water which aggregates 12 person-hours. May entail 1 person for 12 hours, 12 persons for 1 hour, or any equivalent combination of individual or group use, either continuous or intermittent.
† Use of classified archaeological, botanical, geological, historical, memorial, and scenic areas.
Source: US Forest Service, National Forest Recreation Calendar Year 1972.

the other resources: the danger of fire increases greatly especially since the unlimited access policy allows lots of small groups or even individuals to be scattered over a wide area, with scant chance of putting out a fire once it is started. Large recreation developments create few such problems. Visitors too may endanger certain types of wildlife but the scheduling of special management areas for rare species should help to minimize that threat.

Another considerable difficulty in forest management (for recreation or any other use) is the presence of private inholdings in the forests. The number of these may vary from a few sporadic cottage sites to the point where only alternate sections are Federally owned, creating a chequer board pattern. Such complications make any sort of management difficult, especially where large numbers of private individuals are concerned.

193

It is impossible to assess whether the National Forests have more or less recreational potential than units such as the Public Domain and the National Recreation Areas. At any rate, along with them they will form, where made accessible, the main additional sources of supply of recreation resources during the next few decades.[35]

(i) National Wilderness Preservation System

In 1964 Congress approved the Wilderness Act, which authorized the designation of Wilderness areas on Federal lands under the jurisdiction of the National Park Service, the Bureau of Sport Fisheries and Wildlife, and the Forest Service. Every designation has to be made by Congress: at the time of passage of the Act, some 9 million acres (36,423 km²) of Forest Service wilderness areas became the nucleus of the system and other National Forest lands have been added subsequently. At the end of 1970, the system comprised 10·1 million acres (42,000 km²), of which 200,000 acres (805 km²) had been added in the previous year. At that time 9·95 per cent of the National Forests were either wilderness or primitive areas.[36] The latter category is not part of the Wilderness Preservation System, but is withheld from commercial uses pending possible reclassification if it meets the criteria for size and ecological purity. No agency other than the Forest Service has yet scheduled such areas, although the National Parks Service was told to speed up its review.[37] This is based upon an appraisal of the suitability of every roadless area of 5000 contiguous areas or more: a total of 60 units in the system amounting to 27·8 million acres (112,390 km²). In 1970 the first two National Park System's Wilderness Areas had been designated, in Craters of the Moon National Monument, Idaho (43,243 acres, 1732 km²) and in Petrified Forest National Park, Arizona (50,260 acres, 2013 km²).[38] By 1972, some further units had been incorporated but the general progress was slow. In part, the reclassification of Federal lands has been retarded by the requirements of the Environmental Protection Act of 1971, which requires that changes of use shall be accompanied by Environmental Impact Statements.

---

[35] M. Frome, *Whose Woods These Are* (New York 1962); US Dept of Agriculture Yearbook 1949, *Trees*, pp. 299–380; US Dept of Agriculture Forest Service, *Timber Resources for America's Future*, Forest Resource Report 14 (1958), pp. 113–44.

[36] *Seventh Annual Report on the Status of the Wilderness Preservation System*, 92nd Congress, 2nd Session, House Document 92–156 (5 August 1971), appendix V.

[37] Memorandum from Secretary Walter J. Hickel, *op. cit.*

[38] *Seventh Annual Report on the Status of the Wilderness Preservation System*, p. 21.

These have added extra work to, for example, the National Parks Service, who have not only to negotiate wilderness proposals through public hearings but accompany them with an EIS as well.

The System is primarily western in its locations, and consists of areas of forests and mountain land; the Boundary Waters Canoe Area of Minnesota, the Pisgah Wilderness of North Carolina and part of the White Mountains of New Hampshire are also part of the system (Table 3.7). The criteria for designation include a minimum size of at least 5000 acres (2023·5 km²) or 'sufficient size as to make practicable its preservation and use in an unimpaired condition'.[39] The fundamental characteristic suggested by the Act is that the land is undeveloped, primeval (although grazing may have been a use in the west and early logging in the east), and without permanent improvements or human habitation. Later regulations allow a

Table 3.7   USA Wilderness Areas, 30 June 1970

State	Number of units	Total area (acres)
Arizona	6	428,159
California	18	1,908,909
Colorado	5	281,863
Idaho	1	989,179
Minnesota	1	3,089,257
Montana	5	1,486,400
Nevada	1	64,767
New Hampshire	1	5,532
New Mexico	5	679,376
North Carolina	2	20,925
Oregon	10	765,231
Washington	4	1,803,336
Wyoming	4	1,781,582
Total	63	10,236,427

Source: US Department Agriculture Forest Service, National Forest System Areas as of 30 June 1971, 1971, pp. 17–18.

rather wider interpretation of wilderness: areas being studied for inclusion in the system need not automatically be excluded if they contain small boat docks or primitive shelters, for example, or lakes created by water development projects provided the lakes are maintained at a relatively stable level and the shore has a natural ap-

[39] Wilderness Act (3 September 1964), PL 88–577.

pearance. Similarly, underground utility pipelines need not exclude an area from consideration.[40]

The idea behind the system is basically the preservation of very wild areas for back-country recreation travel on foot or horseback, although other reasons were also put forward by proponents of the Bill during its long legislative history.[41] That type of use (and canoe use in the Quetico-Superior area) is the predominant one, although the symbolic idea of wilderness is important too.[42] As an operational reality, the 'untrammelled by man' concept is difficult to maintain since the ecosystem boundaries rarely coincide with the legal ones, although most Wilderness Areas are buffered by stretches of National Forests. In addition, 'previously allowed' uses often remain: aircraft and motorboating, grazing, and development of water resources are delegated to the President if in the public interest. Mining, however, is to cease by 1983 and no new leases will be granted thereafter.

The management of wilderness areas is difficult since certain decisions about, for example, fire control have to be made. Fire is a natural part of the ecology of some of the forests but it is suppressed if large-scale damage is likely or life endangered.

The very nature of the 'wilderness experience' of which one convention is that you see more or less no people other than those of your own party, makes over-use a very narrow constraint. Similarly, the ecology of high mountain areas is very fragile and can easily be altered deleteriously by the grazing of pack stock. Thus the need for careful management of the recreational use of wilderness areas has been established, and Clawson[43] suggested that a form of rationing of visits may be necessary if the present conventions are to be preserved and in the summer of 1972 visitor quotas for some of the most popular back country areas were first established.

The fundamental hope is that the Wilderness Areas will be for all time inalienable except for cases of national emergency. This situation was not accepted by many potential users of mineral and timber resources during the passage of the Act and every addition to the

[40] US Dept of the Interior, *Departmental Guidelines for Wilderness Proposals* (24 June 1972).

[41] I. G. Simmons, 'Wilderness in the mid-20th century USA', *Town Planning Review* 36 (1966), pp. 249–56.

[42] ORRRC Report 3, *Wilderness and Recreation* (Washington, DC 1962).

[43] M. Clawson, 'The Philmont Scout Ranch: an intensively managed wilderness', *American Forests* 74 (1965), pp. 20–23, 57–9. A simulator which mimics the behaviour of wilderness users has been developed by Resources for the Future Inc. See A. C. Fisher and J. V. Krutilla,

System has powerful opponents. Considerable strength will be needed on the part of the System's administration if it is to endure for the length of time envisaged by its proponents, for not only will external forces demand the release of resources into commercial use, but large numbers of visitors will inflict destruction. Most of the latter seem to have 'purist' conceptions of wilderness which will reinforce the Federal managers if they choose to 'consider the value of preserving the richness and diversity of the resources and experiences still available in our American wilderness'.[44]

(j) The future of the public lands

In 1970 was published the Report[45] of the Public Land Law Review Commission, which had been set up in 1964 to make a comprehensive review of public land laws and to compile data on present and future uses of the Federal domain. Its relevance to rural recreation will be easily appreciated from the deep involvement of the Federal government as detailed in sections (a) to (i) above. The tenor of the Report was broadly in favour of a policy of disposal rather than retention of the public domain, summed up in Recommendation 3: 'Public lands should be classified for transfer from Federal ownership when net public benefits would be maximized by disposal.'[46] This type of question-begging recommendation aroused considerable public opposition, as did the proposed swing towards dominant-use rather than multiple-use; and by the end of 1973 the Congress had enacted no legislation based upon the Report. In the narrower field of rural recreation, the Report was less controversial, except perhaps in its insistence that user fees be paid whenever possible, and that the Federal government should cease to acquire land in multiple-use areas other than in buying up inholdings.[47]

'Determination of optimal capacity of resource-based recreation facilities', in J. V. Krutilla (ed.), *Natural Environments. Studies in Theoretical and Applied Analysis* (Baltimore and London 1972), pp. 115–41.

[44] G. H. Stankey, 'A strategy for the definition and management of wilderness quality', in J. V. Krutilla (ed.), *op. cit.*, pp. 88–114.

[45] Public Land Law Review Commission, *One Third of the Nation's Land* (Washington, DC 1970), 342 pp. A relevant background report elicited by the Commission is Herman D. Ruth and Associates, *Outdoor Recreation Use of the Public Lands* (Berkeley 1969).

[46] PLLRC, *op. cit.*, p. 48.

[47] *Ibid.*, p. 215.

3 The contribution of the Federal government of Canada

3.1 THE CANADIAN NATIONAL PARKS

The Federal government of Canada is responsible for her National Parks.[48] In 1972 these totalled 28 in number and 50,503 sq miles (130,803 km²) in area. Of this, 17,300 sq miles (44,807 km²) are in Wood Buffalo NP in the NWT and northern Alberta and thus far from the main recreation traffic of the country. The same applies to the additions (18,630 sq miles/48,252 km²) of the early 1970s in the Yukon and on Baffin Island. Thus about 14,573 sq miles (37,744 km²) of territory are effectively within the recreation system of the nation.

The parks were mostly established between 1885 and 1939, with a revival since 1967, when public opinion in Canada began to press hard upon the Department of Indian Affairs and Northern Development. Much of the system therefore represents a pre-boom set of criteria in terms of their establishment. The first Park, Banff, was designed to protect the mineral hot springs in that area; it and other western Parks were created out of land owned by the Federal government, and indeed the Park preceded the Province in some cases; in later developments the Province has made available the land to the Federal government. In the case of La Mauricie in Quebec, the Province has given Ottawa a 99-year lease, which makes it the first Park not to be owned by the Federal government.

One result of a somewhat piecemeal acquisition policy has been an uneven spread of National Parks over the country (Figure 31). It can be argued perhaps that only the very best areas have been put to Park use and therefore distribution is irrelevant; on the other hand provinces like Quebec manifestly have areas worthy of that status. Ontario, similarly, is under-represented and since the National Parks Policy of Canada is, '. . . to preserve for all times areas which contain significant geographical, geological, biological, or historic features as a national heritage for the benefit, education and enjoyment of the people of Canada', it is a matter for concern that, as Table 3.8 shows, so many of them are where the people are not. Even if it is protested that over-use ruins National Parks, it remains true that a NP as part of a system of parks is a useful entity to have within the intermediate-

[48] The best source of discussion of most aspects of Canadian National Parks is J. G. Nelson and R. C. Scace (eds.), *The Canadian National Parks: Today and Tomorrow*, University of Calgary Studies in Land Use History and Landscape Change, National Park Series 3 (Calgary 1969). The contributions by J. I. Nicol (pp. 35–52), R. C. Brown (pp. 94–110), J. G. Nelson (pp. 111–50), J. S. Marsh (pp. 228–42) and L. Brooks (pp. 869–77) are especially useful.

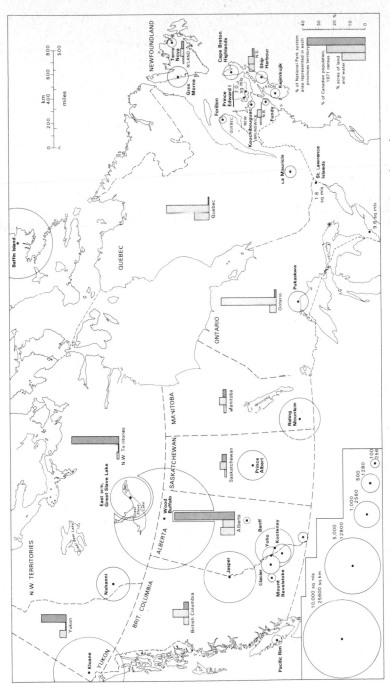

Figure 31 The National Parks system of Canada, showing the location and size of each park, and the relation of the parks to the Provincial proportions of national territory and population, and each Province's share of the total Park system. The relation of the system to resources rather than users is clearly apparent, as would be expected in resource-based areas. *Source:* National and Historic Parks Branch leaflet 1972; and Park use research section. *Provincial Areas and Population in relation to the National Park System,* 1972.

Table 3.8   Canada: relation of National Parks to provincial populations 1966 (Wood Buffalo Park and later additions
excluded)

Province	% of Canadian population	% of NP system
Newfoundland	2·5	1·3
PEI	0·5	0·05
Nova Scotia	3·8	4·2
New Brunswick	3·1	0·7
Quebec	28·9	nil
Ontario	34·7	0·1
Manitoba	4·8	9·5
Saskatchewan	4·8	12·3
Alberta	7·3	58·1
British Columbia	9·4	13·8
Yukon	0·1	nil
North-West Territories	0·1	nil

Source: National Parks Service, Population Trends in Relation to the National Parks System, Planning Report No. 61, 1967, p. 12.

type use zone of a major population centre. However, the role of the
National Parks as resource-based areas is confirmed by Table 3.9
where it can be seen that in Ontario the visitor numbers to NPs are
declining, presumably in the face of alternative choices from provincial and other sources, whereas numbers visiting the mountain
parks of Alberta and BC are rising along with the national trend
(Figure 32). The function of the National Parks, as exemplified in the
quotation above is clearly one in which outdoor recreation has a role,

Table 3.9   Canada: total visitors to National Parks 1965–71 (by province of
park location, thousands of visitors)

	1965	1966	1967	1968	1969	1970	1971
Canada	9,845	11,368	10,918	11,856	12,629	13,607	14,083
Newfoundland	109	180	293	247	308	353	299
PEI	967	1,131	770	1,346	1,288	2,094	1,896
Nova Scotia	729	852	811	749	834	913	901
New Brunswick	679	753	518	632	632	659	738
Ontario	766	859	880	872	865	789	756
Manitoba	688	739	731	760	793	755	745
Saskatchewan	152	147	157	138	138	142	146
Alberta	2,524	2,844	2,935	3,260	3,790	3,920	4,780
British Columbia	2,837	3,377	3,320	3,336	3,507	3,456	3,822

Source: Statistics Canada, Travel, Tourism and Outdoor Recreation: a statistical digest, 1972, Table 8.2.

but it is only part of a multiple-use concept which embraces preservation of scenic, scientific and cultural features untrammelled. Inherent is the concept of natural landscapes untouched by man but as has been shown,[49] many of the emparked areas of the Rockies had in fact undergone considerable exploitation of their economic resources before the enforcement of National Park status.

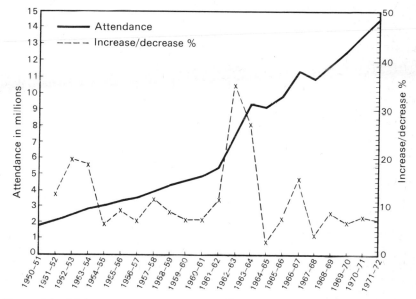

Figure 32 Visitor numbers to the Canadian National Park system 1950–1972. The rate of growth has been falling in recent years but still remains at 7 per cent per annum, a doubling time of 10 years.
Source: National and Historic Parks Branch, *National Park Attendance,* yearly data.

The history of the National Parks in Canada reveals that the role of public enjoyment has often been paramount. The first National Park, Banff,[50] was established to protect an area of hot springs so that they might be developed into a spa. The CPR was instrumental in this endeavour, since its line west passed along the Bow River. Thus it came about that the National Park has within it a townsite

[49] A. R. Byrne, *Man and Landscape Change in the Banff National Park Area before 1911*, University of Calgary Studies in Land Use History and Landscape Change 1 (Calgary 1968).

[50] R. C. Scace, *Banff: A Cultural Historical Study of Land Use and Management in a National Park Community to 1945*, University of Calgary Studies in Land Use History and Landscape Change 2 (1968).

201

housing a 1961 population of 3429, catering to a vastly higher summer influx. The townsite has all the features of an urban settlement and there are continual pressures for growth. Although this scale of activity is not repeated elsewhere in the system, even at Jasper, an emphasis on development of a rather *laissez-faire* nature seems to have characterized the NPs for many years, until the National Parks Service formulated a definite National Parks policy.[51]

This policy admits that 'policies have been piecemeal and have not been adequate to ensure that the real objectives will be maintained or reached',[52] since the interpretation of the purposes of the National Parks, enshrined in the National Parks Act of 1930 have caused conflict of purposes in the administration. Roughly speaking, there has been a revolt against the increasing development of constricted and urban-type recreation facilities, and a demand for a closer return to a wilderness concept (a parallel change happened in the US during the Udall administration at Interior), so that the values of nature no longer take second place to those of summer resort type recreations. With this in mind, the parks have been classified into three groups:

1   Parks which are basically scenic and nature parks, like Banff, Jasper, Yoho and Cape Breton Highlands;
2   Parks basically family holiday parks with a variety of activities in addition to their natural features: Waterton Lakes, Prince Albert, Riding Mountain and PEI are examples of this;
3   Parks which are basically nature resources: Elk Island and Point Pelee, for instance.

So-called 'natural' recreations are to be permitted in all three categories since they are related to Park purposes. Boating, swimming, hiking, trail riding and fishing are examples of such activities. In the (2) category Parks, 'wholesome outdoor recreations'[53] such as 'golf, tennis, lawn bowling and horseshoe pitching'[54] are allowed, to satisfy variations in tastes of family groups. They must not impair the enjoyment of the natural scene by visitors who have come for that particular reason: in Parks where they are already established they may, after due consideration, remain. Commercial entertainments,

---

[51] NPS, Office of the Director, *Requirements of a National Park* (mimeo, Ottawa 1964); NPS, *National Parks Policy* (Ottawa 1964).
[52] NPS, *National Parks Policy*, p. 1.
[53] *Ibid.*, p. 19.
[54] *Ibid.*, p. 19.

spectator sports, roller-skating rinks and the like are not to be permitted except in year-round townsites where they are primarily for the benefit of the residents. It may be noted that the Federal government has no constitutional authority to become involved in the provision of public outdoor recreation facilities.

As a follow-up to the categorization of Parks, the policy introduces the concept of zoning within each Park.[55] This is to facilitate long-range planning, especially the preparation of a Master Plan for each Park (Figure 33). The zones run the gamut from wilderness areas to established townsites, but it is not intended that every Park should have an area of each category. The policy is very firm. 'no violation or exceptions whatsoever should be allowed to occur'.[56] The need for concurrent imposition of zoning and designation in new Parks has been demonstrated at Pacific Rim NP (Vancouver Island, BC, designated 1972), whose visitor pressure already threatens the values for which an initial phase of the Park was set aside.[57]

As plans have developed, the application of zoning has become apparent. At Terra Nova NP, in Newfoundland (created 1961), the plan contains two zones: (1) Nature Preserve. This is accessible to visitors only on foot trails or by boat tours and contains examples of typical Newfoundland habitats; (2) Transition zone. This is the area in which developments are permitted and along which the motorized circulation takes place. Between it and the Nature Preserve, a buffer zone is demarcated. Spatially, the transition zone is linear in character, with thin projecting arms.

A more elaborate zoning has been established for Jasper NP, where older established uses have to be taken into account. The two basic zones are (1) Wilderness and (2) Transition. The first is subdivided into Special Areas, with limited access to ecological preserves or features of historic importance; and Wilderness, with free access to hiking and riding trails, but no other developments. The second category divides into Natural Environment Areas, which serve primarily as buffers between Wilderness and developed areas; general rural recreation areas along existing highway corridors and including the campsites, ski-areas and maintenance facilities; Intensive Use areas for visitor accommodation and service facilities,

[55] *Ibid.*, pp. 25–6.
[56] *Ibid.*, p. 26.
[57] J. G. Nelson and L. D. Cordes (eds.), *Pacific Rim: An Ecological Approach to a New Canadian Park*, University of Calgary Studies in Land Use History and Landscape Change, National Park Series 4 (Calgary 1972).

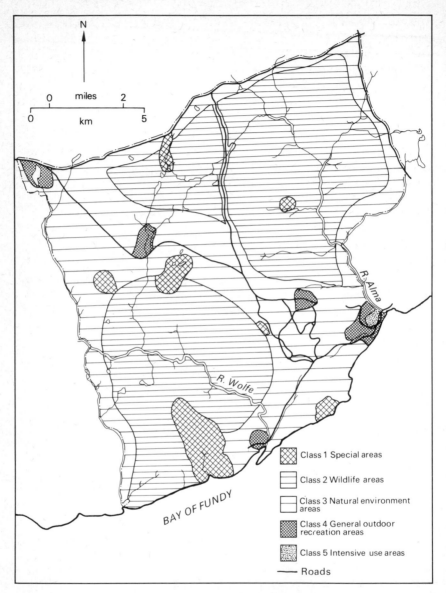

Figure 33 Zoning of Fundy National Park in New Brunswick, Canada. The layout of the zones is dictated to some extent by the course of the roads.
Source: National and Historic Parks Branch, Master Plan public hearings kit.

where careful siting is supposed to allow the surrounding park to preserve a natural dominance over the area. At Jasper NP, the latter two categories dominate the valleys and so, as at Terra Nova, the transition zone is largely linear in nature.

The general policies regarding development appear to have been stretched as far as winter sports are concerned. The official policy encourages the development of more overnight ski accommodation as, for example, in Banff NP; more tows and lifts, and even more *après-ski*, provided it is within the general development of hotel-motel accommodation.[58] Even the sophisticated zoning systems may quail before the impact of the snowmobile which cannot be confined to trails and is very noisy. Their use in thirteen NPs has been officially permitted. The Athabaska Glacier in the Rockies has been used for a 'giant snowmobile rally' publicity stunt in aid of the industry and only after protests was this type of activity forbidden by the Minister.[59]

At present the National Parks of Canada appear to be emerging from a long period of *laissez-faire* development which has impaired their values and, because of its haphazard nature, will not stand the pressures which are being put upon them. Anomalies still remain, and local public and commercial pressures are such that the Superintendents find it difficult to stem the flow of recreational development which was so large a part of the Parks, since these were the only places for public access: the provinces, other than Ontario, did not enter this field significantly until about 10 years ago. As a sign of the times, however, no serviced campgrounds had been built in established National Parks in the five years preceding 1973.

The future of National Parks is being decided upon two lines: firstly, that more of them are needed, and secondly, the identification of criteria by which they can be demarcated. In 1967, the Minister suggested that forty to sixty new National Parks were needed to round out the system and achieve representation of Canadian habitats on a suitable scale.[60] These should be acquired by the year 2000, but at the present rate of progress, it might take 300–400 years to accomplish it. However, it is possible that the current

[58] Dept of Indian Affairs and Northern Development, *Winter Recreation and the National Parks: A Management Policy and a Development Program* (mimeo, Ottawa 1965).

[59] *Park News* 5 (1969), p. 16 (published by the National and Provincial Parks Association of Canada).

[60] Dept of Indian Affairs and Northern Development, Press Release (13 June 1967): see note 3.

tide of vocal public opinion, which is running strongly in favour of National Parks (and other environmental protection measures), will carry the government more rapidly to the high-water mark of Park designation. (It must however be noted that strong opposition to the designation of new National Parks has arisen from local people who would be affected, for example by the loss of fishing rights on the eastern shore of New Brunswick or the compulsory purchase of homes along the eastern coast of Nova Scotia.) Public hearings upon the proposed Master Plan for each Park are now standard practice, and at them there is a preponderance of opinion in favour of lessening the amount of development, leaving more wild country, and if possible extending the boundaries.[61] In cases of Park development, or development within Park controversies, there is considerable pressure upon the authorities to create parks free from present or future threat of commercial exploitation, including recreation. The proposals for a resort complex to be called Village Lake Louise in Banff NP, finally turned down by the Minister in 1972, are an example in point,[62] as is the decision to cut off cars in mid-park Point Pelee NP (which receives heavy visitation from the Detroit region) and permit further access only by 'elephant trains'.[63] In five years' time, all access inside the Park is expected to be by public transport. Such thinking extends to the recently designated Parks in the NWT and Yukon, where access may be by helicopter which, if properly costed, may be cheaper than building roads. Kapuskawa NP in Ontario will have only a 6-mile (9·6-km) spur road used solely by public transport; and the development of a transit system for the Lake Louise area is now a high priority.

The greatest stumbling block to the achievement of this goal, which would place about 2 per cent of Canada in NPs, is jurisdictional. The province must be willing to dedicate the lands to the people of Canada, free of all encumbrances; and secondly, the Federal government must think that the lands are worthy of Park status. The second requirement is less important than the first, for here the

[61] The National and Historic Parks Branch publishes a kit for each Park in which hearings are held, containing maps of the proposed zoning of the Park. The main alterations made as a result of the inquiry are also published, e.g. *Decisions Resulting from the Public Hearing on the Provisional Master Plan for Kejimkujik National Park* (Ottawa 1970).

[62] The National and Provincial Parks Association of Canada was particularly active in campaigning against this development. Its journal, *Park News*, carries statements and reports on this issue through 1970–72. See especially vol. 8 (1972), pp. 8–20.

[63] R. Cahn, *op. cit.* See footnote 19 above.

provinces have a virtual stranglehold on the creation of new Parks, and naturally enough it is the question of finance which is the crux of the matter: who should pay for the lands? This difficulty applies especially in Ontario and Quebec, where there is political disagreement with the idea of the transfer of land to the Federal government, for the 1930 Transfer of Resources Agreement placed responsibility for resource management with the provinces, and they appear anxious to guard their sovereignty. Principally this is because they might just be signing away a large mineral bonanza.[64]

In a long-term sense, it is hoped to create National Parks in each of the recognized Natural Regions of Canada, both terrestrial and marine. Some thirty-nine terrestrial regions and nine marine regions are recognized, and it is hoped eventually to have a National Park in each of these.[65] In the meantime the criteria for identifying parklands, and possibly for trying to have them placed in some 'exploitation-free' category until Park status can be enforced, have been developed.[66] The adjective applied to scenery, fauna, flora or rural recreation facilities is 'outstanding', and it is accepted that the area or part of it will be used for recreational purposes, accommodation and other visitor services. With a sideways glance at the coffers, the policy says that the area must be 'of sufficient value now or for the future to justify the expenditure required for preservation and development'. If it were possible to do that, recreationists and planners in a dozen countries would wear maple leaves in their hair.

3.2 OTHER FEDERAL INVOLVEMENTS IN OPEN-AIR RECREATION

In pursuing primary objectives such as rural development and economic and regional revitalization, the Federal government often finds itself involved with the secondary aim of providing recreation facilities, but it has no responsibility for a co-ordinated approach to the development of the resources, as it has in the case of forestry, agriculture, water, power and minerals.

The programmes of greatest concern have been the 1961 Agricultural and Rural Development Act (ARDA) and the Fund for Rural Economic Development (FRED) programme, both under the aegis of the Department of Forestry and Rural Development. These

[64] Lloyd Brooks 'Planning a Canadian National Park System—progress and problems', in J. G. Nelson and R. C. Scace (eds.), *op. cit.*, pp. 869–77.
[65] Canadian Ministry of Indian Affairs and Northern Development, National and Historic Parks Branch, *National Parks System Planning Manual* (Ottawa 1972).
[66] NPS, *National Parks Policy*, p. 32.

have both realized the virtues of recreation in providing an additional source of income in otherwise marginal rural areas, and both have managed to promote some useful Federal-provincial co-operation.[67] In the interlake area of Manitoba, for example, a programme of resource development will include spending $3 million on recreational development[68] and in the north-east, New Brunswick, which is not an area of high demand, $1 million will be phased over 5 years.[69] Another ARDA contribution, in conjunction with the Canada Land Inventory, has been the development of the recreation resource inventory and evaluation technique referred to in an earlier part of the book. The work of these programmes has now been subsumed into a Federal Department of Regional Economic Expansion (DREE) which is co-operating with the Provinces in particular projects. Recreation can be among these, but more emphasis is given to infrastructure such as road improvements. Items which directly attract tourists are also funded, such as motels, which are more profitable in a short-season region such as the Atlantic provinces, and restoration of historic buildings as in Quebec City. However, the joint Federal-provincial development plan[70] for Prince Edward Island envisages five integrated recreational complexes for visitors to the island. Three major centres will be the focal points of loop drives, and two others will be primarily coastal in their orientation. Associated with these developments will be the accommodation, roads and wharves mentioned above as infrastructural elements. Hand in hand is to go land-use planning and natural environment protection by the province.

The Canadian North of the Yukon and Northwestern Territories is an obvious area for the extension of government influence, since these Crown Lands are directly administered by the Federal Government. *De facto* a certain amount of recreation already occurs, in the form of fishing, hunting and canoe trips, although problems of accessibility generally confine visitors to the very affluent. The road being driven from northern Alberta through to Inuvik will doubtless

[67] Dept of Forestry and Rural Development, *Federal Provincial Development Agreement* (Ottawa 1967); C. S. Brown, 'Federal rural development programmes and recreation resources', in J. G. Nelson and R. C. Scace (eds.), *op. cit.*, pp. 547–62.

[68] Dept of Forestry and Rural Development, *Interlake Area of Manitoba: Federal Provincial Rural Development Agreement* (Ottawa 1967), p. 42.

[69] Dept of Forestry and Rural Development, *Northeast New Brunswick* (Ottawa 1967), p. 36.

[70] Canadian Dept of Regional Economic Expansion, *Development Plan for Prince Edward Island* (Ottawa 1970).

attract summer vacationers, as do other Arctic highways, and if the MacKenzie Valley pipeline is built with a transportation corridor, that also will be popular in summer. Designation of Parks or other forms of protected land is difficult because of the uncertain status of native land claims, both Indian and Eskimo, and since the government of Canada is under severe criticism for its 'sell-out' of native rights in favour of, for example, oil exploration, it is reluctant to incur yet more opprobrium from its native peoples. The cash benefits (if any) to the native people or the government from recreation in the north are scarcely likely to be of the same order as those brought by the oil companies.

Lastly, the National and Historic Parks Branch of the Federal government has announced its intention[71] of formulating a venture, with Provincial and municipal co-operation, to be called the Byways and Special Places programme. It will aim to preserve particular facets of Canadian history and geography such as canal systems, marine parks, national landmarks and wild rivers. These places will be partly recreational in intent, but will have a strong educational content.

4 Resource-based recreation in Europe and Japan

4.1 GENERAL

The nature of the terrain in Europe and Japan and the long history of land occupance under the pressure of increasing populations have brought about the transformation of much of wild nature. In both regions, nevertheless, two outstanding resources are the magnet for longer vacations: mountains and coast. The attractions of the uplands are mainly evident in summer, but extend to winter too, provided there is reliable snow or, as in Scotland, even a good chance of favourable skiing conditions. Even the mountains are not free from land-use competition, and so recreation has often to be part of a multiple-use scheme which includes wildlife, extractive forestry, watershed management, water catchment and power generation (including dams and reservoirs), as well as the mechanized paraphernalia of mass tourism, especially those parts of it designed to carry the visitor uphill without much effort on his own part. The coasts are even more sought after, although most of the urban development

---

[71] Canadian Ministry of Indian Affairs and Northern Development, National and Historic Parks Branch, *Byways and Special Places* (Ottawa n.d. [1972]).

leaves the actual beach as a resort attraction. But away from towns, public access gets restricted by power generating plants, especially atomic installations, private cottage developments which restrict access to if not use of the shore, industrial and port developments, and military installations.

Generalizations about the response to demand for coastal and mountain rural recreation in Europe are difficult to make since there is a variety of national practice. However, much of the coastal proportion is urban-centred and the rest can be catered for by public access roads and paths, to sheltered bays and beaches and by provision of footpaths following the coastline for those who wish to observe the sea *en passant* rather than immerse themselves in it. The coastal paths in Pembrokeshire, and the south-west peninsula of England, are examples of this, as is the recent survey and proposals[72] for the conservation of the coast of England and Wales so that some rural areas may be kept in a wild condition. Norway has imposed a 'development freeze' on all land 1 km from the shore until a national strategy for coastal development can be evolved, and legislation based on the coastal quality of Denmark is being introduced.

In Japan, numerous Quasi-National Parks embrace areas of coastline and confer limited protection on parts of the shore. However as in the Inland Sea QNP, economic pressures force much land reclamation and industrialization to occur; further, the press of people and the ubiquity of public transport tend to urbanize most usable coastlines. The beaches west of Otaru in the Niseko-Shakotan-Otaru Kaigan QNP are the only ones suitable for bathing in Hokkaido, and then only in August, but are nevertheless bounded landward by many urban-type facilities.

In these two crowded regions of the world, therefore, resource-based recreation has relatively few outlets. Combined with the easy weekend accessibility it is therefore not surprising that a lot of international movement takes place to transport people to other regions where new terrain can be explored.

4.2 RECREATION DURING VACATIONS IN JAPAN

National Parks that encompass coast or mountain, and which are relatively remote, form magnets for both Japanese and foreign visitors with time for holiday trips (Table 3.10), especially during

[72] See J. A. Patmore, *Land and Leisure in England and Wales*, pp. 210–20, for an excellent summary.

Table 3.10   Visitors to selected Japanese National Parks

National Park	Location	Area (ha)	Visitors* 1970
Shiretoko	East Hokkaido: very remote	41,375	556,000‡
Akan	Central Hokkaido	87,498	2,938,000
Shikotsu-Toya	South-west Hokkaido, near Sapporo	98,660	11,973,000
Nikko	Central Honshu, 2 hours from Tokyo	140,698	17,464,000
Fuji-Hakone-Izu	Central Honshu, close to Tokyo	122,309	76,817,000†
Hakusan	West Honshu, near Kanazawa	47,402	219,000
Aso	Central Kyushu	73,060	16,626,000
Kirishima-Yaku	Far south of Kyushu	55,231	12,058,000

* The data collection base appears uncertain: compare these statistics with the total population of Japan (107 million in 1973).
† The highest of all the National Parks.
‡ The lowest of all the National Parks.
Source: T. Senge, personal communication.

spring and summer since it becomes desirable to view the *sakura* in spring and to escape the steamy heat in summer. Because of its southerly location, for example, Aso National Park in Kyushu can be visited early in the tourist season, as the active volcanic crater and its environs, including the cable cars and high-altitude bus and car roads, are free of encumbering snow by March. The crater is the focal point of visitation of Aso National Park and the major transfer point between roads and cable cars constitutes a considerable development, especially since it is placed high on a bare mountain and dumps its solid wastes into the nearest gulley. Development in other parks varies considerably: in Towada-Hachimantai it appears to be confined mainly to the roads. In Nikko NP there are several foci which attract development, such as the Kegon Falls near the outlet of Lake Chuzenji. In the mountains are several small settlements, some of them almost entirely recreation-oriented since they comprise the mountain lodges, for example, of industrial corporations and diplomatic missions. In an effort to disperse some of the visitor impact, subsidized development of new groups of *ryokan* and hot-spring hotels is being undertaken on the Nikko plateau but whether these will do other than further crowd the limited access roads remains to be seen.

The coasts of Japan are much sought in summer, both those parts of them which are protected and most of the other parts (except Hokkaido which is too cold for bathing except in August) which are not used by industry or some other exclusive purpose, such as the nuclear power plants constructed on the west coast. The aesthetic pull of the combination of sandy bay, rocky headland and pine trees has long been effective in Japanese culture and some of the busiest areas are where cultural features such as shrines are at or near the coast. Boat transportation to the many small islands is very good and so people can be dispersed over a wide area of coastal resource. This does not, however, prevent crowding and road congestion near to the main accommodation centres.

Hokkaido (Figure 34) forms a special case since its northern and eastern portions are truly remote and snow-bound until May. Its most accessible National Park is Shikotsu-Toya, which has a little over 1 per cent Special Protection Area, mostly the alpine plant zone of Mt Yotei or Ezo-no-Fuji (Ezo was the pre-nineteenth-century name for Hokkaido). Within the Lake Shikotsu section of the park, however, attempts are being made to retard the developments that characterize Lake Toya and the Environment Agency has even called for the removal of a ski-lift on Mt Eniwa which was erected in the service of the 1972 Winter Olympics. The impetus given to road development by the 1972 events and the on-going road building programme of the Hokkaido Development Agency (essentially an arm of the national government) means that with good roads and relatively light traffic, the importance of, and hence sparse development in, Shikotsu-Toya will be very great, the more so since one alternative recreation resource, the south-western coast of Hokkaido, is rapidly being built over by industry. Since there is very little Specially Protected Area, the barriers to unlimited development can confer upon the Environment Agency only limited powers of resistance. In 1969, there were 11·6 million visitors to Shikotsu-Toya rising to 11·9 million in 1972,[73] and rapid increases are expected especially in the middle future when the New Tokkaido Line is completed into Hokkaido (approval in principle was given in 1972) and in the nearer period when the ferry from Honshu is replaced by a tunnel.

It is perhaps the ubiquity of cheap rail transport which has facili-

[73] Hokkaido Prefectural Govt Environmental Dept, *Natural Parks and Wildlife Management of Hokkaido* (Sapporo 1971); T. Senge, personal communication.

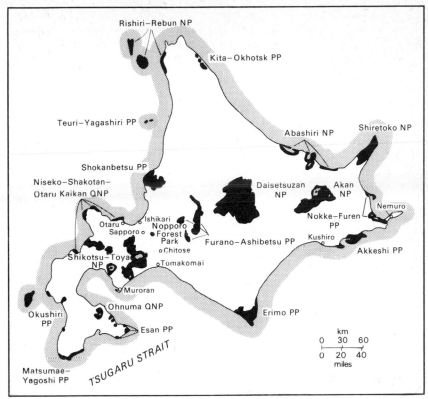

Figure 34 National Parks, Quasi-National Parks and Provincial Parks in Hokkaido, Japan. The northern and eastern coastal areas are the most inaccessible areas in Japan.
Source: Hokkaido Prefectural Government map.

tated the development of winter sports, especially skiing, to the point where some popular runs have all-day queues at both top and bottom. The higher parts of the Japanese Alps are especially popular with Honshu dwellers, and accidents are frequent because of the inattention of fatigued skiers who have sat up all night in crowded trains in order to get 1 or 2 days' sport. In Hokkaido, winter visitor numbers are increasing the most quickly:[74] some come for winter sports, others for events such as the Sapporo snow sculpture festival.

[74] Hokkaido Prefectural Govt Environmental Dept, Visitors Bureau, *Hokkaidō no Kankō-kyaku-irigomi ni kansuru shiryo* (Data on the Concentration of Visitors to Hokkaido) (Sapporo 1971).

213

Air travel makes Hokkaido easily available for weekend use but the relative cost is prohibitive to all but a few, and package holidays are relatively little developed except for excursions arranged by firms for their employees.

4.3 WINTER SPORTS IN BRITAIN: A SPECIAL CASE

The main skiing areas of the British Isles are in the Scottish Highlands and thus outside the scope of this work. A brief mention of them emphasizes the predominance of four areas, especially on the Cairngorms. This is the outstanding reflection of a skiing 'boom' which has come to Britain where until the last 10–15 years skiing was an eccentric pastime unless pursued abroad. The increase in skiers of 10 per cent p.a. (220 per cent membership of the National Ski Federation 1954–64)[75] has resulted in an estimated 25,000 skiers on the Scottish slopes in 1964,[76] with 10,000 beginners in schools in that same year. Millions of pounds have been invested in roads, accommodation and ski-lifts, especially at and around Aviemore in Invernesshire. A certain amount of risk is involved: in 1971–2 there was virtually no suitable snow in the Cairngorms, and a yearly average of 100 days' snow cover is considered necessary for successful commercial business.

In England, the main centres are in the northern Pennines and the Lake District, together with more southerly places like Edale in Derbyshire. The major problem here is that the falls and their lie are unreliable so that demand shifts spatially. The provision of access and parking is very difficult and local authorities are unwilling to invest money because of the intermittent use. Thus a road over the north Pennines may have only a narrow lane cleared in winter and this can easily be blocked by the parked cars of skiers. Of the four areas with annual averages of 100 days' snow cover (totalling 44 km²) in the north Pennines, two lie within remote nature reserves, thus creating a further source of conflict.[77]

4.4 WILDERNESS IN EUROPE AND JAPAN

The long standing economic occupance of Europe has left very little wilderness of the kind found in North America, where large tracts of

[75] J. F. Wager, 'Known demands for outdoor recreation', *The Countryside in 1970*, 2nd Conference (London 1965), p. 6.16.

[76] 'Countryside: Planning and development in Scotland', *The Countryside in 1970*, 2nd Conference, p. 9.28; J. A. Kerr Hunter, 'Access to snow holding mountains in Britain', *The Countryside in 1970*, 1st Conference (London 1964), pp. 219–22.

[77] Northern Sports Council, *Skiing in the North* (Newcastle 1973).

more or less virgin land still remain, and which to the USA form the nuclei of the areas designated as components of the National Wilderness Preservation System. Within western and central Europe, however, the mountainous areas still provide very wild country, especially above the snow-lines. Below that level, economic uses such as forestry and summer grazing have usually altered the natural ecosystems, although their legacy has often provided useful access and shelter in the higher parts of these mountains. Generations of walkers and climbers have however dotted the Alps, Pyrenees, Carpathians and Tatra with alpine huts and chalets and often enough with marked trails. Together with the cable cars and attendant structures which have scaled many of the outstanding peaks in Europe, these have taken away some of the remoteness which the North American wilderness enthusiasts seek to preserve in perpetuity; but the mountains are still wild places, to be avoided by those without the necessary skills for survival in such environments. Where protective measures have been taken, they have generally been aimed at particular kinds of development control, such as preventing ephemeral buildings catering to mass tourism, or at particular forms of wildlife protection, as in the Swiss National Park. An example of more vigorous general control is seen in the Czechoslovak part of the High Tatra Mountains, on the North Slovakian border with Poland. The topography of the isolated mountain massif makes it possible to apportion concentric zones with varying degrees of severity of control. The innermost zone, which comprises the highest peaks with accompanying geomorphological phenomena, flora and fauna, is virtual wilderness with the notable feature that access is limited to certain trails, off which walkers are not permitted to stray. Such restrictions prevent over-frequent disturbance of some animals and trampling of fragile flora. This inner zone is buffered by several others: a mountain zone with freer access but no development; a forest zone in which developments are permitted, for example, for skiing, but where management aim to restore the forest to the ecological condition it had before extraction was practised; a lower forest zone in which the permanent settlement and major transport network are found; and an outer zone where existing agriculture is continued, but where strong development controls are applied. The whole forms an outstanding example of the rational planning of a mountain area to accommodate various kinds of recreation and protection.

215

The outstanding wild areas of Europe are in Scandinavia, and in particular the mountains of Norway and in Lappland. Norway has designated several National Parks in the high Fjell country, and much other *de facto* wilderness exists. In Sweden, mountainous areas of the north have been designated as National Parks, as at Sarek and in the Abisko region, access is restricted in order to protect certain types of habitats; several hydro-electric developments have been pursued within the Parks and Lapp grazing of reindeer still continues, so that the evidence of economic use is fairly strong. Little of Finnish Lappland has been subject to manipulation of any kind other than for reindeer herding, but the terrain is not particularly suited to recreation of any kind except cross-country skiing in winter: the lower levels consist of birch scrub on the drier ridges, with *Sphagnum* bogs in between, and the higher ground of open lichen-moss heath (called *tunturi*) spread across flat plateaux. It would be another useful result of Nordic co-operation to see a co-ordinated series of preserved areas in the north since pressures for development (both for economic purposes and for intensive forms of recreation) are likely to become stronger.

The future of wilderness in Britain can hardly seem promising, but some of the uplands of England and Wales still comprise very wild country, even if the landscapes are largely man-made. In Scotland, especially the north-west, such terrain is the rule rather than the rare. The future designation of wilderness areas, to be kept free of all developments, including those for recreation, would appear to be a useful move. Partly, of course, because there is a demand, albeit of a small group, for wilderness recreation of the simplest kind, and partly (and this is a subjective opinion) because in a small densely populated country like Britain it is good to know it is there, whether visited or not.[78]

A few areas suggest themselves as wildernesses because they are wild, relatively unvisited, and not very accessible except on foot or by pony. The high plateaux of both northern and southern Dartmoor (provided the military could be excluded from the former), parts of the north Pennines, and the high mountains of Wester Ross are 'natural' units, together with much of the western parts of Sutherland.[79] Other areas could be 'zoned' wildernesses: parts of National

---

[78] The writer suspects that the popularity of sitting in cars parked on prominent overlooks into wild country has something to do with this.

[79] I. G. Simmons, 'Wilderness in the mid-20th century USA', *Town Planning Review* 56

Parks which by virtue of that status were kept free of developments of all kinds; very often such areas could be 'core areas' of the parks around which zones of varying degrees of development could be arrayed. Such a suggestion was made in 1974 by some members of the Sandford Committee (see pp. 110–11).

The major conflict in carrying out these suggestions would be with those who wish to halt the rural depopulation which is common to most of the areas mentioned. The population of them is low and as far as wilderness recreation is concerned, the lower the better. There is a substantial body of opinion, which wants to promote economic revival of such places and this, obviously, would be highly inimical to wilderness. No debate has yet ensued but the assumption that rural depopulation is 'a bad thing' is rarely officially questioned.

In England and Wales the possibility now exists of zoning the National Parks to create 'wilderness' areas. The local plans demanded by the Town and Country Planning Act of 1968 might include such areas within the parks. They would be limited in extent and would aim to keep as wild as possible existing rough country, especially moorland and mountain areas. Inaccessibility would be essential: they would be available only to the tough walker. Planning controls would make the land inalienable: in reality this would make marginal farming even more tenuous and so a recreation subsidy for farmers, already suggested by many farmers would be needed. This has been the subject of trial experiments in the Lake District and Snowdonia in 1969 when farmers were paid for marking paths, clearing litter and repairing drainage caused by thoughtless and malicious recreationists.[80]

Wilderness in Japan exists usually only because the area is very remote or because a Specially Protected Area has been declared within a National Park. In Honshu and Kyushu such areas are difficult to find unless the terrain is very rugged. In the mountain spine of Honshu, however, some of the protected areas have wilderness zones, such as the Chibu-Sangaku (Japan Alps) National Park with 38 per cent SPA and Minami Alps with 26 per cent.[81] If near a population centre then wilderness areas receive very heavy use: a

---

(1966–7), pp. 249–56. The wild coast of Scotland will be the scene of considerable development in the cause of North Sea oil exploitation; 'preferred development' and 'preferred conservation' zones have been outlined by the government.

[80] 'Experiment in upland management', *Recreation News* 12 (1969), pp. 3–4.

[81] T. Senge, *op. cit.*, p. 710.

roadless mountain area in Nikko NP has been designated as SPA and is available only to walkers on a particular trail on which there is one overnight stop. It receives 500,000 users per year.[82] Given the increased mobility of the Japanese people and the government policy of dispersing the population away from the Kanto, the outlook for preservation of such areas is not very good.

Hokkaido forms a special case since it is currently quite far from the major population centres of Japan, and within it, the Shikotsu-Toya NP (described above) absorbs a great deal of recreation pressure (Figure 35), having 11·6 million visitors in 1969; by contrast Daisetsuzan NP recorded 2·9 million, Akan NP 2·5 million and Shiretoko NP 0·5 million in that year.[83] The former two parks both have large road-free areas with virgin forest and native fauna such as the Ezo bear, forming wilderness areas which are protected as SPAs

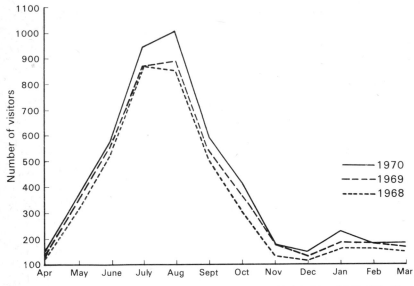

Figure 35 Seasonal distribution of all visitors to Hokkaido, 1968–70. The summer peak is obvious but the growing importance of winter visitors, is apparent, although distorted in 1970 by the Winter Olympics.
Source: Hokkaido Prefectural Government, *Data on the Concentration of Visitors to Hokkaido*, p. 2.

[82] T. Senge, personal communication.
[83] Hokkaido Prefectural Govt Environmental Dept, *Natural Parks and Wildlife Management of Hokkaido* (Sapporo 1971), pp. 2–4.

(6·2 per cent of Daisetsuzan and 9·6 per cent of Akan).[84] A proposal to drive a road through the wildest part of Daisetsuzan was defeated in 1971. The wildest of all the Hokkaido parks is the Shiretoko NP, formed of a volcanic peninsula jutting from the eastern side of the island. It has spectacular lava cliffs and offshore fauna such as sea lions. These are visible from boats but no landing is permitted; in the interior there are no trails through the virgin forest or up the mountain spine of the peninsula. In view of impending developments such as the construction of a tunnel from Honshu to Hokkaido, and the eventual extension of the New Tokkaido Line to Sapporo, the development of other parks in Hokkaido will be necessary if these sanctuaries are to be preserved and it is pleasing to note that the Hokkaido Prefectural Government is one of the most advanced in planning for Prefectural Parks.

Looking overall at Japan, the insidious tenacity with which settlement has penetrated the remote vastnesses of the wilder areas has meant that nature untrammelled is very hard to find, except perhaps where volcanic ash and lava have been added at frequent intervals. It is necessary to realize however that the duality of man and nature which exists in Western culture is much less apparent in that of Japan, and so the evidence of human activity and the changes it brings are viewed with less opprobrium, even in remote and wild places, than in the West. The inroads of Western ideas have been strong, especially since 1945, and the influx of American ideas in park management has included their conception of wilderness.

[84] *Ibid.*

Part 4
Common Themes

1 The roles of government and private enterprise

1.1 GOVERNMENT INVOLVEMENT IN RECREATION PROVISION

It has become apparent that the transfer of land and water resources into recreational use has become a function of government at various levels. The reasons for this vary from country to country but certain common themes emerge. Initially, many environmental management processes are dealt with by government (for example, air and water quality, nature conservation) because these must be organized on a spatially wide basis in order to provide effective control, and either no commercial company would be able to do this or if it could it would be so large as to be politically and socially unacceptable. Secondly, rural recreation can only be made commercially profitable under certain limited circumstances and since it is largely paid for out of taxes, a public agency becomes the obvious avenue of provision. Where strong land-use competition exists, governments with powers of compulsory purchase are the only bodies who can effectively acquire the key resources needed for recreation development. The result has been an evolution of government bodies at all levels, from central to local, concerned with recreation, and the overall structure is remarkably similar both in bastions of free enterprise like the USA and mixed economies with a pink tinge such as those of western and northern Europe.

Some features and examples of government structure are shown in Table 4.1. It can be seen that a usual feature of central government involvement is a bureaucratic body which does not directly engage in resource management, such as the Bureau of Outdoor Recreation in the USA and the Countryside Commission in England and Wales (Scotland has its own Countryside Commission). Frequently their task includes the co-ordination of the programmes of lower echelons of government, the undertaking of research and the provision of advice; almost always the body acts as the extractor of

221

Table 4.1 Government involvement in recreation provision

Government level	Function	Examples (not exhaustive)
Central: bureaucratic	Co-ordination, financial allocation, long-term planning, not usually directly involved in management but Canada is exceptional	Bureau of Outdoor Recreation/USA Countryside Commission/England and Wales/ Scotland Department Environment/UK Department Indian Affairs and Northern Development/Canada [Federal land only] Landsplanudvalgets Sekretariat/Dk Stichting Recreatie/Netherlands
Central: resource managing	Provision and management of resource-based recreation	National Park Service/USA USDA Forest Service/USA [Wilderness areas] National and Historic Parks branch/Canada Staatsbosbeheer/Netherlands Nature Parks branch, Environmental Agency/ Japan Cultuurtechnische Dienst/Neths; HUD in USA
	Provision of resources which may function at both resource-based and intermediate levels, possibly even user-oriented	County Councils/England Wales [National Parks management]
Intermediate (county, province, state): resource managing	Provision and management of areas which are resource-based for some, intermediate for others, depending upon accidents of location	States/USA Provinces/Canada County Councils/England and Wales For Comm/UK
Intermediate resource managing	Provision and management of areas for local region only (but some of which may be resource-based viewed nationally)	Aniter (Counties) Dk
Special single resource-oriented joint government/ private bodies	Provision and management of Intermediate and user-oriented resources	Verenging de Utrechtse Huvelrug/Netherlands Plassenschap Loosdrecht en Omstreken/ Netherlands Derwent Reservoir Advisory Office (advisory only)/ England
Local government: resource managing, single	Providing for own area; may be used as Intermediate areas by outsiders	Metro Toronto and Region Conservation Authority/Canada Counties/USA
Joint authorities	Providing for own area; may be used as Intermediate areas by outsiders	East Bay Regional Park District/USA Lea Valley Regional Park Authority/England

funds from the central treasury and dispenses them in accordance with priorities it has itself determined. In the case of England and Wales some of these functions are shared with the Department of the Environment since the latter has oversight of local authority physical planning, which may generally include recreation provision. In the case of Canada, there is no government body which looks at the nation as a whole: the appropriate central department only looks at the Federal contribution and has no legal power to control or influence the Provinces.

The central governments usually maintain branches of an appropriate agency to acquire and manage resource-based recreation areas, frequently of the kind that are designated as National Parks although such resources may also function at the intermediate level because of their relative proximity to some population centres. The National Park Service[1] of the USA and the National and Historic Parks Branch[2] are examples of this kind: Elk Island NP (Alta) for instance serves mostly as a weekend visitation area for the inhabitants of Edmonton; Banff NP serves both the intermediate needs of Calgary and resource-based demand from eastern Canada. In the USA the Rocky Mountain NP serves both Denver and the nation, the Sierra Nevada parks of Yosemite, Kings Canyon and Sequoia cater for Californians at weekends and everybody else at the same time, but Muir Redwoods National Monument is mostly visited by northern California inhabitants. The importance of scale is shown by the activity of the Netherlands Forest Service in managing recreation resources of all kinds on a nation-wide basis.

Resource-based recreation may also be provided by the intermediate levels of government, such as states, provinces and counties. These tend to cater specifically for their own jurisdictions but cannot of course keep out others. The State Parks of various parts of the USA may thus attract people on longer vacations from other regions, just as the Quetico Provincial Park in Ontario forms a resource-based international zone along with the Superior National Forest in the USA. In England and Wales the counties have always had a leading role in the management of the National Parks (although their designation has been by the then National Parks Commission, albeit with much local consultation), and since the provisions of the Countryside Act 1968 have become involved in the designation and

---

[1] Dept of the Interior.
[2] Dept of Indian Affairs and Northern Development.

management of 'Country Parks' as intermediate or even user-oriented units. National bodies which plan recreation on a regional basis, such as the Forestry Commission of the UK also fall into this category. Lastly, there are the special joint bodies discussed in Part 1 (pp. 90–94) for managing individual resources such as water bodies or heath-forest-farmland areas in the Netherlands; a move towards this organization is seen in the advisory committee for the Derwent Reservoir in northern England but it has no preceptive powers nor does it exercise superseding authority over its constituent bodies.

In the user-oriented zone the local government unit such as the county, or a special conservation district, or a consortium of authorities, is unchallenged. The aim is simple: to provide recreation areas capable of withstanding heavy use easily accessible to the client populations. Budgets may be high and management techniques difficult but aims are more uniform than in intermediate and resource-based areas.

1.2 THE RELATIVE ROLES OF GOVERNMENT AND PRIVATE ENTERPRISE

The study suggests that both governmental and private provision are necessary but that each have their relatively well-defined place. Basic to the whole question is the largely historically determined fact of whether the resources are owned privately or publicly. (We may also include here the factor of access to a resource, such as water, whose ownership may differ from the adjoining land.)

Where there is a mix of both publicly and privately owned land then a fairly clear separation of provision appears to take place. This public concern is manifested even where, as in Britain and Denmark, the ownership of the resources may be private. The Intermediate type of recreation is also largely a government concern, especially where suitable resources are in public ownership, but where suitable resources are in private hands, two alternatives appear. The first of these is their movement into public ownership *via* the process of compulsory purchase or its national equivalent. This can usually only be undertaken where the supply of funds for such purchase is very good and invariably involves some subsidy or matching grant from the national Treasury. Where such funds are not forthcoming then a watered-down form may be present in the form of agreements between government and resource-owner in which recreational use is permitted as a secondary use by the owner, usually in return for a compensation payment. The Access Agreements in the National

Parks of England and Wales and the arrangements for the opening of Dutch woodlands are examples of this.

A second possibility is the development of Intermediate recreation by private enterprise. As we have seen with regard to the US, this involves financial risk, for the economics of such developments are not particularly clear. Proximity to a large population is obviously necessary yet the wild character must be maintained. One field where private enterprise appears to work in this category is that of the specialized attraction which people will travel some distance to see: in Britain the recent flourishing of drive-through 'game-parks' where Savana animals may be seen in a 'wild' habitat of eighteenth-century oak-studded parkland, may be quoted as an example. Rather different, it may be surmised, are the numerous roadside attractions on the highways of the US ('Mysterious Trees', 'Thousand Animals', 'Marine Wonderland') which depend mostly on casual visits from passing traffic.

Although not an activity from which government is absent, the provision of winter sports facilities seems to have become a special area for commercial operators. The reasons are manifold but include factors such as the lack of competing rural attractions in winter and hence the ability to concentrate demand upon a few activities; the willingness of skiers and snowmobilers who have already invested in equipment to pay economic prices for lifts and tree-run areas or trails; the willingness of private resource managers to manipulate their forests and slopes to accommodate ski-runs and skidoo trails to an extent that public authorities, mindful of their environmental responsibilities would not dare; and the desire for on the spot *après-sport* facilities which are scarcely the traditional domain of a public body and which most taxpayers would object to if any loss were incurred. These factors combine therefore to give, in areas such as southern Sweden, Dalarna, the Alps, Ontario north of Toronto, the Laurentides, upstate New York, and northern New England, a galaxy of ski slopes with tows and lifts, snowmobile trail areas, and resorts for which a small but rapidly growing sector of the people is willing to pay a price which ensures a profit to the operator.

Private enterprise appears to have most to contribute in the user-oriented recreation area. Because of locational factors, the profit-ability is likely to be highest and so the operator (or, more likely, his creditor) stands a good chance of a satisfactory return on his capital. Since, however, most operators will want to engage in the most profitable form of enterprise in a given situation (be it day-camping and picnicking, fishing in stocked ponds, or swimming), then there arises a danger of uniformity. Thus government has a clear role to play in the provision of a diversity of recreational opportunity in the user-oriented zone. Where the state of knowledge about the possibilities of recreation as an enterprise is poor, then a well-placed government facility may act as a 'demonstration farm' and show entrepreneurs the opportunities which they might give.

In none of the countries studied was there an entire national lack of public land, but regionally the case may arise where all the land suitable for Intermediate and user-oriented facilities is privately owned. Then the situation described above with regard to Intermediate areas is applicable and the outcome depends very largely upon the supply of finance and possibly also on the articulation of the demand: noisy wheels are likely to get the most grease.

In summary, it appears that the most satisfactory response to recreational demands appears to be provided by a complex interaction of government and private enterprise. On paper a simple structure might look tidy, but in practice the various levels of government together with local entrepreneurs appear to provide the most flexible response system. But since measures of satisfaction are so few and unreliable this conclusion must be viewed with considerable caution.

1.3 LONG-TERM PLANNING BY GOVERNMENTS

The recognition that amenity land use of all kinds is important in a nation's life has led to the incorporation of various types of 'conservation land' into physical planning. Such schemes are undertaken either by central governments or by local units with central governmental co-ordination, and aim to integrate *inter alia*, recreational land use into the overall pattern desired for the area and to identify regions where reaction is likely to be of special importance. Only in very large countries where detailed land-use planning is either absent or very new (as in the USA, where the Congress in 1974 declined to pass a Land Use Planning Act) is a plan for recreation lands likely to be formulated *per se*, without reference to its place in the land-use pattern. The instances discussed below are therefore samples only, to show two examples of approaches to long-term planning for recreation.

226

1 THE ROLES OF GOVERNMENT AND PRIVATE ENTERPRISE

(a) The Netherlands

In the 1966 material on the future planning of the Netherlands, recreation is dealt with as fully as any other land use.[3] Within the context of the structure plan for the year 2000 (with an expected population of 20 million), three basic aims have been followed since 1964: to promote the greatest possible diversity of recreational opportunity; to use the existing recreation space as efficiently as possible; and to develop new space and accommodation for recreation of various types. In the implementation of these policies, day-recreation forms the cardinal point and has the highest priority. The present day-recreation areas for the large cities, even when further developed, will be inadequate (i.e., the coastal dunes, the Utrechtse Heuvelrug, the new lakes in northern and southern Holland, south Veluwezoom, north Drenthe and the Meierij). Therefore, about twenty new 'large-scale elements' for day recreation are to be developed within easy reach of the large cities. The form these will take is not yet finally decided but it seems likely that the Amsterdam Forest will serve as a model for some of them. The cities which it is hoped to serve in this way are, Amsterdam, Rotterdam, Den Haag, Utrecht, Gröningen and Leeuwarden. Landscape protection near large cities is also regarded as important, as is the provision of buffer zones of agriculture or forest between urban agglomerations. It is especially desired to keep open the centre of Randstadt Holland, preferably in agricultural use but with plenty of non-agricultural employment available and land consolidation has a high priority here.

At the other extreme, elements of national importance—the nearest the Netherlands gets to resource-based recreation—are to be recognized and it is possible that the term National Park will be used for areas of national significance in areas such as the coastal dunes, the Drenthe plateau, north-east Twente, south Limburg and the Kempen. Similarly, nationally recognized water-sport areas will be designated in the Frisian lakes, the IJsselmeer polder lakes, the lakes in the Delta and in north and south Holland. The detailed planning for these areas is intended to be zonal in form, with accommodation and services on the periphery and becoming more 'natural' towards the centre; in Drenthe agricultural reclamation in the National Park is envisaged.

[3] Govt Printing Office of the Netherlands, *Second Report on Physical Planning in the Netherlands* (condensed (English) edition, Den Haag 1966), parts I and II.

In between day-use areas closely tied to cities and these national elements, regional day-use facilities are to be encouraged, both water-based (Loosdrecht is singled out as an example of this type) and land-based, such as the Utrechtse Heuvelrug.

The Dutch plan for recreation is designed to cater for both increases in population and increases in demand, though no quantification of the latter is available or contemplated. The aim appears to be to put as much land as practicable to recreational purposes whilst safeguarding landscape and wildlife values and it is all the more impressive for being done as part of an integral plan for all land uses, including urban growth. What happens after 20 million, should the population rise even at its current rate of 0·8 per cent p.a., is another matter.

(b) England and Wales

Physical planning is carried out by the county councils and equivalent metropolitan units, with oversight by the Ministry of the Environment and, in the case of recreation, advice from the Countryside Commission. Since the passage of the 1968 Town and Country Planning Act (the latest in a series of such Acts), the planning authorities have been required to prepare two kinds of plan: structure plans and local plans. The first are regionally indicative of the kinds of development to be permitted or encouraged within the area, i.e., broad strategies for housing or industrial location; the second show the exact proposed locations of the land-use changes. It is apparent that provision for recreation can appear at both scales, for example, in a broad delimitation of the various types of recreation proposed, such as water-based areas in zones of former gravel pits in river valleys and intensive-use areas outside major conurbations in the first instance, and the exact location of country parks in the second. As with all such plans, periodic revision is statutory and so changes in demand and the availability of resources can be reflected in a reasonably flexible manner.

But it is unrealistic to deny that the situation regarding rural recreation is difficult, and likely to remain so particularly if demands increase. The resource base for recreation is on the whole shrinking rather than expanding, as urban growth, industry and agricultural reclamation intensify the use of areas in which recreation formerly had a part.

If England and Wales are to have satisfactory provision for open-air leisure activities then a number of adjustments will have to be made.

1 More Exchequer money is a pre-condition of progress. The geography of England and Wales is such that charging for access to the National Parks, for example, is more or less impossible, and certainly uneconomic. The overriding need at present is for access to land and water and there is little alternative, at the time of writing,[4] to central government finance, and certainly no alternative but to have it paid through the medium of taxation.

2 A yielding of attitudes on the part of land-owners will become essential. Although powers of compulsory purchase by government authorities (local and national) exist, it is preferable to use them sparingly. A more receptive attitude to recreation—which is going to come anyway—will cause fewer ulcers at all levels; just as the land of the National Trust is no longer inalienable as far as building new highways is concerned, then Farmer T's land cannot be inalienable as far as the recreation of City Y's people. But inevitably he will have to be compensated for loss of income.

3 The carrying capacity of our limited lands for recreation is much greater for people than for cars. Thus in very popular areas the nettle of exclusion must be grasped. The powers for this exist, but application of them is more or less non-existent.

4 The popularity of the slogan 'multiple use' seems to have diminished, probably because nobody is quite sure what it means. Some combinations are incompatible and difficult decisions about what is to be permitted will have to be made. Inevitably, heavy pressure will fall on the military to yield up the moorland, beaches and downland that they possess, especially in south England where the recreation demands are so high. Likewise if a minority sport like grouse shooting becomes incompatible with free access to the moors for walkers, then it is likely that the shooters will be dislodged. There will be an element of class warfare here, of course.

5 New management devices for areas of multiple use need to be found and the Derwent Valley Reservoir Committee is a helpful beginning. The example of the *schaps* described for the Nether-

[4] The Report of the Royal Commission on Local Government in England and Wales (the Redcliffe-Maud Report) advocated the setting up of major Provinces which might possibly have handled this type of investment, but its suggestions were replaced with a two-tier system, operative from April 1974, which is less useful from this point of view.

lands (pp. 90–94) may well be a good one. Like the Netherlands, therefore, it is possible that recreation space can become available to many of those who seek it, well into the next 25 years. If demands upon the land and water resources increase *per capita* in that time, then the slower the population growth of the small islands the higher the quality of recreation is likely to be.

2 Rural recreation as a land use

2.1 THE PENETRATION OF RURAL RECREATION INTO THE LAND-USE PATTERNS OF INDUSTRIAL COUNTRIES

The USA exhibits the most highly developed demand and supply system of all the countries examined in this work. Demand is high and the resource and economic conditions for its satisfaction exist. It is interesting therefore to examine recreation as a land use on a par with other land uses, (set out in Table 4.2). Recreation land is nearly all 'parks' or similar protected areas since there is in the USA a considerable identification of 'recreation' with 'parks', i.e., land set aside for the purpose. The unstructured type of use noted for the UK and Holland is less frequently found.

These figures show that although recreation is nowhere a dominant use, it is almost everywhere a significant use, especially when

Table 4.2   Public rural recreation and other land uses: USA sample states (million acres)

State	Wildlife conservation +OR− single use	Wildlife conservation +OR− multiple use and single use	Cropland	Total area of State	Urban area
Maine	0·28	0·32	1·19	19·85	0·17
Massachussetts	0·37	0·37	0·47	5·0	0·75
NY	3·42	3·43	6·98	30·68	1·5
NJ	0·30	0·30	1·00	4·81	0·99
Minnesota	4·54	7·613	22·52	51·21	0·78
Ohio	0·46	0·56	12·43	26·22	1·5
Nebraska	0·24	0·585	23·64	49·03	0·16
NC	0·77	1·92	7·36	31·40	0·60
Louisiana	0·73	1·328	5·05	28·87	0·53
NM	0·82	24·11	2·65	77·76	0·20
Washington	4·09	24·087	8·05	42·69	0·49
California	5·49	41·040	12·60	100·20	2·45

(1 million acres = 4047 km²)

Sources: US Dept of the Interior Bureau of Land Management, *Public Land Statistics 1963,* 1964. R. D. Davidson, Federal and State Rural Lands 1950, *US Dept of Agriculture Circular 909,* 1952. US Dept of Agriculture, Major Uses of Land and Water in the US with Special Reference to Agriculture, *Agr. Econ. Report* 13, 1962.

multiple-use areas are considered. Thus in western states like California and Washington, recreation becomes a very significant element of the land-use pattern. In others where it is not so important, it may nevertheless be equal to about half the cropland area and so deserves attention in any studies of land use patterns.

The upthrust of provision of recreation resources on public land has mainly come about through the reclassification of Federal land and the acquisition of land by the States. The public domain has not altered greatly in areas, but the importance of recreation in it and the need to devote financial resources to the development of facilities are typified in the Multiple Uses Act of the Forest Service and the BLM as well as the host of Federal rural recreation programmes previously discussed. Although no time-series data are available, the shift is continuing as fast as funds will allow, although competition for the latter from the military, NASA, and the urban areas, is strong and it could well be that the flood of conservation and recreation bills which have passed Congress in the last few years may dry up in favour of increased attention to urban matters. The importance of public land is such however, that the Public Land Law Review Commission was set up to examine the whole question of Federal Land use and its legal constraints. The reports included recreational use of public land but no ensuing legislation had been enacted by 1974.

The acquisition of land by the States for their Park systems is another response to the demand for recreation resources. The rapidity with which they have built up systems, using both their own and Federal money, is surprising in a country where endless litigation seems to precede any public acquisition of land or water. Nevertheless the State role in the land-use pattern of its area is now usually dominated by its holdings for recreation: these outpace those for fish and wildlife or forestry, for example.

Private enterprise has added its quota to the land-use shifts. The large areas of development for second homes (not confined to local real estate operators—Weyerhauser Incorporated has for example a vacation home development in Napa County, California), and other 'spot' recreation provisions like marinas and roadside attractions have all taken land out of 'productive' use and put it at the service of leisure, although most land-use statistics do not record it as such—it is most likely to go in some sort of 'miscellaneous' column.

In whatever institutional sector, multiple use is a management goal of some resource managers, whether they belong to the BLM or to Georgia Pacific Timber Incorporated. The term has meant in practice a mosaic of uses rather than different uses of the same piece of land, because of incompatibilities. The mass recreations such as picnics, camping and driving are simply not possible on the same stretch of land (or water) as wildlife, young timber, or domesticated grazing animals. Where people are spread out then there is less problem, so that hunting (whose season is happily outside the main vacation period) is compatible with rather more uses—except that many urban-dwelling hunters tend to confuse domesticated and wild animals in their search for prey.

Fortunately, a good deal of responsibility for the type and quantity of recreation in multiple-use schemes is delegated locally and so the most opportune scheme can generally be evolved.

In Canada the amount of land devoted to recreation in most provinces is puny compared with 'the bush'. Therefore since many Canadians have access to huge areas of wild Crown Land, the impetus to create parks may be somewhat lessened. This applies only to resource-based recreation, and the trend is corroborated by two other factors. There is first the 'frontier mentality' of many Canadians, which applies as much to recreation provision as to most other aspects of resources. Canada is perceived as vast and virtually limitless: the thought of limits or ever running out of supplies is virtual treason. There is therefore little need, it is argued, to create parks in the northlands because the land is so wild and inaccessible. Similarly, the provinces are generally unwilling to give up the rights they possess over Crown Land in order that they might be transferred to the Federal government to make National Parks: where their northlands are concerned they might just be signing away a hitherto untapped economic resource. In the Territories directly under its control, the Federal government is hampered by two sets of pressures: one from the mineral and oil exploration companies anxious not to see any potential profits replaced by parkland, and another from the natives whose land claims are still the subject of dispute.

Perhaps an equally urgent demand is for day-use areas near the major cities of metropolitan Canada, where land prices escalate at very high rates, making acquisition difficult except for the richest urban areas, like Toronto and Montreal. The Conservation Authorities (pp. 140–42) have been very active in Ontario but their primary purpose is flood control and in any case they are found only in that province.

No equivalent of the BOR exists in Canada, only the more advisory work of the Council of Resource and Environment Ministers, which does not itself initiate policy. So no national scale of priorities can be evolved as has happened under the provisions of the Land and Water Conservation Fund Act 1965 of the USA or the Countryside Act 1968 in England and Wales. In the nations of Europe, penetration of rural recreation is scarcely measured by the land use statistics since there is so much informal recreation which does not need 'parks'. The many footpaths and greenways, land to which *de facto* access has been confirmed by centuries of use, and communal resources such as heathland and forest where urban recreationists can scarcely be kept out, are all examples of recreation as the icing of a layer cake of multiple use. The forests of central Sweden for example are officially managed communally for lumber and grazing but in fact the users of second residences are much more effective participants in the resource process so that the saw bites into more trees for fires to cheer the hearts of skiers than for logs for pulping or sawtimber, and summer residents grazing off bilberries are commoner than belled cattle. These shifts are unlikely to appear as such in the official statistics. In Japan the situation is even more difficult to disentangle for even in National and Quasi-National Parks there may be so much Ordinary Area that it is difficult for anybody without a planner's map to tell that he is in a protected landscape. Also, outdoor recreation is less obviously rural-based in Japan, either because the Japanese culture does not demand it or because any spot frequented by large numbers of people tends to become urbanized except in the strongly protected areas of parks. So no estimate of the role of rural-recreation land in the pattern can be made with any confidence.

All the industrial nations seem likely to exhibit shifts towards the designation of more land for rural recreation provided two conditions are fulfilled. Firstly, increased intensification of forestry and more especially agriculture will mean that more marginal land passes out of those uses and becomes available for recreation, as on for example, the moorlands of the UK, the Appalachian foothills of the USA, the sandy sterile moraines of western Denmark, and of south-central Ontario. Only in rare instances will such land be used for urban-industrial expansion. Secondly, the demand for the other

233

resources of wild land must not be increased to the point where they are no longer compatible with recreation: a situation not impossible to conceive in a densely populated country receiving fewer imported resources from abroad because of changed patterns of trade or higher local consumption.

2.2 REGIONAL PROBLEMS

Even such a large and in general well provided for country as the US shows a distinct unevenness of recreation provision, especially in the public sector (Table 4.3). This is scarcely surprising, since there is a

Table 4.3   USA: regional recreation provision 1965 (thousand acres)

	Total area	Built-up area	Population 1965	Public OR area
USA	2,313,772	57,357	193,795,000	491,297,919
New England	42,629	1,863	11,146,000	2,188,288
North Atlantic	65,757	5,479	36,471,000	7,921,436
East-north Central	458,901	11,400	38,231,000	15,270,708
West-north Central	331,038	10,231	15,850,000	15,623,461
South Atlantic	178,534	6,367	28,747,000	16,320,267
East-south Central	116,457	4,268	12,819,000	7,224,139
West-south Central	280,886	8,142	18,540,000	10,430,702
Mountain	552,888	4,513	7,693,000	280,563,091
Pacific	586,682	5,094	24,290,000	135,755,827

(1 million acres = 4047 km²)
Source: BOR, *The 1965 Inventory of Outdoor Recreation Areas*, 1970, Table 2A.8.

broad east-west contrast in population distribution which is the inverse of the east-west diversity of resources. The north-east is probably the worst off, although Megalopolis has both a long, often indented shoreline and the forested mountains of the Appalachian system to the west.[5] The Mid-West is further from those mountains and has only the relatively uniform shoreline of the Great Lakes (where not industrialized or outrageously polluted) as a major water area. Although not so densely populated as many regions, the south is not well provided for. This may be partly due to lack of demand, since income levels are often low, and because of lack of expectation among the black population. Until relatively recently the State Park systems of some southern States were segregated.

A high rate of population increase in a given region can be a source of problems. California is a good example of this: although expansion

[5] The Great Smokey Mountains NP has the highest visitor numbers of any non-urban element in the system.

234

of the SP system has been rapid, the development of user-oriented facilities (especially in the Los Angeles area) has lagged severely.[6] One difficulty is that land is often purchased by private developers long before a governmental agency can acquire it.[7] The price of land[8] may put it beyond the State's (or County's) means, since recreation land will bring in no income—the reverse, in fact: like education it will perpetually be an apparent burden on the taxpayer, and it will similarly be resented by those who do not participate.

Secretaries of the Interior have suggested that new partnership relations involving Federal, State and local governments, and private enterprise, should be explored and encouraged. Joint regional planning for recreation is one way of bringing about a diverse and responsive system and may help to bring extra money to parts of the private enterprise sector: for example, the Department of Housing and Urban Development of the Federal government has given a grant to the State of Pennsylvania to help with planning the area surrounding the Gettysburg National Military Park.[9]

Another major 'regional' problem is the shoreline, including that of the Great Lakes. Although there is of course no absolute shortage, three factors have made it difficult for sufficient of it to be put into public ownership. Firstly, the demand for second (and first) homes has meant that long stretches are in private ownership and there is no public access to the water (the Penobscot Peninsula in Maine is a good example of this); secondly, industrialization has taken up large areas, where access to water and flat land are required, as for steel plants and power stations; thirdly, pollution (especially in the Great Lakes and tidewater lands) renders many forms of recreation undesirable if not downright unhealthy.

As was hinted for California, the major American locational

[6] In 1971–2 the division of the majority of the funds granted to local authorities in California under the Land and Water Conservation Fund Act of 1965 was: Los Angeles area 50 per cent; San Francisco-Oakland-San Jose area 23 per cent; San Diego 6 per cent; non-metropolitan areas 11 per cent (see California Dept of Parks and Recreation, *California Outdoor Recreation Resources Plan* (Sacramento 1972), p. 156).

[7] ORRRC Report 15, *Open Space Action* (Washington, DC 1962) ORRRC Report 16, *Land Acquisition for Outdoor Recreation* (Washington, DC 1962). See also *Open Space Action*, bimonthly journal of the Open Space Action Institute, New York; and numerous other 'how-to-do-it' publications. BOR has a quarterly publication, *Outdoor Recreation Action* (Washington, DC).

[8] BOR, *Recreation Land Price Escalation* (Washington, DC 1967).

[9] Memorandum of Secretary Walter J. Hickel to Director George B. Harzog Jr (18 June 1969).

problem is that of recreation provision for the inhabitants of the major conurbations. Table 4.4 shows that Federal provision increases markedly with distance; traditionally the lower-level agencies and private enterprise have been expected to fill the gap. But as the figures for disbursement of Federal funds in California show (see note 6), the Federal government is becoming very concerned with the urban fringe zone. The parallel activities of the Canadian Federal government in Toronto, and the British government (via the counties) have been noted.

Table 4.4   USA: federal lands suitable for recreation within varying distances of major cities (thousand acres)

Population centre	50 miles (half-day)	120 miles (full day)	500 miles (weekend)
Boston	6	469	1,540
New York	3	37	4,025
Washington, DC	2	548	5,300
Atlanta	—	1,313	10,102
St Louis	—	1,065	7,454
Chicago	—	—	6,754
Minneapolis	150	26	10,290
Denver	1,635	8,530	111,660
Phoenix	2,100	14,560	122,320
Los Angeles	1,200	6,220	117,000
San Francisco	100	3,935	109,650
Seattle	700	8,120	101,600

Source: BOR, *The 1965 Inventory of Outdoor Recreation Areas*, 1970, Tables VIII.10, VIII.11 and VIII.12.

The consumption of near-city rural recreation is shown in the trends observed at various facilities during the 1960–65 period (Table 4.5). The outstanding figure is for overnight use of County

Table 4.5   USA: trends in attendance 1960–65, % change (all positive)

	Total	Day use	Overnight
All areas	52	50	63
Federal	62	60	67
State	43	43	43
County	45	44	113

Source: BOR, *The 1965 Inventory of Outdoor Recreation Areas*, 1970, Table 2A.54.

areas, reflecting an increasing demand for a diversity of facilities (i.e., those other than for simple day use) near to urban centres. Such concerns were often strongly voiced at a series of forums on nation-wide rural recreation planning in 1972.[10]

The fact that 94 per cent of all Canadians live within 300 miles (483 km) of the USA border means that not only do they have their own day-use difficulties, but these and intermediate-zone facilities are also very popular with nearby US residents, especially in areas accessible from Detroit and upstate New York. For example, the commercial resort of Crystal Beach on Lake Erie is mostly used by Buffalonians and the shore is almost all owned by New York State residents, a source of some annoyance and occasional breaches of the peace in a time of upsurging Canadian nationalism. The acquisition of Canadian property by USA citizens has been the subject of official investigation in, for example, Alberta (which saw no objections) and Prince Edward Island (which passed a law prohibiting such sales, which in 1973 was under challenge in the provincial courts).

Most other industrial nations exhibit similar imbalances, since the best recreation resources tend to be where the people are not: an aspect of spatial distributions shared often by water resources. The United Kingdom's disparity between the south-east and most of the rest of the country is apparent to every motorist who has spent a few hours of his summer Sunday in a traffic jam in the suburbs of London. The Tokyo-Osaka axis in Japan is similar; the new govern-ment of late 1972 promised to aid in a programme of population dis-persal but at a population growth of 1·2 per cent p.a. this will probably keep pace only with the extra people. The Danish penin-sula of Jutland acts as a corridor for motorists from Germany going further north, as well as those seeking to vacation there, so that demands for recreation are determined in the first instance by the road pattern. The eventual lay-out of a motorway network is of some importance as shown by J. Humlum's alternative to the official H-shaped layout for the whole of Denmark.[11]

It is probably futile to think of 'solutions' for such regional im-balances but clearly one response must be an increased attention to day-use facilities near large cities; features given an added emphasis in uncertain maritime climates. Since land values are so high in such places, governmental involvement is essential; another response

---

[10] BOR, *America Voices Its Recreation Concerns* (Washington, DC 1973).
[11] J. Humlum, *Landsplanlaegningsproblemer* (Copenhagen 1966).

might be the increased use of public transport for reaching such facilities so as to increase their carrying capacity and incidentally help to make economic the public transport systems which most progressive cities either have or are striving to resurrect.

3 Conflicts and compatibilities in land use

3.1 CO-EXISTENCE WITH RECREATION

(a) Agriculture

When we read of the incidence of malnutrition in the world, the amount of land which is becoming agriculturally marginal in Western countries seems highly paradoxical but in the countries studied, examples can be found of land upon which agriculture is either in a very poor economic position or which has been 'retired' and where the farmer is paid a government subsidy not to grow anything. The hill farms of the British uplands, some of the dairy and pork producers of Jutland, smaller dairy farms on poorer soils in remoter parts of the Netherlands, and semi-arid farmlands in the US are all examples. In such situations, the land released may, if otherwise suitable, be very useful for recreation and so, indirectly, help to counteract any regional economic decline caused by the low returns from farming.[12] In such cases there need, ideally, be no conflict between farmer and recreationist but in reality the adoption of a new activity may be difficult for the affected areas. Particularly is this so for the marginal farmer whose proud independence is threatened by being a member of a service industry and whose education probably fits him badly for a new role as multiple-use manager and outdoor host. In addition, not all the areas released from agriculture may be physically suitable for recreation, nor may they be within the right access zones from major urban centres.

Nowhere is this more so than in the uplands of Britain. The farming here is based on free-range hill sheep and dairy cattle and is economically marginal, especially when the sheep are the mainstay. This is in spite of heavy government subsidies. Although these lands are poor grassland and moorland, there is often competition for their use from interests such as the military, water catchment, forestry, and preservation of landscape for amenity purposes. The farmers (who

[12] For Britain the whole complex of factors affecting land transfer out of agriculture and the possible other uses are discussed in A. M. Edwards and G. P. Wibberley, *An Agricultural Land Budget for Britain 1965–2000*, Wye College Studies in Rural Land Use Report 10 (1971).

are mostly family-farm tenants and owner-occupiers with strong local roots) feel harassed and the influx of recreation is frequently regarded with distinctly mixed feelings. There is the opportunity to make a little extra by providing 'B & B' or teas but on the other hand the congestion of road, trespass, the leaving open of gates, the deposition of litter which may be edible but fatal to stock, and the worrying of sheep by dogs unused to open conditions, all swing the feelings in the direction of hostility.

The recreational use consists mainly of unauthorized picnicking, informal use of fields near roads, and of passing through the enclosures on the way to open land (often moorland) above. Thus part of it may be susceptible to control by the provision of picnic and camp sites by, for example, the County Council under the aegis of the Countryside Act 1968. Other facets of use are less prone to this possible solution and more 'education for the outdoors' may be useful.

In the long run, it seems inevitable that farmers who in some way supply part of the recreation resources should receive a subsidy, just as they receive one for almost every other activity they undertake.

Conflict between agriculture and recreation is most likely to occur nearer the cities. It is commonest at two levels. The first of these is the public confrontation over resource allocation: people want recreation facilities near their homes, the farmers want to farm near cities because it is usually highly profitable and because they like urban amenities (or simply because they have always farmed in that particular place). So conflicts can arise, especially when a local government unit responds to citizen pressure by trying to purchase part of a farm for a camping or picnic site, for example. More sophisticated regional planning can usually avoid this by directing the recreation use to other types of land, for example, around worked-out gravel pits or to land awaiting development for housing or industry.

More serious is the personal conflict of farmer and urban recreationist in the context of damage to farm equipment and operations. Some of this is vandalism, some thoughtlessness or ignorance. Whatever the cause, in densely populated areas it is a significant barrier to the acceptance by the rural community of recreation as an inevitable and fitting use of the areas in which they live.[13]

[13] See the discussions in a British context by A. Phillips and M. Roberts, 'The recreation

239

To return to the world context of agriculture, we can view the movement of land from agriculture to recreation with at least one less misgiving than if it were moving into housing, factories or water reservoirs. Recreational use is unlikely to produce any irreversible ecological changes, and should the need arise the transfer back to farming could be accomplished without too great a cost.

(b) Nature conservation

In many considerations, both in the literature and at a decision-making level, the preservation and management of wildlife and recreation are often lumped together as if they shared the same concerns and purposes simply because they often occupied identical habitats. Sometimes their general aims, in terms of the preservation of diversity in the biosphere, may be the same but in specific cases there is likely to be a considerable variation (often to the point of conflict) in the management aims of the recreation-provider and the nature conserver. Very often the root cause is that the local ecosystem has a carrying capacity for humans which is easily exceeded. The limiting factors may be seasonal (for example, in the breeding season at a ternery which is also a good bathing place) or due to the fragility of the environment (as in high alpine environments easily accessible by vehicle or power lift),[14] or perpetual as in the case of fire risk on heaths and in forests (although mass recreation is less feared than activities involving solitary people).

Careful and sophisticated management (in which the Staatsbosbeheer of the Netherlands excels) may reduce conflicts but inevitably there comes a point in time or a particular place where the public has to be excluded. This causes indignation and vandalism and is not good for the public relations of the resource manager. The relations between these two uses of the outdoors need much more careful understanding than they get at present, and more mutual sympathy from the two publics involved, neither of which are keen to sacrifice any of their interest for the others' good.

In Britain, living organisms and their habitats are generally fragile and the Nature Conservancy (now part of the Natural Environment Research Council) exists to protect and manage both

---

and amenity value of the countryside', *J. Agric. Econ.* 24 (1973), pp. 85–102; M. Dower, 'Recreation, tourism and the farmer', *J. Agric. Econ.* 24 (1973), pp. 465–77.

[14] B. E. Willard and J. W. Marr, 'Effects of human activities on alpine tundra ecosystems in Rocky Mountains National Park, Colorado', *Biol. Cons.* 2 (1970), pp. 257–65.

rare and typical examples of British ecology. But many scientifically interesting ecosystems exist in a matrix of or themselves, form attractive recreational areas. Sand dunes are one example, the heathland valley bog complexes of Hampshire and Dorset another. The potential conflict between waterfowl observers (and shooters) and other water users has been alluded to above.

Management of National Nature Reserves has mostly followed prohibitive lines, except where the public could not be excluded as on rights of way. A more positive attitude, with careful zoning and management of access, is beginning to permeate the Conservancy and reserves with a heavy visitor pressure will undoubtedly need the zoning and interpretive services which SBB provide in the Netherlands. Many reserves are in wild places, where it would be impossible to station attendant staff and here reliance on static interpretive features and education is necessary. Or, in the case of small organisms, keeping very quiet about them.

One area where recreation pressure is causing considerable concern is in the Cairngorm Mountains of Scotland. The ski lifts function in summer and bring unprecedented numbers of people onto the alpine heaths of the summit plateau of these mountains. These heaths are very fragile systems and the trampling leads to denudation and hence probably to soil erosion. The problem is under investigation by the Nature Conservancy since the area forms part of the Cairngorms National Nature Reserve,[15] but no solutions have yet been found. Looking at, and being in, attractive and familiar landscapes is an important part of open-air enjoyment in Britain. Many voluntary bodies place great emphasis on the presentation of rural environments in an unchanged form and to them 'conservation' is equated with 'total preservation'. Recreational use is by no means always consonant with these attitudes for which some types of recreationist are 'environment-oriented' and, within limits, others worry less about the landscape character. Thus the great controversy about the afforestation of moorlands: the walkers, lookers and drivers who are environment-oriented have anathematized the Forestry Commission's changes but those who seek facilities such as car parks, toilets, and places to wander freely in, are unconscious of any deleterious effects of the forests: 48 per cent of first-time visitors to Allerston

---

[15] N. Bayfield, 'Some effects of walking and skiing on vegetation at Cairngorm', in E. Duffey and A. S. Watt (eds.), *The Scientific Management of Animal and Plant Communities for Conservation* (Oxford 1971), pp. 469–84.

241

Forest in Yorkshire (and 81 per cent at Loch Lomond) thought that conifers were more attractive than hardwoods and only 19 per cent (15 per cent at Loch Lomond) held the opposite view.[16] They were not asked about the suitability of the forest *versus* open moorland, however.

Concern with change in rural landscape, especially the upland areas which are such an important recreation resource, runs deep amongst the articulate sector of the population and it is probably the rapidity of contemporary change which provokes the most reaction.[17] Recreation planners, therefore, will need to tread softly if they are not to arouse hostility from a section of the public which, even if not large, has powerful lungs and sharpened pens.

(c) Military land and water use

In Europe, the natural habitat of the soldier seems to be heathland, which is also a valued recreation resource. So are other areas which are in use as military training areas, such as the Dorset coast and part of Dartmoor National Park in Britain. Here there are no conservation plans, as with the US bases which aim at a multiple use management, but a determination to keep the public out and to relinquish none of the areas. Nevertheless a government committee recommended in 1973 that the armed services should relinquish 31,000 acres (12,555 ha) out of the 757,000 acres (306,585 ha) that they control, and the Ministry of Defence decided to abandon 22,500 acres (9112 ha), rejecting the key recommendation concerning 7,000 acres (2835 ha) of the Dorset coast and countryside, although some of the land use for military training within the Dartmoor National Park is to be released.

Apart from training areas, some installations need large tracts of land in rural areas. DEW facilities and the BMEWS stations are examples of these: one of the BMEWS installations is in an English National Park.

Whatever the realities about the security brought by infantrymen and 15-minute warnings, one socio-political fact cannot be ignored. The segment of public opinion, especially in the US, which is most concerned about man-environment relations (and thus which engages in rural recreation to a considerable extent) is also the most

---

[16] W. E. S. Mutch, *op. cit.*, p. 88. (See footnote 26, p. 102.)

[17] I. G. Simmons, 'Britannia deserta', *Landscape* 15 (1966), pp. 27–9; *idem*, 'How do we plan for change?' *Landscape* 17 (1968), pp. 16–18.

anti-military. The taking of more land for military uses is likely to meet very strong opposition and the military authorities will probably experience strong pressure for withdrawal from their present holdings. In an alliance like NATO, where training grounds can be considered on a supra-national basis this need presumably causes no trouble, although some habitats might eventually disappear from the military map. However, neither a large-scale conventional war against the Warsaw Pact nor urban political revolt are likely to be fought out amidst tussocks of heather and the shelter of thickets of regenerating birch.

(d) Multiple use

This term is widely used in land management where recreation is concerned. It seems to offer a millennial position, whereby recreation can be 'fitted in' to other uses and so the cake can both be seen and eaten. In short, it has become something of a 'hurrah-word', rather than a useful resource management concept. This is exemplified by ORRRC's Report 17 (*Multiple Use of Land and Water Areas*), which nowhere arrives at any simple and satisfactory definition of the term.

Basically it can mean, in operational terms, either two or more uses of one piece of land, or the close integration of a mosaic of land uses. Thus the National Forests of the US are managed for several uses, sometimes by multi-use of one unit of land (for example, for timber, grazing, wildlife and water), and sometimes by a single-use unit in close juxtaposition with a different use (for example, a forest campground). The success of multiple use depends on the compatibilities of the different uses, both in ecological and economic terms. The paragraphs above show that in many cases, compatibility is either not very high or at any rate, is thought not to be very high.

The outstanding example in most countries of successful multiple use is forestry. Barring fire and vandal damage, most productive forests appear to be able to withstand a considerable amount of recreation pressure, with the added advantage that their screening effect increases the carrying capacity. Thus second homes, fishing, hunting and observation of wildlife, driving and walking for pleasure and winter sports can all be carried on with very little detriment to timber production, provided skilful management is practised. Where markets are declining for domestic timber, as in the Netherlands, recreation can become a primary aim of the forest but even short of

243

this, it seems a good policy for industrial countries to keep and add to their forest areas whenever possible.

Provided that modern methods of water treatment are used, little recreational use of water is inimical to its use for human consumption. This view is widely held in North America and continental Europe and is at last coming to Britain, where formerly reservoirs were guarded with the sort of intensity normally reserved for CBW research establishments. This applies to both bankside and water surface uses and the major future difficulty is the sub-set of different uses of water bodies, for birds, bathing, boats and bream-fishing are not very compatible. In cool temperate zones, there may be temporal separation, but if not, then sophisticated management is required. A useful solution (as practised in the Netherlands and, for example, on the Derwent Reservoir in the UK) is to have a management committee (preferably executive, but advisory is better than nothing) representing all the different interests. Only rarely then will conflicts remain unresolved.

One factor often inimical to multiple use is lack of co-ordination. Even where land is publicly owned, one management agency may compete with, or act in ignorance of, another. Where government advice is tendered to individuals, different advice may come from different sources. Regional planning may often conflict with farm-by-farm advisory services, for example. No easy solutions can be offered here, but it needs to be clear that lack of co-ordination of the elements of multiple use, where these are not under one management, swiftly negates the potential benefits.

3.2 THE VULNERABILITY OF SPECIAL PLACES

The above discussion has highlighted one particular difficulty. Some places are so outstanding, either on a local, national or even international scale, that they attract myriads of people. Once there, the visitors create two categories of effects. The first is direct and consists of the physical alterations wrought by human feet together with such other phenomena as vandalism, litter and perhaps fire. The second is indirect and comprises the facilities needed to cater to both the metabolism and the cultural whims of the visitor. Increasingly, resource managers are deciding that such places have a limited carrying capacity for people and are beginning to restrict the number of visitors.

Such a course of action is of necessity unpopular but it is interesting to note that there is a vocal segment of public opinion which finds this acceptable. An experimental plan to restrict cars from the Langdale Valley in the English Lake District NP, for example, was obstructed not by visitors but by the residents and catering trade of the valley itself.

It seems a general trend which will become ever more apparent in the next decade, that identification of the vulnerable places, be they scenic, cultural or biotic, is going to occur and that as their true value is realized, most civilized nations will not stop at some form of rationing of visitor numbers in order to ensure the unimpaired perpetuation of the resource.

3.3 CARRYING CAPACITY

Many examples given so far bring out the idea that there is a limit to the number of people who can use a recreation area, either at one particular time or over a period. The concept is usually summarized as the carrying capacity of an area, by analogy with the carrying capacity of an ecosystem for a particular species. Much work has been carried out, of which only a brief summary is given here.[18]

For particular sites, the idea appears to be resolved into two distinct parts. The first is the ecological capacity: the maximum pressure that an area can tolerate without degradation. This is often relatively easily measurable, though only long-term studies can show how quickly some types of vegetation can recover from visitors' foot-pressure. The second part is more difficult and takes into account the attitudes of the recreationists themselves, and leads to definitions like 'the capability of the environment to cater for maximum aggregate user satisfaction while taking into account the views of people already there'. Thus the definition is opened up to the exercise of value systems, with all the possibilities for class conflict, change

---

[18] The literature is large and scattered. Useful beginnings, mostly with bibliographies, are: N. G. Bayfield, 'A review of problems and progress in site management research', *Recreation News Supplement* 9 (1973), pp. 3–5; D. I. Brotherton, 'The concept of carrying capacity of countryside recreation areas', *Recreation News Supplement* 9 (1973), pp. 6–11; J. P. Barkham, 'Recreational carrying capacity: a problem of perception', *Area* 5 (1973), pp. 218–22; T. W. Sudia, 'Recreational carrying capacity of the National Parks', *Guideline* 3(3) (1973), pp. 25–34; D. W. Line and G. H. Stankey, 'Carrying capacity: maintaining outdoor recreation quality', in Northeastern Forest Experiment Station, *Recreation Symposium Proceedings* (Washington, DC 1972), pp. 174–84. A quasi-quantitative method for evaluating recreation capacity in East Europe is given by A. S. Kostrowicki, 'Application of geobotanical methods in appraising fitness of regions for purposes of recreation and rest', *Przeglad Geograficzny* 42 (1970), pp. 644–5 (English summary).

through time and plain ignorance. Measurement of these variables is very difficult and can only be meaningful if undertaken over a long period in order to see if values change in regard to a particular place as management and development of the site proceed. Expense is therefore a consideration. The economic aspects of the capacity idea may be very important at the managerial level, for most of the general ideas mentioned above must resolve themselves into money for the site manager. Thus an optimal carrying capacity will not cause deterioration of a development faster than it can be maintained at a given level of economic resources, i.e., cash input.

At a larger scale, the use of land capability concepts to determine the potential of a region for recreation has been initiated, as in the land classification system and maps produced in Canada by ARDA. A more sophisticated analysis which takes into account the demand for particular recreation activities, both private and public, has been developed for a part of northern England by D. C. Statham.[19] Even here, however, only a rough guide can be produced, not a plan or policy, although criteria for land use policy changes do emerge.

If any general conclusion emerges from these studies, it is that rural recreation resources, like other resources, are finite, and that they are subject to over-use and subsequent degradation. Thus (like the vulnerable places of the previous section) in the long term they can only be perpetuated by limiting the numbers of people who use them.

4 National Parks: a special case

4.1 THE NATIONAL PARK CONCEPT

(a) Purposes of the parks

The resource-management policies of many developed nations include among their different types of protected ecosystems areas of land and water designated as National Parks. The denomination of such Parks arises from the desire to set aside particular areas of terrain from production in the conventional economic sense and to designate these as protected areas. Conservation of wild life, of individual plant and animal species, or more commonly of assemblages of species, of habitats and groups of habitats, are often a major reason for the setting up and subsequent management of a National

[19] D. C. Statham, 'Capability analysis for recreation in the North York Moors', *Recreation News Supplement* 7 (1972), pp. 23–7.

246

Park. The needs of education and research are another function of such areas since unaltered or little manipulated ecosystems provide datum lines in which the structure and function of pristine ecosystems provide a reference point for man. There is also the Parks' capacity as wilderness areas used for back-country recreation, usually on foot or with the help of horses or mules, together with the symbolic, cultural and ecological values of terrain which is virtually unaltered by human activity.

The preservation of entire landscapes which are particularly valued is another concern of National Park management. Such landscapes are frequently natural but they may also be cultural, in which case there are generally some productive uses. The last major use is that of rural recreation, where the park is the setting for informal activities in a rural setting, the most popular of which are driving, walking, swimming, and cycling.

Of the various goals for management, rural recreation presents the developed countries with the strongest and most easily quantifiable social demand of all the possible management aims for National Parks. Rural recreation is the most akin to production in the conventional economic sense; the more so because of all the alternatives it is the most easily priceable. Because of their outstanding qualities of interest and beauty, National Parks are special magnets for recreationists and the number of visitors to them has been doubling every 6–7 years since the 1950s. There is thus considerable scope for conflict between recreation and the other, protective, roles of National Parks, even leaving aside the demands for productive uses in some of them.

(b) Criteria for selection[20]

A feature common to the selection of National Parks in most countries is that it is undertaken by the national government of the state

[20] The criteria laid out by Steven Mather for the USA are found in J. Ise, *Our National Park Policy* (Baltimore 1961), and the more recent versions in NPS, *Criteria for Selection of National Parklands and National Landmarks* (Washington, DC 1971), p. 11; for Canada, see National and Historic Parks Branch, Dept of Indian Affairs and Northern Development (n.d. but is from late 1960s), *National Parks Policy*; a concise version in English of Japanese policies is in National Parks Association of Japan, *National Parks of Japan* (Tokyo 1966); for England and Wales see J. Dower, *National Parks in England and Wales*, Cmnd 6628 (London, HMSO 1945), and also H. C. Darby, 'British National Parks', *Advmt Sci.* 20 (1963), pp. 307–18, and W. A. Johnson, *Public Parks on Private Land in England and Wales* (Baltimore 1971); the international viewpoint can be found in IUCN, *UN List of National Parks and Equivalent Reserves* (Brussels 1971). J. G. Nelson and R. C. Scace (eds.), *op. cit.* (see footnote 73, p. 135) contains a historical summary by

concerned. The criteria used, however, are not necessarily constant through time: at some periods the demands for recreation may be paramount, at others the desire for the protection of landscapes and ecosystems may be the dominating feature.

In the USA, for instance, one of the founding fathers of the National Parks system, Steven Mather, intimated that the parks should contain scenery of a supreme and distinctive quality with some natural features so extraordinary or unique as to be of national interest or importance, and further that the system should not be lowered in standard, dignity or prestige by the inclusion of areas which expressed in less than the highest terms the particular class or kind of exhibit which they represent. These criteria are little changed today except in language.

Likewise in Canada the overall purpose of the system has been stated to be to preserve the Canadian heritage: this somewhat indefinable concept is amplified by criteria which develop the notion that a National Park must be an outstanding example of the best scenery in the nation or must possess unique scenic, geographical or geological features of national interest or have outstanding examples of fauna or flora, again of national interest, or must provide outstanding opportunities for non-urban forms of rural recreation in superb surroundings. The parks must be large enough to support indigenous flora and fauna and it is desirable that part of the park is suitable for recreational purposes and for the provision of the services which those demands create.

In England and Wales there is no public domain but this did not prevent John Dower, in his Report which was largely the foundation of the 1949 National Parks and Access to the Countryside Act, from defining National Parks as extensive areas of relatively wild country in which the characteristic landscape beauty is strictly preserved, in which access and facilities for enjoyment are amply provided, and in which wildlife, buildings and places of historic interest are preserved. He also maintained, and this principle has been enshrined in legislation and management, that farming, rural industries and afforestation should continue to function.

The theme of the inclusion of cultural phenomena, particularly

---

J.-P. Harroy, 'The development of the national park movement', pp. 17–34; see also J.-P. Harroy, 'A century in the growth of the "National Park" concept throughout the world', *Background papers of the Second World Conference on National Parks* (1972), and comments on IUCN criteria by I. G. Simmons in Nelson and Scace, *op. cit.*, pp. 738–41.

ancient buildings, in National Parks is also carried through in the National Parks of Japan. Here, a long tradition of the harmony of man and nature (not now evident in many parts of those densely populated islands) is expressed in the criteria for selection of National Parks in which areas distinguished by superlative scenic beauty are accompanied by cultural relics that blend with nature.

Together with examples from other countries, these examples of national policies have been incorporated by IUCN into criteria which must be satisfied if the area is to be included in the UN List of National Parks and Equivalent Reserves. Most importantly, it must have protected status in which the legislative machinery exists to preserve the park from resource development, although where only a part of a park is under strict protection as with Daisetsuzan National Park in Hokkaido (Japan), it may still qualify for inclusion in the list. Secondly, there must be 'minimum superficies'. This does not preclude from the list Parks which are subject to manipulation and management policies but such areas of terrain as have permanent inhabitants and on-going programmes of resource development are therefore excluded from the IUCN definition. The National Parks of England and Wales, therefore, are not included although some of the National Nature Reserves of the UK qualify on the grounds of their supposedly natural status. Thirdly, there must be effective enforcement of status, and conditions are laid down for wardening, expenditure, and boundary establishment, all of which must be seen to be enforced.

(c) Management for protection
The critical first phase in the history of a National Park is protection from economic development and this is enshrined in many legislative acts, whether it be complete protection from all forms of activity such as grazing, mining, building of roads and the development of water storage facilities, or partial protection involving the acknowledgement of the compatibility of some production provided that its ecological and aesthetic effects are consciously minimized. In areas where National Parks have been created upon terrain formerly used for economic yields, particularly timber extraction, it has not always been possible to persuade the agency concerned with lumbering to cease their more obvious practices, such as clear-felling; thus in Japanese parks such as Nikko National Park and the Shikotsu-Toya

249

National Park in Hokkaido, clear-felling has been a cause of some contention between the Forest Agency and the National Park Agency. Similarly in the Krkonose National Park in the northern Bohemia region of Czechoslovakia, clear-felling has been permitted after the designation of the area as a National Park and is a source of conflict in management policies. In the National Parks of England and Wales, most economic activities, including wholesale landscape change by agricultural reclamation of moorland, or afforestation, are permitted. This is partly because the legislation exempts agriculture and forestry from the development controls which are a major feature of the 1949 Act, and partly because it was always intended that the ordinary everyday activities included in the National Park should continue. Activities such as the building of roads, and the extraction of minerals have all continued, subject only to cosmetic landscaping by virtue of their effects upon the landscape.

A second phase is the protection of ecosystems and landscapes within areas of National Park status. There exists here the dichotomy of management technique which may be expressed as *laissez-faire* versus manipulation. *Laissez-faire* management is rarely successful because the boundaries of the natural ecosystems do not usually coincide with the legal limits of the Park; therefore if the managers desire to protect either rare or typical biota it is unusual to find that they are components of an ecosystem confined to the protected area. The simplest example is of an insect which is a part of the natural ecosystem within the Park but which becomes a pest in ecosystems manipulated for economic yield outside the Park area. Examples are to be found in the Gypsy Moth and the Spruce Budworm in the coniferous forests of the western cordillera of the USA. The problem for the Park manager is then whether he should continue to manage for a pristine set of ecosystems or whether he is to be accused of providing the source area for pests that damage the economic resources of peripheral forests. Again, the role of fire in natural ecosystems has been little understood, and efficient, indeed ruthless, fire suppression has been a feature of park management. In the case of the Sierra redwood (*Sequoiadendron giganteum*), suppression of fire has led to the shading out of the seedlings of this rare species by other coniferous forest taxa and hence a lack of regeneration. The discovery that light burning was a normal feature of the forest ecosystem has led to the introduction of prescribed burning as a management technique in such places as King's Canyon—Sequoia National

Park and Yosemite National Park in California, and regenerative levels have been improved.

A third phase is the restoration of ecosystems and landscapes which were disturbed by economic use prior to emparkment. This process is obviously not much employed in cultural landscapes, but in the National Parks of England and Wales, the enhancement of landscapes by the removal of eyesores such as military installations and relics of former periods of industrial activity is provided for, and indeed encouraged by the financial structure of the legislation. Elsewhere there have been attempts to reconstruct a natural environment in which certain elements of the biota which had been eliminated either deliberately or accidentally by management for economic gain are restored. We may quote the examples of woodland management in the High Tatras National Park of Slovakia, designed to restore the multiple-dominance mixed forest of the middle and lower slopes of the mountain which had been regulated as a virtually single-species unit, and the re-introduction of animals which had either been hunted out or had been victims of habitat change. The re-introduction of the wolf in parts of Europe is an example of this as is the re-introduction in 1968 of the caribou into Cape Breton Island National Park in Nova Scotia.

There are two reasons for these planned reversions. There is firstly the need for increasing scientific knowledge of ecosystems both of the present and the past, and this is allied to a desire for a better understanding of the principles of ecosystem management which might enable the re-introduction of species, and secondly there is increasing public concern in the developed countries that ecosystems and landscapes should be maintained in a wild condition and with high biotic diversity. The sentimental, total-preservationist attitudes of the past are also giving way to an increasing willingness to accept management as a feature of National Parks.

(d) Management for development

Of the several kinds of development which can take place within National Parks, recreation is generally held to be compatible with protection. The role of recreation is usually enshrined in most acquisition and management legislation and regulations and is often accorded equal status with protection. It is held to be ethically right in the sense that it is no use having National Parks if people cannot enjoy them: the apotheosis of this idea was probably in the slogan

251

used in the USA in the 1950s and 1960s: 'Parks are for people.'

An early phase of tourist-oriented development existed in some places before the Parks attained the full flowering of their present conceptual basis. There are instances of development of resorts, particularly at hot-spring areas in the Rocky Mountains of Canada, and in many parts of Japan where luxury resorts, along with roads, railways, hotels and golf courses, eventually became an integral part of large National Parks.

The major phase of development has been under the impetus of the demand for rural recreation facilities in the industrial countries in the post-1945 era. Because of the generally wild areas in which National Parks are situated, statistics of visitor numbers are often of doubtful validity except as general guides. On this basis we may note that in 1971 Shenandoah National Park in Virginia, USA, recorded 2·4 million visits, Yosemite National Park (California) 2·4 million, and Yellowstone National Park (Wyo-Mont-Idaho) 2·1 million. The total National Park system of the USA, (which includes National Monuments, National Recreation Areas, and some historic sites) received c. 200 million visits in 1971. In Britain the increase in visitors to National Trust properties in the decade 1952–62 was estimated at 50 per cent, and overnight visitors to National Forest Parks increased 130 per cent (no statistics are collected for the National Parks). The annual average increase in the developed countries has been in excess of 10 per cent, rising to approximately 15 per cent in Japan, thus testifying to the popular appeal of the attractions that the Parks have to offer.[21]

The demand thus exhibited has made itself felt in the landscapes of the Parks in many ways. Since one of the triggers of the rural recreation explosion is the possession of the private automobile, then the provision of roads, gas stations and all the infrastructure associated with road transport, on a vastly greater scale than hitherto, has been the most noticeable effect. Park managers have been led to construct roads into formerly wild areas of the parks in order to spread the existing load and thus of course have created even greater demand for the future. Following the existence of the visitors has been the creation of numerous facilities for their accommodation and

[21] The statistics for the USA are from NPS, *Public Use of the National Parks, December 1971* (Washington, DC 1971); for Britain, from J. Wager, 'Known demands for outdoor recreation', *The Countryside in 1970*, 2nd conference, Royal Society of Arts (London), Paper 6; for Japan, T. Senge, in J. G. Nelson and R. C. Scace (eds.), *op. cit.*, pp. 706–21.

comfort. Urban-type developments create urban problems of the disposal of solid wastes and sewage, and the contamination of air (Yosemite Valley may have a smog problem in summer); campsites in forests permit no regeneration of trees and on grass are quickly reduced to a quagmire in wet conditions.

In some National Parks, therefore, whole townships have been established. At Banff and Jasper, (Alta, Canada), for example, the permanent populations are above 3000 people, not unexpectedly creating demands for facilities of an altogether urban kind for these long-term residents.

All these developments have been thought to have followed the right course of events for National Parks, either because the existing facilities were crumbling under the strain of increased demand or because it was thought good to enhance the use of the National Parks by the public: even in 1971 the Canadian government was mounting holiday travel campaigns based on National Parks as if they were commercial resorts. In the last few years there have been distinct signs of a retreat from this maximum phase of development. Public opinion expressed through vocal citizen groups is swinging in favour of wildness and the holding down of development.[22]

(e) Retreat from development

In the National Parks of industrial countries, protection and development appear as divergent trends in spite of attempts to combine them by the use of zoning. In this section the management of some National Park systems will be examined in the light of their dominant trends since inception.

In the USA development of the Parks in the pre-1940 years was confined to a few roads and trails, together with accommodation facilities of varying degrees of splendour, from permanent canvas camps through to wooden cabins to luxury hotels like the Ahwahnee in Yosemite Valley. The justification for such developments was that the 1916 Act made enjoyment of the parks a legal purpose of their management and that at that time they were in rather inaccessible

[22] For a general sequential model, see M. Clawson, 'Park visitation in the coming decades: problems and opportunities', *Background papers of the Second World Conference on National Parks* (1972); see esp. pp. 4–7. A somewhat similar approach is taken in I. G. Simmons, 'National Parks in developed countries', in A. Warren and F. B. Goldsmith (eds), *Conservation in Practice* (London 1974), pp. 393–407.

places. Fraser Darling and Eichorn contend[23] that the years 1935–40 were probably the peak of achievement and enjoyment of the National Parks: visitors could gain the experience of National Parks that had been the goal of the founders of the movement, and there was much less pressure than at present from other visitors and cars. The post-1945 boom brought pressure to bear on facilities, including roads, of an altogether new dimension and the response of the parks service was a 10 year (1956–66) programme entitled 'Mission 66' to open up more of the parks and enlarge visitor facilities. This movement was mainly for people rather than parks because more development led almost immediately to increased numbers of recreationists.

The retreat from development was catalysed by the Leopold Report[24] (see p. 184) in which the Parks policy to date was said to have been too heavily weighted in favour of visitors rather than the Park resource, and which proposed a management goal to preserve these 'vignettes of primitive America'. In a remarkable redirection of aims, the service adopted a new classification for their entire system in which the major part of the National Parks is classified as a natural area and management plans formulated on an ecosystem basis. De-development is being undertaken, so that for example private cars are being excluded from Yosemite Valley, being replaced with shuttle minibuses, (used for 60,000 rides on a day in 1972 when 20,000 people visited Yosemite Valley[25]) to be followed by the removal of built structures to a service area outside the gates. Eventually even camping will be outside the Park itself. At Yellowstone, it is planned to reduce the developed zone from 5 per cent to 2 per cent of the park area, and restrictions on various kinds of vehicles are planned on existing roads at Mesa Verde, Glacier and Grand Canyon National Parks. The master plans for each park are now becoming public documents and under pressure of vocal public opinion, more wilderness proposals under the authority of the National Wilderness Preservation Act of 1964 are being submitted to

[23] F. Fraser Darling and N. Eichorn, *Man and Nature in the National Parks: Reflections on Policy* (Washington, DC 1967).

[24] A. S. Leopold, *Wildlife Management in National Parks* (Washington, DC, US Dept of the Interior Advisory Board on Wildlife Management 1963), reprinted as *Study of Wildlife Problem in National Parks, Trans 28th North American Wildlife Conference* (1963), pp. 28–45. See also N. P. Reed, 'How well has the United States managed its National Park system? The application of ecological principles to park management', *Background papers of the Second World Conference on National Parks* (1972).

[25] R. Cahn, 'Touring the undersea parks around the world', *Christian Science Monitor* (30 September 1972), quotes these statistics.

the Congress. These events chronicle a strong retrocession of development which currently makes the US National Parks probably the most protected in the world; undoubtedly the most important factor in the changes of policy has been the shift in public opinion due to increased awareness of environmental matters.

The development of Canadian National Parks has taken place under the same pressures as those of the USA, mitigated only by the smaller population of Canada, although the 'overflow' from the US National Parks finds Canada especially appealing. Commercial development was encouraged in the parks to attract tourists into areas otherwise economically marginal and some Canadian National Parks function also as regional parks for nearby cities. Development pressures are still high, as shown by the proposal to alter the visitor facilities at Lake Louise in Banff National Park by removing the old hotel development (a relic of the grand days of railroad travel) and replacing it on a different site with a multi-purpose resort area to be known as Village Lake Louise, to cost $30 million, and 50 per cent owned by Imperial Oil Ltd. This proposal was strongly opposed by organizations like the National and Provincial Parks Association of Canada which spearhead the anti-development movement for National Parks and was rejected by the minister in July 1972.

The decision to formulate Park master plans and then to submit them for approval by public hearings has produced a movement strongly in favour of protection rather than increased development. Such development as is undertaken will be confined to clearly defined zones in the parts where they will not offend, aesthetically or visually, the scenic and ecological values of the region.

In Japan the visitor pressure which brings about considerable development is inexorable since large numbers of Japanese visit the cultural features of many parks (such as the Kasuga shrines at Nikko) as well as those who venture away from the roads. Parks such as Nikko and Fuji-Hakone-Izu are very close to Tokyo and Shikotsu-Toya is close to a large proportion of the population of Hokkaido. The ubiquity of cheap public transport in Japan means that most of the National Parks are within weekend range of most of the population (excepting only Hokkaido, but those that can afford to fly can be there in $1\frac{1}{2}$ hours from Tokyo), and those near central Honshu are available for day-use by 60 million people. The result is an immense urbanization of the settlements and routeways of the parks. Winter-use of the parks is also gaining strength as skiing gains hold on a population whose disposable incomes are rising rapidly.

A major trend towards protection is the commencement in 1971 of a funded programme to buy up private holdings in National Parks, especially where these are in critical areas. Its progress depends simply upon the amount of money the Diet will provide. A straw in the wind is possibly provided by the insistence of the Environment Agency that one of the chairlifts built in a Specially Protected Area of the Shikotsu-Toya National Park for the 1972 Winter Olympics must be removed now that the games are finished.

Ten National Parks totalling about 9 per cent of the surface of the two countries, were established in England and Wales following the 1949 National Parks and Access to the Countryside Act and have experienced relatively little development for public enjoyment. On the other hand the Act provided strong measures of development control and the authorities have given priority to their implementation. Finance for development has also been in short supply since such uses of money are the first to be culled in every financial crisis, of which there has been no shortage since 1949. However, several long distance footpaths, of which the Pennine Way is the best known, have been established and numerous lay-bys and picnic sites constructed. Most noticeable are the car parks designed to relieve pressure on narrow roads or in small villages such as Hawkshead in the Lake District National Park.

The development control measures have been quite firmly applied and have aroused considerable opposition from local residents since they restrict, *inter alia*, the building of new houses and the conversion of old structures, and regulate the spread of caravan sites. Nevertheless they generally enjoy public support since they are also applied to potential eyesores and sources of land dereliction. On the positive side, the Countryside Commission has carried out experiments in traffic control, such as the exclusion of cars from the Goyt Valley in the Peak District National Park. There is as yet no formal zoning of National Parks but since the Town and Country Planning Act 1968 requires local authorities to produce structural (broad-scale) and local (more detailed) plans for their areas, then it is conceivable that zoning could be applied under the aegis of a local plan. These plans will be public documents.

England and Wales differ from the other examples, therefore, in having the balance of their trends on the side of protection: whether

256

more development is to come or whether the prevailing trend will even increase their degree of protection is not yet foreseeable. Much depends upon whether the government accepts the recommendations of the Sandford Committee (pp. 110–11).

4.2 IMPORTANCE OF THE NATIONAL PARKS

Possibly the most important role of these wild areas in developed lands is their symbolic value, providing a sense of 'otherness' or 'of the wild beyond' where man has not yet been a force; or in Luten's terms[26] 'wilderness as helmsman', functioning as an inertial reference point of a cybernetic nature for man's activities. Curry-Lindahl[27] is even more emphatic: 'they will have . . . a role of paramount importance, namely to serve as ecological sample areas for our guidance in managing the world's renewable natural resources'. Such a capacity is hard to define, measure and price but finds its way to the surface in the political espousability of National Parks which generally transcend party loyalties: the setting up of a system is a useful piece of publicity which enables a government to say that it is keenly concerned about the environment.

In the developed countries wildlife is valued *per se* and National Parks inevitably form one of the larger reservoirs for biota, especially large mammals. The Parks are thus outdoor biological gardens where the bird, beast or flower may be observed and recorded in either its natural habitat or a little-altered version of it. Populations can also be trimmed of surplus members to re-introduce them to areas from which they have disappeared.

Wild areas are important too as preservers of pools of genetic diversity. As plant breeding tends towards greater genetic uniformity of crop plants, the necessity of preserving reservoirs of potential genetic diversity becomes greater.

Rural recreation is, without doubt, the most important current social role of National Parks. The difficulties which it can cause in management goals and programmes have been discussed and it is now becoming clear that de-emphasis of the recreational use of the National Parks is coming about and other resources are being developed to take some of the strain off National Parks in this regard.

[26] D. B. Luten, 'Resource quality and the value of the landscape', in S. Ciriacy-Wantrup and J. J. Parsons (eds.), *Natural Resources: Quantity and Quality* (Berkeley and Los Angeles 1967), pp. 19–34.

[27] K. Curry-Lindahl, 'Projecting the future in the worldwide National Parks movement', *Background papers of the Second World Conference on National Parks* (1972).

We may quote the Country Parks of England and Wales, National Recreational Areas, State and Regional Park systems in the USA, some Provincial Parks in Canada and Prefectural Parks in Japan, as examples of resource development with rural recreation as a primary aim.[28] Nevertheless the increase of recreational demand, together with even slow increases in population (which mean high absolute numbers in nations like England, Japan and the USA), coupled with the high values put upon their qualities, mean that pressure upon National Parks for recreation will continue for the foreseeable future and that the general movement in favour of protection which emerges from the above discussion will need to be sustained by continued strong public opinion if it is to be maintained; unless alternative recreation areas are developed, those who are at present less vocal will probably start to press for a reversal of the trend.

4.3 THE ROLE OF PUBLIC OPINION IN FORMULATING POLICIES FOR PROTECTED LANDSCAPES

It is interesting to note that the master plans for parks in the USA and Canada are public documents, open to hearings at which criticisms may be made, and that if National Parks become the subjects of local plans in England and Wales, then roughly the same procedure will apply. The outcome of most public participation exercises so far seems to have been a strong movement towards protection at the expense of development, a not unexpected trend in view of current environmental awareness. The same themes are evident in hearings conducted before the establishment of National Parks[29] in the USA: those who want the park, want it as wild as possible. The question which comes most strongly to mind is whether the vocal and the articulate who obviously play such a large role in the formulation of policies arrived at publicly are representative of all the users. Are they not in fact an elite group whose tastes and acceptabilities are very different from those of most park users? Should their views prevail in the absence of others or simply because they are the best

[28] Other general categories of alternative are given by J. L. Fisher, 'Population and economic pressures on National Parks', *Background papers of the Second World Conference on National Parks* (1972).

[29] See for example the hearings on the then proposed Redwoods National Park, conducted in Crescent City, California in 1968. S. Crowe, 'The master plan for National Parks and their regional setting', *Background papers of the Second World Conference on National Parks* (1972) does not mention public participation in Park planning at all. A fairly typical British perspective.

informed about the alternatives, or ought there to be a positive effort on the part of the authorities to seek the views of those who would not normally come forward?[30] There are no absolute answers to such questions, for they operate in particular social and political contexts, but they serve to remind us that although squeaky wheels get the most grease, the bed of the cart is an important component of the whole.

5 Problems of prognostication

5.1 GAPS IN KNOWLEDGE

The recent nature of the rural recreation phenomenon and the ad hoc nature of much of the managerial response to it has meant that many areas of information needed for planning have had to be neglected until the last few years. Identification of problems for research have now emerged with greater clarity, even if the answers are as muddily complex as they always were. The first area of needed facts centres around demand which is an extremely intricate social and economic issue and even in very sophisticated studies can only be tackled on the basis of assumptions about other social trends. The interaction of all the factors discussed in Part 1, may continue to produce a linear increase in recreation demands, or the whole scene may at some threshold move to an entirely different order of pressure. Demand and supply are often inextricably linked, especially in Europe: the opening of a new recreation area will bring in many people who had never thought to express an interest when they filled in their latest questionnaire.

Even though state of knowledge about rural recreation is probably greater in the USA than anywhere else, there are still many gaps which are thought to impair the introduction of a much improved system. Not only is there insufficient cash (a problem which is shared by most other countries) but a lack of understanding of how best it can be applied: is the present grants/loan structure the best, or should for example much more money go directly to cities to establish their own recreation area systems: is the best policy for urban-fringe areas for the Federal government itself to get involved, as appears to be happening,[31] and is apparently to come about in

[30] See I. G. Simmons, 'How do we plan for change?', pp. 16–18; and 'The evolution of a landscape', in I. G. Simmons (ed.), *The Yorkshire Dales* (London 1971).

[31] Memorandum from Secretary Walter J. Hickel to Director George B. Harzog, Jr (18 June 1969).

Canada since the announcement of a Federal park for Toronto's waterfront. The responsiveness to demand of the countryside system is, as said above, partially dependent on an active private sector but here there is a deficiency of knowledge about what makes an enterprise profitable: there is not very much accumulated know-how about this type of enterprise compared with, for example, gasoline stations or movie houses. Again, there is a serious lack of reliable projections of demand. In spite of the sophistication of the ORRRC projections,[32] a few years proved them to be inadequate. Is it in fact possible to make adequate forecasts of the numbers of people who will want to sail boats or hunt quail in 1993? How far are such predictions likely to be self-fulfilling[33] and how deep is the desire for rural recreation as a leisure activity? Is much of it a current fad which will exhaust itself when people turn to other forms of time-consuming endeavours? Similarly it is not known at what thresholds the poor will begin to participate more actively: since they tend to form distinctive sub-cultural groups, will this mean that outdoor activities are unlikely to be part of their life-style as it is for the WASP? At the other extreme where does satiety set in for the rich: after the second boat and the third trail buggy, or well before those points? And overriding these concerns in the minds of resource manager and financial officials alike, is the realization that the benefits of recreation are unclear (except in the very narrow sense of profit to those engaged in service activities which encompass recreation) and thus little objective basis for decision in the allocation of material and financial resources exists.

In most countries there is often a lack of understanding between the administrator and participant about the use of the park or other resource. The flood of new-comers has meant a lot of people ignorant of or unwilling to observe the conventions of the use of the outdoors, together with some administrators unsure of the purpose for which they were managing the area. Even the expensive and often very thorough interpretive programmes have sometimes failed to cope with this and perhaps there is, basically, no answer except the course of time, although increased environmental education in schools might help greatly.

Another imponderable is the possibility of changes in life-style.

[32] ORRRC Report 23, *Projections to the Years 1976 and 2000: Economic Growth, Population, Labor Force and Leisure, Transportation* (Washington, DC 1962).
[33] D. B. Luten, 'Parks and people', *Landscape* 12 (1962–3), p. 4.

The whole of the discussion so far has accepted the division between work and leisure which is implicit in the so-called 'protestant work ethic'. Whether this ethic will endure is perhaps questionable although confident predictions are likely to be unreal. But these are straws in the wind, such as the refusal of some middle-rank white-collar workers to accept promotion either because they do not think that the extra income is worth the sacrifice of their leisure time, or an extra ulcer; also the problem of fewer jobs because of cybernetic developments which force people to accept a welfare income provided by the state, a trend which could no doubt be accelerated if the labour unions were willing. After all, if work is not necessary to produce wealth, merely to distribute it in the service industries, why should anybody give his soul to the assembly line? This trend is carried to a fair extreme in Reich's[34] Consciousness III stage, where a turning away from material acquisition forces a re-evaluation of what is work and what is leisure, and the value to the society and the individual of both. But any of these changes could produce a flood of extra 'non-work' time, some of which would inevitably be directed towards using a recreation resource; but quantities are impossible to foretell.

Parallel with this is an ignorance of the ecological repercussions of park management. Studies are beginning to emerge on this topic[35] but it is likely to be a long time before the ecological effects of, say, establishing a 20-acre campground in virgin territory, can be predicted with any degree of confidence. The impact on the immediate site is not too difficult an estimation but the reaction of the wild fauna, for example, to the people, their circulation patterns, and their garbage, may be difficult to judge in advance. Landscape management is another thorny thicket. Until a landscape has been altered (consciously or unwittingly), the resource manager never knows how many people will object to the change. How much change is acceptable in order that the recreational carrying capacity of a park can be enhanced? And just how compatible are the combination of uses under multiple-use schemes: the brief mention given this topic above barely scratches the surface of the complexity of this problem where every situation is likely to be unique.[36] And in every country

---

[34] C. Reich, *The Greening of America* (New York 1970).
[35] R. P. Gibbens and H. F. Heady, *The Vegetation of Yosemite Valley*, California Agric. Exper. Man. 36 (Berkeley 1965).
[36] ORRRC Report 17, *Multiple Use of Land and Water Areas* (Washington, DC 1962).

which does not have the space to devote large areas to parks, as have Canada and the USA, almost every act of designation of recreation land is the adding of a new multiple use element, because of the repercussions it must inevitably have upon the adjoining pieces of property.

5.2 THE LIMITS TO GROWTH

The title of a somewhat controversial computer-based study[37] of the future interactions of resources, population and pollution, reminds us of some of the basic characteristics of recreation and its resources. Like other natural resources, there is a finite supply of recreation land and water which can be stretched according to the price people are willing to pay. Happily it creates few waste products and is, ideally, a non-consumptive resource: even after use it is still there, although not always in an unaltered condition. The equation of supply and demand is a difficult matter however, for the free market does not operate because of the heavy involvement of government. It is difficult to envisage the diversity and quantity of recreation areas now enjoyed in the West having been provided by free enterprise and so it may be thought that the present situation, though far from ideal, is probably about the best that could have been achieved given the particular institutional and financial constraints. Undoubtedly there is in all countries a considerable slack in the supply: there are many areas which could be diverted to all categories of resource use, but it is interesting to note the restrictions being applied in the USA to wilderness travel, in order to satisfy the psychological and ecological conventions of wilderness areas in that culture. Perhaps it is likely that the first major check upon the transfer of resources to recreation will come as more and more governments at all levels decide upon detailed land-use planning. Once recreation is contained within the framework of an official plan it will be more difficult for it to seek territorial gains than for the interests representing for example industry or housing. The second check will then be a function of carrying capacity. Given the adaptability of man it is probable that the ecological aspect of capacity will be the first to set limits, when managers see that irreversible damage is being done. Even given a higher level of environmental consciousness than at present prevails, it is difficult to see demand falling because

[37] D. Meadows *et al.*, *The Limits to Growth* (London 1972).

of perceptual inacceptance of a damaged area: in the user-oriented zone, people are accustomed to a high degree of alteration, and in resource-based areas they have invested a great deal of time and money getting there and so are not going to be put off because the resource is over-used.

The time dimension to such a progress is difficult to estimate, and must inevitably vary with unknowns such as economic and population growth, as well as changing life-styles. But the model will serve to remind us that in this area of resources there must be for all practical purposes a finite supply which is certainly insufficient to match all the potential demands. Within that envelope there is a good deal of scope for manoeuvre and expansion but its presence will inevitably lurk in the background. The shortfalls in energy supply experienced in the West and Japan in 1973–4, and their effects upon recreational motoring, remind us that the whole rural recreation phenomenon is an outgrowth of the intensive-use-of-cheap-fossil-fuel syndrome. If that syndrome disappears, then this book's interest will be very largely as historical geography.

6 Rural recreation in a wider environmental context

6.1 RECREATION AS AN ELEMENT OF ENVIRONMENTAL QUALITY

The environment of man has to supply all his resources, both those which are necessary to his metabolism and those for which demand is culturally motivated. Within the latter category there are both consumptive resources whose use physically transforms them, and non-consumptive resources such as nature conservation, rural recreation areas, and regions of protected landscapes. Together with freedom from gross pollution of air, land and water, these protective uses of land and water form the complex of values known in the West as 'environmental quality'. Recreation is probably no more important than any of the others and shares with them the property of being largely an extra-market resource whose supply is controlled by governmental action. Whether such environmental quality is a necessity for human life or merely one of the luxuries available to rich industrial nations is arguable. Dubos[38] argues for the plasticity of man in accepting all kinds of undesirable conditions and so if industrial nations had no recreation space, little wild nature and

[38] R. Dubos, *Man Adapting* (London and New Haven, Conn. 1967).

263

highly polluted surroundings they could doubtless survive, as indeed do most of the people of the large cities of Japan today. But the success of the environmentalist movement shows that an increasingly large segment of the population is unwilling to accept such conditions and wishes to maintain or enhance the quality of its local or regional environment. The disappearance of some wildlife habitats and the pollution of air and water can usually be traced to the processes of economic growth and so, it is argued, a steady-state economy will ameliorate the present situation. Pressure upon recreation resources is presumably a facet of the same problem since it is economic growth which has created the time, income and mobility which have under-pinned the demand. But a steady-state economy would presumably increase leisure time considerably, which would exacerbate the demand for recreation space without any guarantee that the same type of economy would lessen competing demands for space: indeed any moves towards greater national self-sufficiency in many re-sources would,[39] in the industrial countries, create much greater demands for space and recreation would undoubtedly be the loser. The only 'answer' seems to be in the fundamental restriction of demand which would come from a population which was not growing. Not only would the absolute number be no greater but in time the redistribution of old and young might tend to lessen the impact of people upon recreation space. Although a 'spaceship earth' economy may in the long-run be the only way to preserve rural recreation as we know it in industrial nations, the transition phase may well be as difficult as with other more crucial resources. Those who reject the environmentalist model of man-biosphere relations must predicate their argument upon a sufficiency of energy supply to run the man-controlled systems which will replace natural ones.[40] In view of the inevitable if not imminent demise of fossil fuels, nuclear power is expected to be the major supplier, initially from variations of the currently available fission reactors and eventually (but probably not for at least 30 years) from fusion reactors. The effects upon recreation of the technological solution to environmental difficulties are too difficult to foretell, since the land and water require-

---

[39] See for example the trends desired by E. Goldsmith *et al.*, Blueprint for Survival, *The Ecologist* 2(1) (1972), and subsequently reprinted as *Blueprint for Survival* (Harmondsworth 1972).

[40] See for example A. M. Weinberg and R. P. Hammond, 'Limits to the use of energy', in S. F. Singer (ed.), *Is There an Optimum Level of Population?* (New York 1971), pp. 42–56.

ments of the energy supply plants of a nation using mostly atomic fuels (which would presumably apply to the countries discussed in this work with the exception of Canada), are not accurately predictable. But atomic power stations, unless placed below ground, are likely to be where towns and cities are not, and near large bodies of water thus competing with recreation space, as they already have done at Dungeness in England and on the west coast of Japan. If sea water is used as the raw material for fusion reactors then European countries with short coastlines may find that a great proportion of the unbuilt sections need to be devoted to power stations. There will be secondary effects of cheap nuclear energy, such as the possibility of working mineral deposits hitherto uneconomic[41] and so more land-use competition is brought about. On the other hand, waste heat from the cooling processes might be used to produce a high biomass of warm-water fish to delight the anglers, and warmed lakes for swimmers and sailors. The prospect of a version of Waikiki beach somewhere near Worthing is not altogether unattractive.

Although a continued growth model might produce all the material wants of a greatly increased number of people, it would not of itself produce any more recreation resources unless it were so intensively industrial as to free most farmland, forests and grazing land from production. But the industry and the increased population would also require land and water and it is impossible to predict whether the swings would be larger than the roundabouts. On balance, therefore, it looks as if those who value their own rural recreation and those who plan it for others would do best to join the advocates of equilibrium economics.

6.2 RURAL RECREATION AS PART OF THE BIOSPHERIC MANAGEMENT MATRIX

In a much-quoted paper, E. P. Odum[42] notes that one of man's problems is not to upset too drastically the stability of the biosphere, a condition which is apparently maintained in nature by a complex matrix of ecosystems, some of which are inert and emit gases and dust, such as volcanoes; others are at an early stage of succession and exhibit a simple structure and some instability but are nevertheless highly biologically productive; a third category is complex and stable ('climax') although perhaps with a lower biological produc-

[41] A. M. Weinberg, 'Raw materials unlimited', *Texas Quarterly* 11 (1968), pp. 90–102.
[42] E. P. Odum, 'The strategy of ecosystem development', *Science* 164 (1969), pp. 262–70.

tivity than some of the earlier stages. Man's manipulation of eco-systems[43] has produced analogous formations: cities, and agriculture correspond to the first two categories, the latter being highly productive but unstable. The unmanipulated areas of the world form the third category, which Odum labels as 'protective' are essential for the stability of the whole earth system in various ways, including an important role in the CO_2/O_2 balance of the atmosphere. It will be apparent that the wildlands sought for recreation areas fall into this latter category, along with the mixed productive and protective unit which Odum erects for areas of land use such as intermingled forestry and agriculture. So it is possible that the social forces in the industrial nations which are pressing for the preservation of wild lands and natural environments for recreation space are also acting in a way which will help to ensure biospheric stability and hence human survival.[44] Thus environmental quality as discussed above becomes an essential part of man-environment relations rather than a frill, provided that man decides to continue to depend upon natural bio-environmental systems for life support. If he chooses to erect man-made systems to replace these then the necessity for protective ecosystems will disappear, as most probably will the sort of rural recreation which has been the subject of this book.

[43] The present author has explored the intensity of these manipulations in 'Land use ecology as a theme in biogeography', *Canadian Geogr.* 14 (1970), pp. 309–22; in *The Ecology of Natural Resources* (London 1974) and (with C. M. Simmons) in *Resource Systems* (London 1974).

[44] For two rather different reviews with the same title, see P. Toyne, *Recreation and the Environment* (London 1974), and J. G. Nelson and R. W. Butler, 'Recreation and the Environment' in I. R. Manners and M. W. Mikesell (eds), *Perspectives on the Environment* (Washington, DC 1974), pp. 290–310.

Bibliography

This list is intended as a complement to the footnotes. Not all the items included in the notes are in this section, especially those dealing with local or very specific details; likewise this Bibliography includes material of more general interest that may bear upon the work and approaches to it but which was not used at any specific point. A few items appear twice, under both their author and their publisher.

ALDSKOGIUS, H., 1967: Vacation House settlement in the Siljan region, *Geogr. Ann.* **49**, 250–61.

1968: *Studier i Siljansomradets Fritidsbebyggelse,* Uppsala University Studies in Regional Geography **4**.

ABRAHAMS, H. M. (ed.), 1959: *Britain's National Parks,* London.

ALLIANCE INTERNATIONALE DE TOURISME, 1966: 1st International Congress on Leisure and Tourism, Rotterdam.

AMERICAN ACADEMY OF ARTS AND SCIENCES, 1967: America's Changing Environment, *Daedalus* **96** (4), 1003–225.

ALGEMENE NEDERLANDSCHE WIELRIJDERS BOND, 1964: Picknick-platsen, *Recreatie-Memorandum* **1**, 's-Gravenhage.

1964: Caravanparken, *Recreatie-Memorandum* **2**, 's-Gravenhage.

1966: Ligplatsen, *Recreatie-Memorandum* **4**, 's-Gravenhage.

1967: *Iets over de Recreatie Capacitiet van Meren en Plassen,* 's-Gravenhage (mimeo).

[n.d.]: *Iets over de Bruikbaarheid voor de Waterrecreatie van Kleine Kunstmatige Meren,* 's-Gravenhage (mimeo).

ARVILL, R., 1967: *Man and Environment,* Harmondsworth.

BARKHAM, J. P., 1973: Recreational carrying capacity: a problem of perception, *Area* **5**, 218–22.

BEAUFORT, J., (ed.), 1966: *The Call of the Vanishing Wild,* Christian Science Monitor, Boston.

BENTHEM, R. J., 1969: Changing of the countryside by land consolidation, *Biol. Cons.* **1**, 209–12.

BIELCKUS, C. L., ROGERS, A. W. and WIBBERLEY, G. P., 1972: *Second Homes in England and Wales*, Wye College Studies in Rural Land Use **11**.

BJERKE, S., 1967: *Landscape Planning and Nature Parks*, Copenhagen (mimeo).

BRITISH TRAVEL ASSOCIATION-KEELE UNIVERSITY, 1967: *Pilot National Recreation Survey Report* **1**.

1969: *Pilot National Recreation Survey Report* **2**.

BROADS CONSORTIUM, 1971: *Broadland Study and Plan*, Norwich.

BROOKS, L., 1962: The forces shaping demand for recreation space in Canada, *Resources for Tomorrow* **2**, Ottawa (Queen's Printer), 1957–68.

BROTHERTON, D. I., 1973: The concept of carrying capacity of countryside recreation areas, *Recreation News Supplement* **9**, 6–11.

BROWER, D. (ed.), 1960: *The Meaning of Wilderness to Science*, San Francisco.

(ed.), 1964: *Wildlands in Our Civilization*, San Francisco.

BUCHANAN, COLIN, *et al.*, 1966: *South Hampshire Study*, London HMSO.

BULTENA, G. L. and TAVES, M. J., 1961: Changing wilderness images and forestry policy, *J. For.* **59**, 167–70.

BURCH, W. R., 1964: Two concepts for guiding recreation management decisions, *J. For.* **62**, 707–12.

1965: The Play world of camping: research into the social meaning of outdoor recreation, *Amer. J. Sociol.* **60**, 604–12.

1966: Wilderness—the life cycle and forest recreational choice, *J. For.* **64**, 606–10.

BURDGE, R. and HENDEE, J., 1972: The demand survey dilemma: assessing the credibility of State outdoor recreation plans. *Guideline* **2**, 65–8.

BURTON, I. and KATES, R. W. (eds.), 1965: *Readings in Resource Use and Management*, Chicago.

BURTON, T. L., 1966: Caravan sites for holidaymakers, *Town and Country Planning* **34**, 113–19.

1966: Outdoor recreation in America, Sweden and Britain, *Town and Country Planning* **34**, 456–61.

(ed.), 1970: *Recreation Research and Planning*, University of Birmingham Centre for Urban and Regional Studies Publication 1.

BURTON, T. L. and WIBBERLEY, G., 1965: *Outdoor Recreation in the Countryside*, Wye College Studies in Rural Land Use Report 5.

BYRNE, A. R., 1968: *Man and Landscape Change in the Banff National Park before 1911*, University of Calgary Studies in Land Use History and Landscape Change 1.

CAHN, R., 1968: *Will Success Spoil the National Parks?* Christian Science Monitor, Boston.

1972: People, traffic, noise: can parks survive? *Christian Science Monitor*, 18 September.

CALDER, N., 1967: *The Environment Game*, London.

CALIFORNIA [UNIVERSITY OF] WATER RESOURCES CENTER, 1956: Contribution 4, *Recreational Use of Impounded Water*, Los Angeles.

CALIFORNIA [STATE OF] RESOURCES AGENCY, 1960: *California Public Outdoor Recreation Plan*, Sacramento, 2 Parts.

DEPT. OF PUBLIC HEALTH, 1962: *Recreation on Domestic Water Supply Reservoirs*, Berkeley.

DEPT. OF PARKS AND RECREATION, 1965: *Accelerated Development Program, projecting through 1980*, Sacramento.

1968: *California State Park System Plan*, Sacramento.

1970: *Report on a Decade*, Sacramento.

1971: *California Coastline Preservation and Recreation Plan*, Sacramento.

1972: *California Outdoor Recreation Resources Plan*, Sacramento.

CANADA, DEPARTMENT OF INDIAN AFFAIRS AND NORTHERN DEVELOP-MENT, NATIONAL AND HISTORIC PARKS BRANCH, 1964: *Requirements of a National Park*, Ottawa (mimeo).

1964: *National Parks Policy*, Ottawa.

1965: *Winter Recreation and the National Parks: a management policy and a development program*, Ottawa (mimeo).

1967: *Population Trends in Relation to the National Parks System*, Planning Report 61, Ottawa.

1967: *The Outdoor Recreation Resource and the Federal Role*, Ottawa.

1972: *Byways and Special Places*, Ottawa.

1972: *National Parks System Planning Manual*, Ottawa.

BIBLIOGRAPHY

CANADA, DEPARTMENT OF FORESTRY AND RURAL DEVELOPMENT, 1966:
    The ARDA Program in Relation to Recreation and Tourism,
    Ottawa.
    1967: *Federal-Provincial Development Agreement*, Ottawa.
    1967: Canada Land Inventory, Field Manual: *Land Capability
    Classification for Outdoor Recreation*, Ottawa.
CANADA, DEPARTMENT OF REGIONAL ECONOMIC EXPANSION, 1970:
    Development Plan for Prince Edward Island, Ottawa.
CANADA, STATISTICS CANADA, 1972: *Travel, Tourism and Outdoor
    Recreation. A Statistical Digest*, Ottawa.
CANADIAN FACTS CO. LTD, 1967: *Park Visits and Outdoor Activities of
    Canadians*, Ottawa (mimeo).
CENTRAL COUNCIL OF PHYSICAL RECREATION [OF GREAT BRITAIN],
    1964: *Inland Waters and Recreation*, London.
CHRISTIAN, G., 1966: *Tomorrow's Countryside*, London.
CIRIACY WANTRUP, S. V. and PARSONS, J. P. (eds), 1967: *Natural
    Resources: quantity and quality*, Berkeley and Los Angeles.
CIVIC TRUST, 1964: *A Lee Valley Regional Park*, London.
CLAWSON, M., 1959: *Methods of Measuring the Demand For, and Value Of,
    Outdoor Recreation*, Reprint **10**, Resources for the Future Inc.,
    Washington.
    1967: *The Federal Lands since 1956*, Washington.
CLAWSON, M. and HELD, R. B. 1957: *The Federal Lands, their use and
    management*, Baltimore.
CLAWSON, M., HELD, R. B. and STODDARD, C. H., 1960: *Land for the
    Future*, Baltimore.
CLAWSON, M. and KNETSCH, J. L. 1967: *Economics of Outdoor Recreation*,
    Baltimore.
Commentaur, Special issue on open-air recreation (No. 591),
    's-Gravenhage, May 1967.
CONSERVATION FOUNDATION, 1972: *National Parks for the Future*,
    Washington, DC.
COPPOCK, J. T., 1966: The recreational use of land and water in rural
    Britain, *Tidj. Econ. Sec. Geogr.* **57**, 81–96.
    1968: Changes in rural land use in Great Britain, *Trans. Inst.
    Brit. Geogr.* **44**, 111–25.
COSGROVE, I. and JACKSON, R. T., 1972: *The Geography of Recreation
    and Leisure*, London.
COUNCIL FOR THE PRESERVATION OF RURAL ENGLAND, STANDING

270

COMMITTEE ON NATIONAL PARKS, 1965: *Afforestation in National Parks*, Study 1, London.

CROSETTE, G. and OEHSER, P. H., 1973: The Adirondacks, *American Forests* **79**, 25–40.

DAHL, K., 1966: *Naturfredninger i Nordjylland*, Copenhagen.

DARBY, H. C., 1963: Britain's National Parks, *Adv. Sci.* **20**, 307–18.

DARLING, F. FRASER and EICHORN, N., 1967: *Man and Nature in the National Parks*, The Conservation Foundation, Washington.

DARLING, F. FRASER and MILTON, J. (eds..), 1966: *Future Environments of North America*, N.Y.

DARTINGTON AMENITY RESEARCH TRUST [DART], 1968: *The Great Western Canal*, Totnes.

1970: *The Recreational Use of Disused Railways*, Totnes.

DASMANN, R., 1968: *A Different Kind of Country*, N.Y.

DAY, L. and DAY, A., 1964: *Too Many Americans*, Boston.

DENMAN, D. R., ROBERTS, R. A. and SMITH, H. J. F., 1967: *Commons and Village Greens*, London.

DENMARK, LANDSPLANUDVALGETS SEKRETARIAT, 1962: *Introduction to the National Zoning of Denmark, 1962*, Mimeo Document **A-9-3**, Copenhagen.

1965: *Danish Planning Legislation, a survey*, Copenhagen.

1966: *Strandkvalitet og Fritidsbebyggelse*, Copenhagen.

FRILUFTSRADET (annually): *Arsberetning*, Copenhagen.

DENMARK, MINISTERIET FOR KULTURELLE ANLIGGER, 1967: *Betoekning om Naturfredning*, Statnings Trykningskontor Betoekning **461**, 2 vols., Copenhagen.

DRIVER, B. L. (ed.), 1970: *Elements of Outdoor Recreation Planning*, University of Michigan School of Natural Resources, Ann Arbor.

DOWER, M., 1965: The Fourth Wave: the challenge of leisure, *Architects' J.* (Jan.), 122–90.

1970: Leisure: its impact on man and the land, *Geography* **55**, 253–73.

1973: Recreation, tourism and the farmer, *J. Agric. Econ.* **24**, 465–77.

DUBOS, R., 1967: *Man Adapting*, London and New Haven.

DUFFIELD, B. S. and OWEN, M. L., 1971: *Leisure + Countryside =* , Dept. of Geography, University of Edinburgh. (2 vols.)

EAST BAY REGIONAL PARK DISTRICT, (annually): *Stewardship Report*, Oakland, Calif.

ECOLOGIST, THE, 1972: *Blueprint for Survival*, Harmondsworth.

EDLIN, H. L., 1963: Amenity values in British forestry, *Forestry* **36**, 65–89.

EDWARDS, A. M. and WIBBERLEY, G. P., 1971: *An Agricultural Land Budget for Britain 1965–2000*, Wye College Studies in Rural Land Use No. **10**.

FROME, M., 1962: *Whose Woods These Are*, Garden City, N.Y.

FURMIDGE, J., 1969: Planning for recreation in the countryside, *J. Town Plg. Inst.* **55**, 62–7.

GIBBENS, R. P. and HEADY, H. F., 1965: The Vegetation of Yosemite Valley, *Calif. Agric. Exper. Manual* **36**, Berkeley.

GITTINS, J. W., 1973: Recreation and resources, III: Conservation and capacity. A case study of the Snowdonia National Park, *Geogr. J.* **139**, 482–6.

GREAT BRITAIN, 1964: *The Countryside in 1970, Proceedings of the Study Conference November 1963*, London, HMSO.

1966: *Proceedings of the 2nd Conference*, November 1965, London, Royal Society of Arts.

1970: *The Countryside in 1970. Proceedings of the 3rd Conference*, October 1970, London, Royal Society of Arts.

GREAT BRITAIN, BRITISH WATERWAYS BOARD, 1967: *Leisure and the Waterways*, London, HMSO.

GREAT BRITAIN, COUNTRYSIDE COMMISSION, 1968–: *Annual Reports*, London.

(monthly): *Recreation News*.

(quarterly): *Recreation News Supplement*.

(annually): *Recreation Research Register*.

1968: *Investment in Recreation in National Parks*.

1968: *Planning for Leisure and Recreation*.

1968: *Rural Planning Methods*.

1968: *The Coasts of England and Wales, Measurements of Use, Protection and Development*, London, HMSO.

1968–9: *The Coasts of Great Britain* (A series covering the major coastal units of England and Wales), London.

1969: *Digest of Countryside Recreation Statistics*.

1969: *Policy on Country Parks and Picnic Sites*, London.

1969: *Resource Planning*.

1970: *Disused Railways in the Countryside of England and Wales*, London, HMSO.

1970: *The Coastal Heritage*, London, HMSO.

1970: *The Planning of the Coastline*, London, HMSO.

1971: *The Evolution of a Country Park Policy*.

1973: *Second Homes in England and Wales*, a report prepared by P. Downing and M. Dower.

1973: *Transport for Countryside Recreation*.

GREAT BRITAIN, COUNTRYSIDE COMMISSION AND ENGLISH TOURIST BOARD, 1974: *Tourism and Conservation*, London.

GREAT BRITAIN, COUNTRYSIDE COMMISSION AND PEAK PARK PLANNING BOARD, 1972: *The Goyt Valley Traffic Experiment*.

GREAT BRITAIN, DENBIGH COUNTY COUNCIL, 1972: *Second Homes in Denbighshire*, Ruthin.

GREAT BRITAIN, DEPARTMENT OF THE ENVIRONMENT, 1974: *Report of the National Park Policies Review Committee*, London, HMSO.

FORESTRY COMMISSION, *Annual Reports*, London, HMSO.

1972: *Forestry Policy: a consultative document*, London, HMSO.

HAMPSHIRE COUNTY COUNCIL, 1968: *East Hampshire Area of Outstanding Natural Beauty: a study in countryside conservation*, Winchester.

1972: *Disused Railways in Lindsey—Policy for After-Use*, Lincoln.

LINDSEY COUNTY COUNCIL, 1970: *The Lindsey Coast, a Policy for Conservation*, Lincoln.

1973: *The Lindsey Coast, a Policy for Holiday Development*, Lincoln.

NATIONAL PARKS COMMISSION, 1949–68: *Annual Reports*, London.

THE NATIONAL TRUST FOR PLACES OF HISTORIC INTEREST OR NATURAL BEAUTY, *Annual Reports*.

THE NATURE CONSERVANCY, 1949–64: *Annual Reports* (thereafter subsumed in the *Annual Reports* of the Natural Environment Research Council).

1959: *The First Ten Years*, London.

1965: *Report on Broadland*, London.

ROAD RESEARCH LABORATORY, 1967: *Revised Forecasts of Vehicles and Traffic in Great Britain*, London.

ROYAL COMMISSION ON COMMON LAND 1955–58, 1958: *Report*, Cmnd. **462**, London, HMSO.

SOCIAL SURVEY, 1969: Planning for Leisure, *Report* **SS388**, London, HMSO.

WATER RESOURCES BOARD, 1963–74: *Annual Reports*.

WEST RIDING OF YORKSHIRE COUNTY COUNCIL, 1969: *Caravans for Recreation*, Wakefield.

1974: *The South Pennines: an Interim Report*, Wakefield.

273

GRETTON, J., 1971: The hours we work, *New Society*, 7 Jan., 15–17.

GROFFEN, W. H., 1966: The importance of open-air recreation, First AIT Congress on Leisure and Tourism, Theme 1, *Report* **4**, Rotterdam.

HAINES, G. H., 1973: *Whose Countryside?*, London.

HALL, J. M., 1972: Leisure motoring in Britain: patterns and policies, *Geographia Polonica* **24**, 211–25.

HARDY, E. and MCGILLY, F. J., 1962: The hierarchy of government and public agencies in park development, *Resources for Tomorrow*, Ottawa, (Queen's Printer), vol. 2, 1037–46.

HARVIE, C. C., *The provincial parks of Alberta* in NELSON, R. C. and SCACE J. C. (eds.), *op. cit.*, 461–72.

HAULOT, A., Evolution et prévisions du mouvement touristique dans les régions tempérées, in IUCN, *see below*, 60–71.

HELLIWELL, D. R., 1969: Valuation of wildlife resources, *Reg. Stud.* **3**, 41–7.

HENDEE, J. C., 1969: Rural-urban differences reflected in outdoor recreation participation, *J. Leisure Res.* **1**, 333–91.

HERFINDAHL, O. C. and KNEESE, A. V., 1969: *Quality of the Environment*, Baltimore.

HEYTZE, J. C., 1965: *Recreation on the Roadside*, English abstract of Publication of the Sociological Institute of the State University at Utrecht (mimeo).

　　1968: *Het Recreatieverkeer in Enkele Boswachterijen van het Staatsbosbeheer*, SBB, Utrecht.

　　1969: *Recreation in the forest of Nunspeet*, SBB, Utrecht.

HODGE, E. W., 1969: Whose coast? *Town and Country Planning* **37**, 99–102.

HOLECEK, D. F. (ed.), 1974: *Proceedings of the 1973 Snowmobile and Off The Road Vehicle Research Symposium*, Michigan State University Department of Park and Recreation Resources Recreation Research and Planning Unit Technical Report **9**, East Lansing.

HOLST-HANSEN, A., 1968: Danske campingpladser i 1967, *Kulturgeografi* **107**, 239–42.

HUMLUM, J., 1966: *Landsplanlaegningsproblemer*, Copenhagen.

INSTITUTION OF WATER ENGINEERS [OF G.B.] 1963: *Recreational Use of Waterworks*, London.

ISE, J., 1961: *Our National Park Policy*, Baltimore.

IUCN, 1967: *Towards a New Relationship of Man and Nature in Temperate*

Lands, Part I: Ecological Impact of Recreation and Tourism upon Temperate Environments, Morges.

1971: *UN List of National Parks and Equivalent Reserves*, Brussels.

JACKSON, J. N., [n.d.]: *Recreational Development and the Lake Erie Shore*, Niagara Regional Development Council.

JAPAN, HOKKAIDO PREFECTURAL GOVERNMENT ENVIRONMENTAL DEPARTMENT, 1971: *Natural Parks and Wildlife Management of Hokkaido*, Sapporo.

1971: *Hokkaidō no Kankōyaku-irigomi ni Kansuru Shiryo* (Data on the concentration of visitors to Hokkaido), Sapporo.

JAPAN, MINISTRY OF AGRICULTURE AND FORESTRY, FORESTRY AGENCY, 1971: *Forest management in Natural Park Areas upon the Multiple Use Basis*, Tokyo.

JAPAN, OFFICE OF THE PRIME MINISTER, 1972: *Yoka ni Kansura yoron Chosa* (Public Enquiry into Leisure, 1971), Tokyo.

JENSEN, SV. A., *et al.*, 1966: *Egnsplan for Århusregnen*, Århus.

JOHNSON, W. A., 1971: *Public parks on Private Land in England and Wales*, Baltimore.

KILGORE, B., (ed.), 1966: *Wilderness in a Changing World*, San Francisco.

KNETSCH, J. L., 1963: Outdoor recreation demands and benefits, *Land Economies* **34**, 387–96.

KNOPP, T. B., 1972: Environmental determinants of recreation behaviour, *J. Leisure Res.* **4**, 129–38.

KRUTILLA, J. V. (ed.), 1972: *Natural Environments. Studies in Theoretical and Applied Analysis*, London and Baltimore.

LAPAGE, W. F., 1967: *Camper characteristics differ at public and commercial campgrounds in New England*, US Forest Service Research Note **NE-59**.

1967: *Some observations on campground trampling and ground cover response*, US Forest Service Research Note **NE-68**.

1972: Characterizing the forest user, in US DEPARTMENT OF AGRICULTURE FOREST SERVICE NORTHEASTERN EXPERIMENT STATION, 105–48.

LAPAGE, W. F., CORMIER, P. L. and MAURICE, S. C., 1972: *The Commercial Campground Industry in New Hampshire*, US Forest Service Research Paper **NE-255**.

LAZUCHIEWICZ, W., 1966: The importance of open-air recreation, First International AIT Congress on Leisure and Tourism, Supplement to Theme 1, *Report* **2**, Rotterdam.

275

LEOPOLD, A. S., *et al.*, 1963: *Wildlife Management in the National Parks*, US Dept. Interior Advisory Board on Wildlife Management, Washington DC.

LEUTZBACH, W., 1966: *Traffic and transport for touring*, First International AIT Congress on Leisure and Tourism, Rotterdam, Theme IV.

LEWIS, R. C. and WHITBY, M. C. 1972: *Recreation Benefits from a Reservoir*, University of Newcastle upon Tyne Agricultural Adjustment Unit Monograph **2**.

LITTLE, A. D., INC., 1966: *Tourism and Recreation*, Cambridge, Mass.

LOWENTHAL, D. and PRINCE, H. C., 1965: English landscape tastes, *Geogr. Rev.* **55**, 186–222.

LUCAS, R. C., 1964: Wilderness perception and use: the example of the Boundary Waters Canoe Area, *Nat. Res. J.* **3**, 394–411.

1964: Recreational Use of the Quetico-Superior Area, *US Forest Service Research Paper* **LS-8**.

1964: The Recreational Capacity of the Quetico-Superior Area, *US Forest Service Research Paper* **LS-15**.

LUTEN, D. B., 1962–3: Parks and people, *Landscape* **12**, 3–5.

1962: Human values in wildland recreation, in *Recreation in Wildland Management*, 14th Univ. of California Extension Forestry Field School, Berkeley, 1–12.

1966: Engines in the wilderness, *Landscape*, **15**, 25–7.

1967: Resource quality and the value of the landscape, in CIRIACY WANTRUP, S. V. and PARSONS, J. J. (eds.), *op. cit.*, 19–34.

LUTZ, H. J., 1963: Forest ecosystems, their maintenance, amelioration and deterioration, *J. For.* **61**, 563–9.

MACINKO, G., 1965: Saturation: a problem evaded in planning land use, *Science* **149**, 516–21.

1968: Conservation trends and the future American environment, *The Biologist* **50**, 1–19.

MEADOWS, D. H., MEADOWS, D. L., RANDERS, J. and BEHRENS, W. W., 1972: *The Limits to Growth*, London and New York.

MERCER, D., 1971: The role of perception in the recreation experience: a review and discussion, *J. Leisure Res.* **3**, 261–76.

MERRIAM, L. C., 1963: *A Land Use Study of the Bob Marshall Wilderness Area of Montana*, Montana State Univ. School of Forestry Bull. **26**, Missoula.

MEYERSOHN, R., 1969: The sociology of leisure in the United States:

introduction and bibliography 1945–65, *J. Leisure Res.* **1**, 53–68.

MICHIGAN DEPARTMENT OF CONSERVATION, 1966: Outdoor Recreation Planning in Michigan by a System Analysis Approach. *Technical Manual* **1**: *A Manual for Program RECSYS*, East Lansing.

MILES, J. C., 1972: *The Goyt Valley Traffic Experiment*, Countryside Commission and Peak Park Planning Board.

MINNESOTA, MORRC, 1965: *A Study of Private Enterprise in Outdoor Recreation, Report* **6**, St Paul.

MORSE, N. H., 1965: *An Economic Evaluation of A National Park*, Acadia Univ. Inst., Wollville, NS.

MØLLER, I., and WICHMANN, SV. E. 1967: *Dispositionsplan for Samsø*, Århus.

MOON, F., 1972: Angling and pleasure boating on inland waterways, *Recreation News Supplement* **6**, 27–9.

MUTCH, W. R. S., 1968: Public Recreation in National Forests: a factual survey, *Forestry Commission Booklet* **21**, London, HMSO.

NASH, J. B. (ed.), 1965: *Recreation: pertinent readings*, Dubuque.

NASH, R., 1967: *Wilderness and the American Mind*, New Haven.

NATIONAL ASSOCIATION OF COUNTIES OF THE U.S., 1964: *County Parks and Recreation*, Washington and New York.

NATIONAL PARKS ASSOCIATION OF JAPAN, 1966: *National Parks of Japan*, Tokyo.

NELSON, J. G. and BUTLER, R. W., 1974: Recreation and the environment, in MANNERS, I. R. and MIKESELL, M. W. (eds.), *Perspectives on the Environment*, Association of American Geographers Commission on College Geography Publication **13**, 290–310, Washington, DC.

NELSON, J. G. and CORDES, L. D. (eds.), 1972: *Pacific Rim: an Ecological Approach to a National Park*, University of Calgary Studies in Land Use History and Landscape Change, National Park Series **4**, Calgary.

NELSON, J. G. and SCACE, R. C. (eds.), 1969: *The Canadian National Parks: Today and Tomorrow*, University of Calgary Studies in Land Use History and Landscape Change National Park Series **3**, Calgary (2 vols.).

NETHERLANDS, CENTRAL STATISTICAL OFFICE, 1965: *Leisure Activity in the Netherlands*, 's-Gravenhage.

1966: Ministry of Agriculture and Fisheries, *Open-air recreation and rural development*, First AIT Congress on Leisure and Tourism, Rotterdam.

NETHERLANDS, MINISTRY OF AGRICULTURE AND FISHERIES, SERVICE FOR LAND AND WATER USE, [n.d.]: *Rural Development in the Netherlands*, Utrecht.

FOREIGN INFORMATION SERVICE, 1965: *Land Consolidation in the Netherlands*, Pub. **E125**, Utrecht.

GOVERNMENT PRINTING OFFICE, 1966: *Second Report on Physical Planning in the Netherlands*, Parts I and II, Den Haag (Condensed version in English).

MINISTRY OF CULTURE, RECREATION AND SOCIAL WORK, 1966: *Increased Leisure, What Use is Made of It?*, Rijswik.

STAATSBOSBEHEER, 1966: *The Task of the State Forest Service in the Netherlands*, Utrecht.

(annually): *Jaarverslag*, Utrecht.

NEWBY, F., 1972: Understanding the visual resource, in US DEPARTMENT OF AGRICULTURE FOREST SERVICE NORTHEASTERN EXPERIMENT STATION, 68–72.

NEWCOMB, R. M., 1967: Geographical aspects of the planned preservation of visible history in Denmark, *Ann. Ass. Amer. Geog.* **57**, 462–80.

1972: Has the past a future in Denmark? The preservation of landscape history within the nature park, *Geoforum* **9**, 61–7.

NIERING, W. A., 1960: *Nature in the Metropolis*, Regional Plan Assoc., New York.

NISHIO, H. K., 1972: The changing Japanese perspectives and attitudes towards leisure, *Humanitas* **3**, 367–88.

ODUM, E. P., 1969: The strategy of ecosystem development, Science **164**, 262–70.

OLSON, S., 1961: The spiritual aspects of wilderness, in D. BROWER (ed.), *Wilderness: America's Living Heritage*, San Francisco, 16–25.

ONTARIO, CONSERVATION COUNCIL, 1965: *A Conference on Parks and Outdoor Recreation*, Toronto.

DEPARTMENT OF INTERGOVERNMENTAL AFFAIRS, 1968: *Toronto-centered Regional Plan*, Toronto.

DEPARTMENT OF LANDS AND FORESTS, 1967: *Classification of Provincial Parks in Ontario*, Toronto.

1968: *Methodology for Ontario Recreation Land Inventory*, Toronto (mimeo).

DEPARTMENT OF LANDS AND FORESTS, 1972: *Algonquin Provincial Park: economic impact study*, Toronto.

1972: *Killarney Provincial Park: options for the future*, Toronto.

(annually): *Provincial Parks of Ontario Statistical Report*, Toronto.

DEPARTMENT OF LANDS AND FORESTS/HOUGH STANSBURY ASSOCIATES LTD., 1970: Lake Alert Phase 1: *Data Analysis*, Toronto.

1972: Lake Alert Phase 2: *Methodology*, Toronto.

DEPARTMENT OF TOURISM AND INFORMATION, 1972: *Ontario Winter Facilities*, Toronto.

MINISTRY OF NATURAL RESOURCES [succeeds Dept of Lands and Forests], 1972: *The Sandbanks, Hallowell Township, Prince Edward County*, Toronto.

QUETICO PROVINCIAL PARK ADVISORY COMMITTEE, 1972: *Quetico Park*, Toronto.

OOSTERKAMP, H. P., 1966: National, Regional and local planning for open-air recreation, First AIT-Congress on Leisure and Tourism, Rotterdam, Theme II, *Report* 4.

PARSONS, J. J., 1972: Slicing up the open space: subdivisions without homes in northern California, *Erdkunde* 36, 1–8.

PATMORE, J. A., 1970: *Land and Leisure in England and Wales*, Newton Abbott.

1973: Recreation and resources, 11: Patterns of supply. *Geogr. J.* 139, 473–82.

1973: Recreation, in DAWSON, J. A. and DOORNKAMP, J. C. (eds.), *Evaluating the Human Environment*, 224–48, London.

PERRY, N., 1972: Recreation activity in the Netherlands: four recent use studies, *Recreation News Supplement* 6, 2–5.

PETERSON, G. L. and NEWMANN, E. S., 1969: Modeling and predicting human response to the visual recreation environment, *J. Leisure Res.* 1, 219–45.

PHILLIPS, A., and ROBERTS, M., 1973: The recreation and amenity value of the countryside, *J. Agric. Econ.* 24, 85–102.

PLEVA, E. G., 1961: Multiple purpose land and water districts in Ontario, in H. Jarrett (ed.) *Comparisons in Resource Management*, Lincoln, Neb., 189–207.

1969: Ontario's parks, in NELSON, J. G. and SCACE, J. C. (eds.), *op. cit.*

279

POLITZ, ALFRED, RESEARCH INC., 1957: *Life Study of Consumer Expenditures*: A background for marketing decisions, New York.

PRATT, F., 1973: Informal recreation on inland waterways in 1972, *Recreation News Supplement* **9**, 41–3.

QUARTERLY REVIEW, THE, (Special issue, April 1966): *The Countryside*, 121–235.

RAGATZ, R. L., 1970: Vacation homes in the North-eastern United States: seasonality in population distribution, *Ann. Assoc. Amer. Geogr.* **60**, 447–55.

RAMBLER'S ASSOCIATION [OF GREAT BRITAIN], 1963: *Motor Vehicles in National Parks*, London.

REES PRICE, W. T., 1967: The location and growth of holiday caravan camps in Wales, *Trans. Inst. Brit. Geogr.* **42**, 127–52.

REICH, C., 1970: *The Greening of America*, New York.

REVELLE, R., 1967: Outdoor recreation in a hyper-productive society, *Daedalus* **96**, 1172–91.

ROBERTS, K., 1970: *Leisure*, London.

1971: Sociology and recreation planning, *Recreation News Supplement* **4**, 2–6.

RODERKERK, E. C. M., 1961: *Recreatie, Recreatieverzorging en Natuurbescherming in de Kennermerduinen*, Delft.

RODGERS, H. B., 1969: Leisure and recreation, *Urban Studies* **6**, 368–84.

1972: Problems and progress in recreation research. A review of some recent work, *Urban Studies* **9**, 223–8.

1973: Recreation and resources, I: The demand for recreation, *Geogr. J.* **139**, 467–73.

RUBINSTEIN, D. and SPEAKMAN, C., 1969: *Leisure, Transport and the Countryside*, Fabian Research Series **277**, London.

RUTH, H. D. and ASSOCIATES, 1969: *Outdoor Recreation Use of the Public Lands*, Berkeley, Calif.

SEHLIN, H., 1966: The importance of open-air recreation, First AIT-Congress on Leisure and Tourism, Rotterdam, Theme I, *Report* **1**.

SENGE, T., 1969: The planning of National Parks in Japan and other parts of Asia, in NELSON, J. G. and SCACE, R. C., *op. cit.*, 706–21.

SEWELL, W. R. D. and BURTON, I. (eds.), 1971: *Perceptions and Attitudes in Resource Management*, Dept of Energy, Mines and Resources, Resource Paper **2**, Ottawa.

SCACE, R., 1968: Banff: *A Cultural Historical Study of Land Use and*

Management in a National Park Community to 1945, University of Calgary Studies in Land Use History and Landscape Change **2**, Calgary.

SIDEWAY, R. M., 1970: Estimation of day use recreation by the Forestry Commission, *Recreation News* **20**, 1–2.

SILLITOE, K. K., 1969: *Planning for Leisure*, Social Survey Report **SS388**, London, HMSO.

SIMMONS, I. G., 1965: Americans for open space, *Town and Country Planning* **33**, 255–9.

1966: Britannia deserta, *Landscape* **15**, 27–9.

1966–7: Wilderness in the mid-20th century USA, *Town Planning Review* **56**, 249–56.

1967: Outdoor recreation as a land use in the USA, *Tidj. Econ. Soc. Geogr.* **59**, 183–92.

1968: How do we plan for change? *Landscape* **17**, 16–18.

1969: The Ninetieth's fall special, *Town and Country Planning* **37**, 127–8.

1970: Land use ecology as a theme in biogeography, *Canad. Geogr.* **14**, 309–22.

1970: (ed.), *The Yorkshire Dales*, London, HMSO.

1974: National Parks in developed countries, in WARREN, A. and GOLDSMITH, F. B. (eds.), *Conservation in Practice*, 393–407, London.

1974: *The Ecology of Natural Resources*, London.

SIMMONS, I. G. and C. M., 1974: *Resource Systems*, London.

SINDEN, J. A. and SINDEN, L. B., 1964: A forest recreation survey: implications for future development, *Scottish Forestry* **18**, 120–27.

SINGER, S. F. (ed.), 1971: *Is There an Optimum Level of Population?*, New York.

SOET, F. DE, 1965: Groenvoorziening en recreatie, *Bouw* **3**, Jan. 2–6.

SONNENFELD, J., 1966: Variable values in space and landscape: an enquiry into the nature of environmental necessity, *J. Social Issues* **22**, 71–82.

1967: Environmental perception and adaptation level in the Arctic, in LOWENTHAL, D. (ed.), *Environmental Recreation and Behaviour*, Univ. Chicago Dept. of Geog. Res. Paper **109**, Chicago, 54–9.

STATHAM, D. C., 1972: Capability analysis for recreation in the North York Moors, *Recreation News Supplement* **7**, 23–7.

281

STICHTING RECREATIE, (annually): *Jaarverslag*, Den Haag.
   1965: *Oeverrecreatie*, Den Haag.
   1966: *De Tweede Woning*, Den Haag.
   1968: *Autokerkhoven*, Den Haag.
SWEDEN, KOMMUNIKATIONSDEPARTEMENT, 1964: *Friluftslivet i Sverige*, Del **I**, Stockholm.
TANNER, M. F., 1973: Recreation and resources, IV: The recreational use of inland waters, *Geogr. J.* **139**, 486–91.
   1973: *Water Resources and Recreation*, London, Sports Council.
TAYLOR, G. D., *Techniques in the Evaluation of Recreational Use*, Canada Department of Indian Affairs and Northern Development, Ottawa, 1967.
THOMAS, D. J. and ROBERTS, J. T., 1970: *Tyne Recreation Study 1969*, University of Manchester Centre for Urban and Regional Research.
TOMBAUGH, L. W., 1970: Factors influencing vacation home locations, *J. Leisure Res.* **2**, 54–63.
TORONTO, METROPOLITAN TORONTO AND REGION CONSERVATION AUTHORITY, 1959: *Plan for Flood Control and Water Conservation*, Woodbridge, Ont.
   1963: *Pollution Control and Recreation in the Metropolitan Toronto Region*, Toronto.
   1967: *Conservation*, Woodbridge, Ont.
TOWELL, W. F., 1968: *Forestry and the Human environment: landscape quality*, Address at 68th Annual Meeting, Society of American Foresters, Philadelphia (mimeo).
TOYNE, P., 1974: *Recreation and the Environment*, London.
TROTTER, J. E., 1962: *State Park System in Illinois*, Univ. Chicago Dept of Geog. Research Paper **74**, Chicago.
UDALL, S. L., 1963: *The Quiet Crisis*, New York.
   1968: *1976—Agenda for Tomorrow*, New York.
UNITED STATES ARMY CORPS OF ENGINEERS, 1971: *National Shoreline Study: California Regional Inventory*, San Francisco.
* UNITED STATES DEPARTMENT OF AGRICULTURE, 1962: *A New Family-farm Business*.
   1966: Farmers' Home Administration, *Handbook of Outdoor Recreation Enterprises in Rural Areas*.
   1967: Yearbook of Agriculture, *Outdoors USA*.

* All UNITED STATES publications are published by the Government Printing Office, Washington, DC.

UNITED STATES DEPARTMENT OF AGRICULTURE FOREST SERVICE, 1965:
Outdoor Recreation in the National Forests.
1965: The American Outdoors—*Management for Beauty and Use,*
Miscell. Pub. **100**.

UNITED STATES DEPARTMENT OF AGRICULTURE FOREST SERVICE,
NORTHEASTERN FOREST EXPERIMENT STATION, 1972: *Recreation
Symposium Proceedings.*

UNITED STATES DEPARTMENT OF COMMERCE, 1965: *The Skier Market in
NE North America.*
1969: *Second Homes in the United States,* Current Housing Reports,
Series H-21, **16**.

UNITED STATES DEPARTMENT OF THE INTERIOR BUREAU OF OUTDOOR
RECREATION,
(quarterly): *Outdoor Recreation Action.*
(occasional): *Outdoor Recreation Reesearch: a reference catalog.*
1966: *Federal Credit for Recreation Enterprises.*
1967: *Outdoor Recreation Trends.*
1967 and 1971: *Federal Outdoor Recreation Programs.*
1967: *Financing of Private Outdoor Recreation.*
1967: *Northern New England Vacation Home Study 1966.*
1967: *Outdoor Recreation Space Standards.*
1968: *Co-ordination of Federal Outdoor Recreation Assistance
Programs.*
1968: *Private Assistance in Outdoor Recreation.*
1968: *Federal Assistance in Outdoor Recreation.*
1970: *The 1965 Outdoor Recreation Survey.*
1972: *ORRV. Off Road Recreation Vehicles.*
1972: *The 1970 Survey of Outdoor Recreation Activities.*
1973: *America Voices Its Recreation Concerns.*
1973: *Lake Tahoe: a Special Place.*
1973: *Outdoor Recreation. A Legacy for America.*
1973: *The 1965 Nationwide Inventory of Publicly Owned Recreation
Areas and an Assessment of Private Recreation Enterprises.*

UNITED STATES DEPARTMENT OF THE INTERIOR/UTAH UNIVERSITY,
1966: *National Conference on Policy Issues in Outdoor Recreation,*
Logan.

UNITED STATES DEPARTMENT OF THE INTERIOR NATIONAL PARKS
SERVICE,
(annually): *Public Use of the National Parks.*
(bi-annually): *Areas Administered by the National Park Service.*

283

1961: *Land Use Survey: proposed Point Reyes National Seashore.*

1961: *Economic Feasibility of the proposed Point Reyes N.S.*

1962: *First World Conference on National Parks.*

[n.d.]: *Our Vanishing Shoreline.*

1965: *Parks for America.*

1967: *Criteria for Parklands.*

1968: *Administrative Policies for Natural Areas of the National Park System.*

1968: *Administrative Policies for Recreation Areas of the National Park System.*

1971: *Criteria for Selection of National Parklands and National Landmarks.*

1971: *Forecast of Visits to the National Park System 1971–75 and 1980.*

1971: *Winter Activities in the National Park System.*

UNITED STATES NATIONAL ACADEMY OF SCIENCES/NATIONAL RESEARCH COUNCIL, 1963: *A Report by the Advisory Committee to the National Park Service on Research.*

UNITED STATES OUTDOOR RECREATION RESOURCES REVIEW COMMISSION, 1962: *Recreation for America.*

1962: *Study Reports* (27 vols.).

UNITED STATES PRESIDENT'S COUNCIL ON RECREATION AND NATURAL BEAUTY, 1968: *From Sea to Shining Sea.*

UNITED STATES PUBLIC LAND LAW REVIEW COMMISSION, 1970: *One Third of the Nation's Land.*

UNIVERSITY OF WISCONSIN, COLLEGE OF AGRICULTURAL AND LIFE SCIENCES, 1972: *Some Organizational and Income-Determining Features of the Wisconsin Outdoor Recreation Industry*, Madison.

WAGAR, J. A., 1964: *The Carrying Capacity of Wild Lands for Recreation,* Forest Science Monographs **7**.

WAGER, J. F., 1967: Outdoor recreation on common land, *J. Planning Inst.* **53**, 398–403.

WEDDLE, A. E., 1965: Rural land resources, *Town Planning Review* **35**, 267–84.

WIBBERLEY, G. P., 1969: *The British Countryside in the Year 2000,* Address to the Council for the Preservation of Rural Wales, April (mimeo).

WOLFE, R. I., 1951: Summer cottagers in Ontario, *Econ. Geogr.* **27**, 10–32.

1952: Leisure: the elements of choice, *J. Human Ecology* **2**, 1–12.

1954: *Recreational Land Use in Ontario*, Ph.D. thesis, University of Toronto (2 vols.).

1964: Perspective on outdoor recreation: a bibliographical survey, *Geogr. Rev.* **54**, 203–38.

1966: Recreational travel: the new migration, *Canad. Geogr.* **10**, 1–14.

1967: A Theory of Recreational Highway Traffic, *Ontario Dept. of Highways Report* **RR34**, Downsview, Ontario.

1967: A Use-classification of Parks by Analysis of Extremes, *Ontario Dept. of Highways Report* **RR134**, Downsview, Ontario (4 vols.).

YATES, E. M., 1972: The management of heathlands for amenity purposes in south-east England, *Geographia Polonica* **24**, 227–40.

Index

Prepared by Brenda Hall, MA, Registered Indexer of the Society of Indexers

Note: References will be found in the index to authors whose work is commented on in either the text or the footnotes; purely bibliographical material is not indexed.